Sports Media

Planning, Production, and Reporting

Sports Media

Planning, Production, and Reporting

By Brad Schultz, Ph.D.

ELSEVIER

AMSTERDAM • BOSTON • HEIDELBERG • LONDON
NEW YORK • OXFORD • PARIS • SAN DIEGO
SAN FRANCISCO • SINGAPORE • SYDNEY • TOKYO

Focal Press is an imprint of Elsevier

Focal
Press

Acquisitions Editor: Amy Jollymore
Project Manager: Paul Gottehrer
Assistant Editor: Cara Anderson
Marketing Manager: Mark Hughes
Cover Design: Eric Decicco
Interior Design: Julio Esperas

Focal Press is an imprint of Elsevier
30 Corporate Drive, Suite 400, Burlington, MA 01803, USA
Linacre House, Jordan Hill, Oxford OX2 8DP, UK

Recognizing the importance of preserving what has been written, Elsevier prints its books on
acid-free paper whenever possible.

Library of Congress Cataloging-in-Publication Data
Application submitted

British Library Cataloguing-in-Publication Data
A catalogue record for this book is available from the British Library.

ISBN 13: 978-0-240-80731-7
ISBN 10: 0-240-80731-6
ISBN 13: 978-0-240-80731-6 (CD-ROM)
ISBN 10: 0-240-80732-4 (CD-ROM)

The first edition of this book was authored by Brad Schultz and titled *Sports Broadcasting*, © 2002,
Butterworth-Heinemann.

For information on all Focal Press publications
visit our website at www.books.elsevier.com

11 12 13 14 15   10 9 8 7 6 5

Printed in the United States of America

My sincere thanks to the many industry professionals who contributed invaluable insights to this book, including Gary Kicinski at USA Today, *Ron Franklin of ESPN, Rick McCabe, Jeff Price, and David Bauer of* Sports Illustrated, *Michael Wallace of the* Jackson Clarion-Ledger, *Gregg Ellis of the* Northeast (MS) Daily Journal, *Mike Lageschulte at the University of Utah, Angela Renkowski of Drake University, and Howard Schlossberg of Columbia College.*

Thanks also to all our sports heroes we've enjoyed through the media, past and present, especially mine: Jack Nicklaus and Roger Staubach. You've given me countless hours of enjoyment, and continue to do so even today, thanks to ESPN Classic.

Contents

Contents

About the CD-ROM

This book's companion Sports Video Tutorial CD-ROM was designed by Buzz Hoon as an instructional tool for college sports live event productions. Hoon originally created the CD-ROM for his Western Illinois University students.

College productions present special challenges, since each semester brings with it a new student crew. While many students watch sports, they rarely recognize the responsibilities of the various cameras shooting a particular game. The tutorial includes suggestions for camera layout at basketball and football games. From the layout section, you can select a camera and see recommendations on field of view, framing, and other shot assignments. Several video examples are included on each camera. The narrative next to each video explains how the cameras work in unison for effective storytelling and a quality sports production. The tutorial also includes suggestions for shooting video at team practices. Enjoy!

Preface

At the annual convention of journalism educators in Toronto in the summer of 2004, a movement began. Several educators and researchers met privately during the convention to discuss the state of sports media, and how to create a *Journal of Sports Media*. The journal would fill a niche in the academic and research community by focusing on all areas of sports media, including broadcasting, print, and the Internet.

Several interesting observations came out of the meeting. No one can disagree that in the U.S. sports media touches almost every aspect of life. For example, the firestorm over Janet Jackson's appearance at the 2004 Super Bowl eventually involved several issues, including popular culture, politics, government regulation, ethics, and economics.

This is why the sports media are important in this country. From an economic perspective, the sports media are multi-billion dollar industries. Broadcast and cable networks currently have an 8-year, $17.6 billion contract to televise National Football League games to U.S. audiences. Other professional sports contracts for baseball, basketball, and hockey run into the hundreds of millions of dollars. The Entertainment and Sports Programming Network (ESPN) is a good example of the growth of sports media within the past 20 years. ESPN started as an obscure cable outfit in 1979, but has since grown into a powerful sports media conglomerate. ESPN now has 25 domestic and 6 international networks, and programs more than 10,000 hours of sports each year reaching into more than 200 million homes worldwide. In 2003, ESPN had revenues in excess of $2.8 billion.

These high dollar figures indicate the importance American culture places on sports and sports media. The late sportswriter Leonard Koppett wrote, "As mass entertainment, sports plays a larger role in American culture than in any other society, past or present." This is reflected in the fact that of five of the ten highest rated shows in television history are sporting events.

What happens in the sports media can have profound consequences in American society, as witnessed by events of the 2004 Super Bowl. When Janet Jackson exposed part of herself during the halftime show, it focused national attention on the issue of sports media and culture. Jackson, the National Football League, and the CBS network all received a tremendous amount of criticism for showcasing the event in prime-time network television. "I am outraged at what I saw during the halftime show of the Super Bowl," said Michael Powell, then chairman of the Federal Communications Commission (FCC). "Like millions of Americans, my family and I gathered around the television for a celebration. Instead, the celebration was tainted by a classless, crass and deplorable stunt. Our nation's children, parents and citizens deserve better." Powell and the FCC opened hearings into the matter, prompting Congress to consider tougher legislation on televised sex and violence.

But also coming out of the Toronto meeting was the sense that the sports media will always be considered relatively unimportant by the academic community. There is still a strong feeling among journalism educators and researchers that most people still believe "it's just sports." Veteran sportswriter and author Roger Kahn remembers that when he began writing sports for the *New York Herald-American*, news editors at the paper advised him to get out of the "toy department."

Yet, the study of sports media is important, both in a theoretical and practical perspective. From a theoretical standpoint, we must try to come to a better understanding of the tremendous impact of sports and sports media on our society. I live in Oxford, Mississippi, which is generally a sleepy little town of about 12,000 people. But five or six times a year, the town swells to five times that many for football Saturdays. "Tailgating in the Grove" on campus is not just an event; it's a social and cultural phenomenon. All those people are also bringing in money to spend in local restaurants, hotels, and bars. For a really big game, such as when LSU came to Oxford in the fall of 2003, the entire community revolves around a single sporting event.

The focus on sports can also have tragic consequences. After a football game in 2004, a student was struck and killed by a car while she was trying to cross a busy four-lane highway. One of the things that contributed to the accident was the fact that cars were allowed to use the shoulder of the road as overflow parking. Shortly after the accident, the city council met and banned parking on the highway shoulder for all football games. Again, the situation reflects how sports can affect so many different aspects of life.

This book will get into many of these issues, at least from a sports media perspective, but most of the text will concentrate on the practical application of sports media. The first edition which came out on 2001 was called *Sports Broadcasting*, but I felt that given the changing nature of the industry that approach was too limited. The emphasis today is on converged media, where television, radio, newspaper, and Internet coverage all blends together in a coherent mix. The newspaper reporter not only writes his or her game story for the paper, but also contributes to a local radio show and writes a different version for the paper's web site. It is hoped that this book addresses many of these issues which face today's sports media practitioners.

As this book goes to press, we're working on the first issue of the *Journal of Sports Media*, now scheduled for publication in March of 2006. We are now more than ever convinced of the appropriateness of our efforts, for the issues related to sports media are more important than ever—even if not everyone is willing to admit it.

Introduction

I truly believe that this edition represents a significant improvement over the first edition of *Sports Broadcasting*, which came out in 2001. While the first edition covered several important topics that had never been addressed before, I believe this edition expands and improves on the original in many areas.

Primarily, it goes beyond sports broadcasting to take a converged look at the new sports media environment. Today's students rarely concentrate solely in sports broadcasting or print, and they must be able to write and perform across a variety of media platforms. Even someone hired as a 'sports broadcaster' will likely be expected to make contributions to a web site, newspaper, or magazine. I believe this edition better addresses the new realities of the industry by incorporating those media.

The book also has much more practical advice from industry professionals. Media veterans from *Sports Illustrated, USA Today*, and ESPN have contributed, and students will benefit greatly from their experience. Not only will students learn more about the craft, but they will also get a better understanding of what it's like to work in today's sports media environment.

There is also an instructor's manual version of this edition, which will help educators in several ways. There are theoretical and practical syllabi, developed on a week-by-week basis. It also includes lesson plans, suggestions for assignments, and exam questions. Hopefully, it will help educators create a converged approach to teaching sports media.

This edition is also important for what it doesn't have. Educators and instructors reviewed the first edition and suggested that some parts were not necessary. The sections on the history of sports broadcasting and famous sports broadcasters were interesting, but not necessarily relevant to the subject. Those sections have been removed or drastically reduced, and there is much more effort spent on the practical teaching of sports media. Instructors who enjoyed the first edition will be pleased to know that the emphasis on 'doing'—writing, producing, editing, and creating—remains unchanged.

In addition to reinforcing those important areas, this edition also goes into new territory. The Internet is included, and industry professionals discuss the best ways to create an effective sports web site. Sports magazines are also featured, and executives at *Sports Illustrated* talk about the changes going on in the sports magazine industry. There is also a new chapter on economics, which is perhaps the fastest growing area of the sports media field. Finally, there is much more attention paid to job skills and especially getting an internship.

I hope you find what you're looking for in this edition, whether it's as a student, instructor, or someone simply interested in the sports media business.

Brad Schultz, Ph.D.
Coordinator, Broadcast Sequence
Department of Journalism
University of Mississippi
July 2005

1

Foundations

A Look Back

It's hard to pinpoint exactly when sports media became an important player in American society and culture. By the late 1800s, professional sports leagues and college sports programs had succeeded to the point that they had created a high level of interest in the general public. In 1893, Joseph Pulitzer created the first separate sports page at the *New York World*, and he was quickly followed by William Randolph Hearst at the *New York Journal*. In addition, newspapers began running special weekend sports sections, which helped increase the popularity of sports like college football.

The important relationship among sports, sports media, and the public began to develop during this time period. Author and researcher Michael Oriard stated that football entrenched itself deeply into the American soul, but the effect would not have occurred without the help of the new metropolitan newspapers and their large circulations. Sports coverage was similarly important in the infancy of major league baseball. Hall of Famer Connie Mack began his career as a player in the late 1800s and managed until the 1950s. "How did baseball develop from the sandlots to the huge stadiums—from a few hundred spectators to the millions in attendance today?" he asked. "My answer is: through the gigantic force of publicity. The professional sports world was created and is being kept alive by the services extended the press."

From Victoria to Jazz

The close relationship between sports media and culture also became evident, as early sportswriters reflected the dominant cultural themes of the times. In the Victorian and post-Victorian period of the early 1900s, athletes reinforced the cultural values of selfless heroism, self-sacrifice, duty, and honor. The fictional Yale football star Frank Merriwell was the embodiment of these ideals, not only studious and diligent, but "honest, brave, steady, generous and self-sacrificing" according to Oriard. During this time, real-life baseball pitcher Christy Mathewson "made the invention of Merriwell superfluous," wrote Donald Honig. "In addition to being a star athlete, he was also class president, a member of the glee club, a member of several literary societies, (and) he even found himself a campus sweetheart. This was America's first Golden Boy." Mathewson's image was further embellished by his volunteering to fight in World War I at age 37, and by his premature death at 44.

While Merriwell and Mathewson were celebrated for honor and duty, a different kind of hero emerged in the 1920s. Babe Ruth, Jack Dempsey, and Bobby Jones were all characterized in the sports media as larger than life performers who symbolized the excess and achievements of the "Roaring Twenties." One of the more celebrated athletes was football star Red Grange, described in 1924 by sportswriter Grantland Rice as

> A streak of fire, a breath of flame,
> A gray ghost thrown into the game
>   Eluding all who reach and clutch;
> That rival hands may never touch;
> A rubber bounding, blasting soul,
>   Whose destination is the goal -
> Red Grange of Illinois!

During the Depression years of the 1930s, the values of self-sacrifice, humility, and hard work were especially important in the American culture. One of the athletes that came to symbolize these values was Joe DiMaggio of the New York Yankees. DiMaggio certainly had humble beginnings, growing up the son of an immigrant fisherman in San Francisco. His talent, grace, and natural humility further endeared him to the sporting public and raised him to icon status. Popular songs celebrated his achievements and he still held a special place in the sporting consciousness even after his death in 1999. "He was the perfect Hemingway hero, for Hemingway in his novels romanticized the man who exhibited grace under pressure," wrote Pulitzer Prize winning author David Halberstam. "DiMaggio was always that kind of hero; his grace and skill were always on display, his emotions always concealed."

Changing Times

The 1960s marked a time of great social upheaval in America when traditional values came under increasing attack. Many younger Americans embraced new cultural values associated with civil rights, women's rights, the sexual revolution, and a rejection of duty as represented by the Vietnam War. During this time, a new breed of athlete emerged; one unafraid to challenge traditional assumptions of culture and society.

Athletes such as Jim Brown, Muhammad Ali, and Joe Namath were very outspoken about their own nontraditional beliefs. In the 1968 Olympics, American sprinters Lee Evans and Tommy Smith shocked U.S. television audiences by celebrating their gold medals with a "black power" salute.

In the face of such challenges, the sports media did their best to preserve the old order and reinforce traditional values. They certainly could not ignore the athletic successes, but they could and did subvert the cultural contexts. According to writer Marty Ralbovsky, "Namath (and Ali) . . . looked tradition in its overbearing eye and poked a finger into it. Traditionalists answered them by removing them from the mainstream and by clouding their accomplishments in controversy. Much of America, it seemed, wanted its athletes dished up on celibate platters with no side orders of humanity."

But at some point during the past 20 years the relationship between sports media and culture began to change, and the sports media abandoned their role as enforcers of traditional cultural values. Oriard suggested that sports and sports media exist to create heroes, especially those heroes lacking in American culture. But it can be argued that the modern sports media mainly exist as an outlet for nontraditional cultural values such as voyeurism, sensationalism, celebrity, and, most importantly, entertainment.

Witness the tabloid-type coverage of the Tonya Harding–Nancy Kerrigan skating saga in 1994 or recent coverage of athletes such as Dennis Rodman, Terrell Owens, or Joe Horn. It was Owens who pulled a pen out of his sock and signed the football after scoring a touchdown in an NFL game in 2002. Not to be outdone, a year later Horn pulled a cell phone out from under the goal post padding and pretended to make a call after scoring a touchdown. Both games were televised nationally and the events received significant media exposure. "The biggest currency athletes now have is celebrity," says sportswriter Mitch Albom. "It's not important what you do on the field anymore."

If we accept the argument that there has been a fundamental change in the relationship among sports, sports media, and American culture, what has caused it?

The New Media Environment

There are certainly changes going on within the media that have contributed to this situation. Beginning in the 1970s with the advent of cable television and satellites, the media began to experience changes that are still accelerating today. Growing technological sophistication significantly increased the number of sports media options. Where once consumers could find sports content only in newspapers, radio, and broadcast television, today there are literally thousands of sports media outlets. "Nobody could have predicted that cable TV in the 1980s exploded geometrically

Figure 1-1

Recent years have seen the tremendous growth of technology in sports media at outlets such as ESPN. *Courtesy of ESPN/Rich Arden.*

rather than arithmetically, and that's what exploded us," says ESPN's Chris Berman (Figure 1-1).

An important result of the satellite and cable revolution is the growth of the superstation. Stations such as WGN in Chicago and WTBS in Atlanta broadcast a full schedule of major league games for their local teams. For the most part, only local audiences could see these games until the advent of the new technology. Satellite and cable made it possible to beam games from the Cubs and Braves into almost every home in America, which opened up new markets for advertisers and, of course, increased profits.

The rise of the superstations points out the changing landscape of sports broadcasting. The key is technology and choice. Now viewers can have satellite signals brought directly into their homes, bypassing cable completely. The Internet makes sports information available 24 hours a day, 7 days a week, and digital television promises to deliver even more programming and more viewing options. With all this new technology, it's not really correct to call it "sports broadcasting" anymore because the term broadcasting implies the limited delivery of over-the-air signals to a mass audience. Sports programming delivery is now highly sophisticated and aimed more at specialized "niche" audiences than the captive mass audiences of the 1950s and 1960s.

But technology has also increased the cost of doing business and fewer media outlets are actually making money. One of the major findings from a 2004 study conducted by the Project for Excellence in Journalism was that in the long term, media organizations will face a myriad of problems, most of them economic. Given that large companies can bear the costs and difficulties of media ownership most easily, consolidation is a reality of the modern media environment, thanks in part to deregulation of ownership rules. In the summer of 2003, the FCC sought to raise ownership limits for a single media company from 35 to 45% of total television households. Even though there was strong objection, Congress ultimately voted to raise the limit to 39%.

The change in ownership limits means more media outlets will be in the hands of fewer companies. The largest media companies, such as Paxson (73 television stations), Viacom (62), General Electric (42), and News Corp. (38), now own a significant portion of the broadcasting industry. Consolidation has made broadcasting, especially the news business, much more bottom-line oriented. For example, in 2003 Viacom decided to end local news operations at two of its stations in Detroit, potentially saving the company as much as $10 million per year. According to media attorney Henry Baskin, "It's an admission that local broadcasting can't compete with cable and other national products." Several stations, including those in Tampa and Las Vegas, have eliminated some of their locally produced sports programming.

Increased competition and audience fragmentation have also shrunk the stage for national sporting events. Ratings, the lifeblood of multimillion dollar television rights fees, continue a downward slide to record low levels. Even high profile events like the Super Bowl, World Series, and Olympics have lost viewers in recent years. For example, the NCAA basketball championship game has seen audiences and ratings decline steadily to their lowest levels ever (Table 1-1).

"Ratings are smaller than ever, and the sports world is the exaggerated tip of it," said advertising media officer Peter Gardiner. The obvious result is declining revenue and rights fees, and a strain on network sports budgets. For example, NBC has drastically scaled back its sports commitment, dropping the NFL, NBA, and World Series. "If we were still in baseball, football and basketball right now, our losses

Year	Rating[b]	Teams
2004	11.0	Connecticut–Georgia Tech
2003	12.6	Syracuse–Kansas
2000	14.1	Michigan State–Florida
2002	15.0	Maryland–Indiana
2001	15.6	Duke–Arizona

Table 1-1

All-Time Lowest Rated NCAA Basketball Championship Games[a]

[a] From CBS, Nielsen Media Research.
[b] One ratings point equals just over 1 million homes.

would be substantial, in the range of $400 million per year" said Ken Schanzer, NBC Sports President. "It's not that we don't want to be involved in those sports, but not at that price." Fox Sports, which spent heavily on sports rights fees, wrote off $909 million in losses in just 3 months for its NFL, NASCAR, and major league baseball packages.

These changes have created a situation in which the media, and particularly sports media, have put much more emphasis on profit than public service. According to Oriard, part of the public service function of the sports media was to create heroes and reinforce traditional cultural values. But today the sports media have largely abandoned this function and serve primarily as a revenue stream for large media conglomerates. And it is much easier to make money by pandering to the lowest desires of the consuming public. According to media researchers Gerbner, Mowlana, and Schiller, corporate control has all but destroyed the public interest element required of the media.

But if the sports media are pandering for economic gain, does that not indicate a fundamental shift in American culture? After all, the demand for content must exist on a large scale to make the media outlets profitable. The last two decades have seen the rise of a "celebrity" culture in America, where people are honored not for their achievements, but simply for their star power and media attractiveness. A media personality such as Princess Diana fit the new definition of "hero" in the modern context: entertaining, accessible, and disposable. *Washington Post* media critic Howard Kurtz wrote, "(It's) a news culture that runs through celebrities like Kleenex and nothing is more important than being wealthy or famous. The media play a crucial role in marketing these larger-than-life personalities."

Implications

The current direction of sports media has important implications, both practically and culturally. From a practical standpoint, the stronger emphasis on profit and revenue is changing the very nature of sports in America. Sociologists Frey and Eitzen call it the "commercialization" of sport. This includes changes in rules or formats, such as college basketball adopting a shot clock and three-point line in the 1980s. Game times and venues are commonly changed to accommodate broadcast networks. It also includes aesthetic changes to make sports more pleasing to broadcast audiences, such as new color combinations for team uniforms. And there is the growing professionalism of sport and a corresponding decline in amateurism, especially in the Olympics. Olympic events were opened to professional athletes in the 1990s primarily to attract higher television ratings from American audiences. "Television drastically altered the character of sports events," said Jim Spence, who worked 25 years at ABC Sports. "Anyone who thinks television is not going to ensure its economic investment pays off is being naïve."

Sports media outlets also find it profitable to control their own programming, a major reason that companies such as Cablevision, News Corp., Comcast, and Disney have owned professional sports teams in recent years. Outlets that don't own teams outright have found other ways to influence sports programming and make it more entertaining and engaging. In 2000, NBC and World Wrestling Entertainment combined to produce a new football league called the XFL. The XFL featured high-intensity action and lots of scantily clad cheerleaders, but never caught on with viewers. A more modest success has been Slamball, a combination of basketball and trampolining. Slamball was created in 2002 specifically to appeal to young, "extreme sports" fans on the TNN network and now airs on Spike TV.

Made-for-TV sports such as Slamball, the X Games, and the XFL are examples of how changes in sports media have changed the sporting landscape. Perhaps more important is the effect of the changes on the American culture as a whole. Gerbner, Mowlana, and Schiller argue that media corporations have the power to shape or reshape culture. It would seem that sports media now have the ubiquity and influence to create such changes. Frey and Eitzen acknowledge the power of sports media to socialize youth and young adults through image management, the manipulation of symbols, and commentary.

What will be the effect on culture and on today's youth in an environment where the sports media have abandoned traditional cultural values in favor of revenue and profit? Consider LeBron James, who is the prototypical athlete-celebrity of the current generation. In high school, James was hyped by the national sports media as the second coming of Michael Jordan, considered by many the greatest basketball player of all time. James had his high school games nationally televised by ESPN, affording him instant celebrity status. After he decided to skip college and turn pro, he signed a $90 million dollar shoe contract before he ever played his first professional game.

And there's no doubt James was reveling in his newfound celebrity. He received numerous gifts from people who wanted to be part of his inner circle, including an expensive automobile, even though his family was living on public assistance. When one of the gifts became public knowledge, James was suspended by his state high school athletic association. The issue finally went to court and James won back his eligibility and finished out his senior season. Many portrayed James as a victim in the episode, but not sportswriter Phil Mushnick:

> The James saga has less to do with LeBron James than with everything that now passes as sports and popular culture, starting before James was kicking slats out of his cradle. He was raised in a world that purposely instills hideously warped values—even criminal values—as a matter of commerce. The rationalists, the apologists and the race-selective tell us that James is a victim of antiquated rules. LeBron's not a victim of the rules; he's a victim of his senses that long ago began to be filled with junk. Kids can't even watch the Super Bowl without steady commercial reminders to have plenty of sex with their beer and assault rifles. And as long as these kinds of proud "push the envelope" sells persist and grow bolder—and they have, and they will—the number of what sociologists call "at risk children" will escalate. What would make such a trend suddenly stop? Or even begin to reverse itself?

The trend certainly appears to be going full steam ahead. More and more high schoolers are forsaking the traditional values of hard work and education for the promise of quick riches in professional athletics. In 1995, Kevin Garnett became the first high school basketball player selected in the first round of the professional basketball draft. By 2003, 17 high school players had been drafted in the first round, with dozens more picked in later positions or entering the pros as free agents. Similarly, college freshman Maurice Clarett sued the National Football League in 2004, hoping the courts would let him enter the league's amateur draft. The courts rejected his arguments, in part because it was believed other teenagers would follow suit and skip college for the NFL.

These changes are not simply limited to high school-aged players. ESPN's decision to televise the Little League World Series in Williamsport, Pennsylvania, has created some disturbing scenarios. Several 12-year-old players have used the national stage to imitate behavior they see in the big leagues, such as posing for home runs, pointing at beaten players in exultation, and preening around the bases. Sportswriter Jeremy Gottlieb attributes the behavior directly to television. "I'll bet that kid that called his shot a la Babe Ruth the other night never does that when his team plays at the middle school playground down the street from his house. Or that every 12-year-old that has showboated after a big play in apparent homage to his favorite bloated, overpaid major league star doesn't do that in his hometown."

There are also numerous ancillary examples of how the sports media are affecting children by transmitting different cultural values. Since its games began appearing on ESPN, the Little League World Series has been rocked by scandals involving both gambling and ineligible players. Several players in the 2003 Pop Warner football championship game were seen sporting tattoos similar to the ones favored by pro athletes, even though the league is for pre-teens. Again, the game was televised nationally by ESPN.

The Future

Growth

One thing that has not changed is the nation's growing interest in sports media content, whether it's on television, radio, the Internet, or in print. It's important to remember that this explosion of sports media took place not just because it was possible, but because there was and is demand. Sports have always been some of the most highly watched formats in all of television. The highest-rated single show in the history of television is the last episode of M*A*S*H, which aired in 1983. But ranking number four is the 1983 Super Bowl game between San Francisco and Cincinnati. Five of the top 10-rated shows and 11 of the top 20 are all sports events (Table 1-2). It's not that demand has suddenly increased, but rather that technology has finally caught up with demand.

This would suggest that the number of sports media outlets will continue to increase in the near future. ESPN is a perfect example of the explosion of sports media in the past generation. The Entertainment and Sports Programming Network started in 1979 as a modest cable outfit, reaching just over a million homes with programming that no one else wanted, such as college lacrosse. Today, ESPN is a media conglomerate that runs 40 business entities and has estimated revenues of more than $2 billion per year (Table 1-3).

Table 1-2

All-Time, Top-Rated Television Programs[a]

Program	Date	Rating[b]	Number of TV households
1. M*A*S*H	2/28/83	60.2	50,150,000
2. Dallas	11/21/80	53.3	41,170,000
3. Roots	1/30/77	51.1	36,380,000
4. Super Bowl XVI	1/24/82	49.1	40,020,000
5. Super Bowl XVII	1/30/83	48.6	40,480,000
6. Winter Olympics[c]	2/23/94	48.5	45,690,000
7. Super Bowl XX	1/26/86	48.3	41,190,000
10. Super Bowl XII	1/15/78	47.2	34,410,000

[a]From A.C. Nielsen (www.nielsenmedia.com).
[b]Rating indicates percentage of all U.S. television sets.
[c]Women's figure skating final involving Tonya Harding and Nancy Kerrigan.

Table 1-3

The ESPN Empire[a]

Media/business	ESPN involvement
Television	Seven domestic networks/25 international networks
Radio	ESPN radio
Internet	Five online entities, including espn.com
Publishing	Two magazines, ESPN books
Emerging technology	Video on demand, broadband, interactive TV, ESPN HD
Wireless	Scores, headlines, games
Restaurants	ESPN Zones
Consumer products	Home videos, digital games, compact discs
Merchandise	ESPN Zone
Event management	X Games, Outdoor Games, ESPY awards, bowl and basketball games

[a]ESPN corporate fact sheet (http://sports.espn.go.com/espn/news/story?page=corporatefactsheet).

Convergence

The ESPN empire also suggests that sports media in the future will exist in a converged environment. It's no longer enough just to be a "print" journalist or a "television personality." In a world where one company owns several different media outlets, journalists who write for newspapers or magazines will also be expected to contribute to radio, television, and the Internet. Consider someone like Tony Kornheiser (Figure 1-2). Kornheiser works primarily as a sports columnist for *The Washington Post*. But he also has a sports talk radio show in Washington DC, hosts the ESPN

Figure 1-2

Tony Kornheiser (R) used to work with Andy Pollin on ESPN radio, but left in 2004 to host a local sports talk show in Washington, DC.
Courtesy of ESPN.

television show *Pardon the Interruption*, and contributes to other outlets such as *ESPN The Magazine*. ESPN gets more value for its dollar by having Kornheiser and other journalists contribute content across different media.

Similar efforts are taking place at media outlets all across the country. Even the smallest stations and newspapers can afford to create their own Internet content, even if it means simply duplicating material in both media. However, most stations try to create value by incorporating material unique to each medium.

There is still great debate over exactly what convergence is and how it works. Forrest Carr, news director at WFLA-TV in Tampa, says that convergence isn't just telling one story on three platforms. "Each is very different in sight, sound, and depth of analysis and interactivity," Carr said, explaining that not every story can be used in print, on air, and online. And there's a great sense that many media outlets are into convergence because everyone else is, not because it saves money. "Convergence is not an expense-saving operation," said Gil Thelen, president and publisher of the *Tampa Tribune*. "It's not antennas up with a digital backpack."

The bottom line on convergence is ... well, the bottom line. Large media corporations see it as the wave of the future and eventually a way to reduce the growing costs of providing all that sports content. Thus, any future of sports media will necessarily focus on economics and revenue.

In addition to convergence, media companies are looking at other ways of boosting profit and reducing cost. One way is for the company to buy into a sports franchise, thereby owning both content and distribution. Ted Turner bought the Braves as a showcase for his growing media empire, giving him a ready-made outlet to market his product. In the following years, the Tribune Company would buy the Chicago Cubs, Disney would take over the Anaheim Angels *and the NHL's Anaheim Mighty Ducks*, and Fox would spend millions to buy the Los Angeles Dodgers (although Fox eventually sold the team). Ed Snider of Comcast-Spectacor, which owns the Flyers and 76ers, said "Sports programming can make a (media) company stronger. Ownership gives the company control of (its) own destiny in terms of broadcasting rights."

Competition

If anything, tomorrow's sports media environment will be even more competitive than it is today. Advances in technology, such as cable, home satellite, the Internet, and digital delivery, have increased the amount and quality of sports media greatly. Today, the radio airwaves are filled with sports talk shows, while the cable and satellite universe is saturated with sports content of all types. Sports media content has also splintered into niche offerings, such as "extreme" sports, outdoors, and classic. Each of these groups is large enough to support its own cable network, such as ESPN Classic or Outdoor Life, suggesting that the money to be made in sports media will not come so much from the big network contracts of years past as it will from the hard-core, segmented, niche audiences.

A key factor in the growth of competition has been new technology, especially digital and satellite. Content providers are using technology to reach new audiences and to increase revenue. In 2004, Major League Baseball signed a deal with digital radio company XM Satellite that gave XM the right to broadcast all major league games for 11 years. In addition to carrying live games, XM also created a channel featuring original content and classic Major League Baseball game broadcasts and another channel to broadcast select games in Spanish. The deal pays Major League Baseball $470 million, and it could reach $650 million if the contract is extended. Competitor Sirius Satellite Radio signed rights deals with the NFL and the men's NCAA basketball tournament.

Not only are sports media outlets competing against each other, they also must now compete with powerful sports entities wanting to control distribution of their own content. In 2002, the New York Yankees abandoned long-time television partner MSG Network to form their own cable outlet (YES Network) and showcase their own games and programming. The National Football League created its own satellite network in 2003 and could soon challenge the broadcast networks and start televising live NFL games. "Live games are a possibility for the NFL Network," said NFL Commissioner Paul Tagliabue. "This is something that clearly has strategic value for us. The question is whether we start (putting on live games) sooner rather than later."

Profit is the name of the game for today's sports media. Large corporations that own media entities demand that those outlets make money, often forsaking other considerations such as public service. Consider the case of *Playmakers*, the controversial ESPN original series that aired in 2003. The show was a realistic look at life in professional football, focused mainly on such off-field issues as drugs, sex, and violence. The show didn't have great ratings, and it received a very poor reaction from the NFL, which considered it damaging to the league's image. Coincidence or not, ESPN has a multimillion dollar contract to televise NFL games, so the network bowed to league pressure and cancelled the series. Dusty Saunders of the *Rocky Mountain News* wrote, "Producing revenue (at ESPN) overrides any other consideration." As if to confirm that decision, ESPN immediately began selling the entire series on DVD.

Entertainment

Playmakers is an excellent example of how the emphasis on profit and competition has pushed all media toward an entertainment-oriented focus. Critics have a derisive name for it—"infotainment." The growing numbers of stations that emphasize infotainment typically use the same formula, including an emphasis on sensational stories mixed with pretty anchors and lots of music and graphics. Even as far back as 1977, Pulitzer-Prize winning television critic Ron Powers wrote, "TV journalism in this country—local TV journalism, in particular—is drifting into the sphere of entertainment."

Certainly this trend has not escaped televised sports. If anything, sports led the way because of its very nature. Events were not considered hard news, yet they weren't pure entertainment, either. Wrestling and boxing became a staple of sports television on Friday and Saturday nights. And when eventually eclipsed by other professional sports, wrestling reinvented itself in the 1980s. Now, World Wrestling Entertainment and its contemporaries dominate the cable ratings with high-energy music, laser-light shows, and soap-opera plots. Wrestling routinely makes millions of dollars in pay-per-view specials.

Such success spawned a host of other similar shows, mixing sports and entertainment. These include a variety of formats, including professional athletes competing in nontraditional events (the *Home Run Derby* shows of the 1960s, *Superstars* of the 1970s, and *The Skins Game* of the 1990s) and amateur athletes engaging against each other in contests of strength or skill (*The World's Strongest Man* and *American Gladiators*).

Another interesting format is the "Battle of the Sexes" match, which became quite popular during the women's rights movements of the 1970s. Tennis players Billie Jean King and Bobby Riggs showed the popularity of this kind of event with their match in 1973. Thanks to heavy preevent promotion and publicity, the match drew a huge crowd inside the Houston Astrodome and attracted millions of viewers on national television. The popularity of such events waned a bit in 1975 after a made-for-television horse race involving "Foolish Pleasure" and the filly "Ruffian." The popular Ruffian broke a leg during the race and had to be destroyed. ABC revived the format in the 1990s, involving golf pros from the PGA, Senior PGA, and LPGA tours. But nothing yet has matched the success and staying power of professional wrestling, perhaps because it makes no pretense of legitimate competition and instead focuses on promotion, entertainment, and marketing.

Sports announcers also started becoming more entertaining. ABC introduced two watershed concepts in sports entertainment—*Wide World of Sports* and Howard Cosell. More than any other announcer, Cosell's brash and bombastic style shifted the focus of the event squarely on him and institutionalized the role of an entertaining sports broadcaster on a national level. According to Dave Kindred of *The Sporting News*, Cosell "had no abiding interest in the game itself, but he certainly loved the stage it gave him. And no one entertained more sports fans than Cosell on Monday nights. Not in the sense that people loved him, but entertained in that fans listened to every word he said."

Figure 1-3

Dan Patrick (R) once
worked with former major
league pitcher Rob Dibble
on ESPN radio and
television. *Courtesy of
ESPN/John Atashian.*

Cosell has left the stage, but he set in motion the age of the entertaining sportscaster. According to *Electronic Media*, "Somewhere along the line, sportscasts became less important for substance than style. They became diversions that could be used to entertain viewers and hold on to people who didn't care about the information they heard." ESPN seemed to lead the way with a stable of young, irreverent sportscasters, many of whom had far stronger backgrounds in entertainment than sports. Craig Kilborn always dreamed of a job in television entertainment and went to ESPN because it offered him a national showcase for his talents. After a few years, he left to host a late-night interview and comedy show on CBS.

The trend really picked up steam in the mid-1990s with the pairing of Dan Patrick and Keith Olbermann on ESPN. Their humorous interplay created more fans than the sports events they covered and eventually led to a book (*The Big Show*). The party ended for Olbermann and Patrick when the former left ESPN after a contract squabble and eventually resurfaced on Fox Sports Net (Olbermann has since moved on to MSNBC). Patrick had a similar relationship with Rob Dibble on ESPN Radio (Figure 1-3).

On any stage and in any format, sports as entertainment has a strong foothold in the media. Although the experiment ultimately failed, ABC hired comedian Dennis Miller as an announcer for Monday Night Football in 2000. According to Tim Keown of *ESPN The Magazine*

The network acknowledged one salient fact. The game isn't enough anymore. It doesn't matter whether the game features a compelling story line or a storied rivalry or a quarterback every woman in America loves. It doesn't matter because on UPN there's wrestling with all its homoerotic, daytime soap-opera permutations. There are shirtless men being handcuffed and hauled out of rusted trailers on Fox. There's a guy up for murder describing his multiple-personality disorder on *Dateline*. That's the new world order.

The biggest collision of sports and entertainment in recent years happened during the Olympic ice skating trials in 1994. Nancy Kerrigan was attacked by an unknown assailant and immediately the attention focused on competitor Tonya Harding, who denied any part in the incident. But just days later, her bodyguard was arrested as the prime suspect. Kerrigan recovered enough to skate in the Olympics, which set up a soap-opera showdown with Harding and fueled unparalleled media frenzy. "We basically ignored every other athlete in the Olympics," said Albom. "We were too busy covering Tonya and Nancy's practice sessions." Jim Nantz helped anchor the CBS Olympic coverage and noted, "This is a tabloid-crazy society. We love nothing more than a good scandal."

Harding skated poorly in the finals and eventually confessed to "obstructing the investigation," although she never admitted any direct involvement in the attack. That fueled another round of intense media scrutiny, as did her suspension from sanctioned skating events. Kerrigan skated very well and just narrowly missed a gold medal. The medal ceremony should have ended the media's fascination with Kerrigan, but they just couldn't get enough. In the days that followed, they reported on Kerrigan's complaints about the judging and her subsequent critical comments at a Disney parade. "The media used me for months," she said later. "And then they just threw me away."

Media critic Tom Shales now says preoccupation with entertainment and hype makes today's sports coverage looks more like a production of the *Young and the Restless*. "The Olympics may simply have become a victim of television's incredible sports glut," he says, "something that has grown exponentially and geometrically in the years since ESPN first signed on." Such is life in the hi-tech, high demand world of sports media in the 21st century.

References

Chylinski, Patrick. (2003, July 3). Preps to the pros. *InsideHoops.com* http://www.insidehoops.com/nba-from-prep-070303.shtml

Connor, Anthony J. (1982). *Voices from Cooperstown*. New York: Macmillan. Eight-year deal would be worth $470 million. (2004, October 19). *ESPN*. http://sports.espn.go.com/mlb/news/story?id=1905454

Einstein, Charles. (Ed.) (1987). *The fireside book of baseball*. (4th ed.). New York: Simon & Schuster.

Frey, James H. and Eitzen, D. Stanley. (1991). Sport and society. *Annual Review of Sociology*, 17, 503–22.

Gerbner, G., Mowland, H., and Schiller, H. (Eds). (1996). *Invisible crises: what conglomerate control of media means for america and the world*. Boulder, CO: Westview.

Gottlieb, Jeremy. (2002, August 25). Has expanded TV coverage exploited the little league world? *Lawrence Eagle-Tribune*. http://www.eagletribune.com/news/stories/ 20020825/SP_006.htm

Halberstam, David. (1989). *The summer of '49*. New York: Avon.

Headline central. (2004, October 21). *Sports Business News*. http://www.sportsbusinessnews.com/ index.asp?story_id=40295

Hipsman, Barbara. (2004, February 23). Journalists to J-schools: forget the backpack. *The Poynter Institute*. http://www.poynter.org/column.asp?id=56&aid=61304

Keown, Tim. (2000). It's more than a game—it's a TV show. *ESPN*.

Kindred, Dave. (1999, July 7). Top 5 ornery charmers: number one, Howard Cosell. *The Sporting News*.

Kurtz, Howard. (1993). *Media circus*. New York: Times Books.

Martzke, Rudy. (2004, September 14). NFL network making run for TV deal. *USA Today*. http://www.usatoday.com/sports/columnist/martzke/2004-09-14-martzke_x.htm

Martzke, Rudy. (2003, February 25). Deals affirm NBC's direction. *USA Today*. http://www.usatoday.com/sports/columnist/martzke/2003-02-25-martzke_x.htm

Moretti, Anthony. (2004, August 6). *ESPN and playmakers: business and programming decisions*. Presentation at national convention of Association for Education in Journalism and Mass Communication, Toronto, ON.

Mushnick, Phil. (2003, February 3). He's all the rage! *New York Post*. http://www.nypost.com/sports/ 54036.htm

Oriard, M. (1982). *Dreaming of heroes: American sports fiction, 1868–1980*. Chicago: Nelson-Hall.

Postman, Neil. (1985). *Amusing ourselves to death*. New York: Penguin Books.

Ralbovsky, Marty. (1971). *Super bowl*. New York: Hawthorn.

Red Grange changed the shape of American sports. (1981). *DuPage County Heritage Gallery*. http://www.dupageheritage.org/yps/grange.html

Sandomir, Richard. (2003, September 10). The decline and fall of sports ratings. *The New York Times*. http://www.nytimes.com/2003/09/10/sports/10ratings.html

Shales, Tom. (2000, September 25). Oh, the tragedy: Olympics coverage is just too sad. *Electronic Media*, p. 4.

Smyntek, John. (2002, November 20). Viacom-WXYZ deal made to cut costs. *Detroit Free-Press*. http://www.freep.com/entertainment/tvandradio/via20_20021120.htm

Spence, Jim. (1988). *Up close and personal*. New York: Atheneum.

SportsCenter of the decade, the 90s. (1999, December 14). *ESPN*. [Television program].

The state of the news media 2004. (2004). *The Project for Excellence in Journalism*. http://www.stateofthenewsmedia.org/narrative_localtv_audience.asp?cat=3&media=6

Top holding companies. (2003). *The Center for Public Integrity*. http://www. openairwaves.org/telecom/ contacts.aspx?action=top

Turano, Cara. (2001). *The rise of intercollegiate football and its portrayal in American popular literature*. Paper presented at the Center for Undergraduate Research Opportunities Symposium, Athens, GA.

U.S. Congress passes TV ownership cap compromise. (2004, January 22). *Reuters*. http://story.news.yahoo.com/news?tmpl=story&u=/nm/20040122/media_nm/media_congress_fc c_dc_1

2 Reporting

Before we can discuss the basics of sports reporting, we must first decide on our approach and style. Both issues relate to presentation rather than actual content. Approach is how we define our overall philosophy of presenting sports to our audiences and relates more to the policies of media outlets taken as a whole. Style is a little narrower perspective, in that it deals with presentation of individual stories, and is more related to the personalities of the people delivering the content.

Approach

Types of Approaches

There is an ongoing debate in journalism regarding how to view the sports media. In general, the issue centers on whether the media should present sports in a serious or a nonserious manner.

There are several arguments for both sides. Those that favor the serious approach point to the tremendous amount of money involved in sports. There are literally billions of dollars spent every year in activities related to professional, college, and amateur sports. The economic impact is staggering and can have important consequences in a variety of ways. For example, whether a professional sports team decides to build a new stadium or relocate to a new city can literally make or break a local economy. In 2004, the Dallas Cowboys of the NFL reached a tentative agreement with the suburb of Arlington to build a new stadium at a cost of $650 million. The money will come from an increase in local sales taxes, which voters approved in a special referendum. The new stadium will take 4 years to build and will have obvious economic consequences for Arlington, which will gain around 2000 new jobs and more than $2 million per year in revenue. The suburb of Irving, where the Cowboys currently play, stands to lose millions of dollars.

Not only are stories like this important economically, they also point out how sports involve a variety of important social and political issues. In recent years, the sports media have focused more on issues such as drugs, crime, and discrimination based on race or gender. One issue that has become extremely important is the relationship between sports and gambling. Legal gambling is an enormous business, as witnessed by the record $81.2 million bet on the 2004 Super Bowl. But there was also an estimated $6 billion bet illegally on the game. *U.S. News and World Report* did a study of gambling in the late 1990s and estimated illegal action in the United States at $100 billion a year, more than twice the country's illegal drug trade. The magazine also noted that "both legal and illegal gambling have grown tremendously as the number of athletic events on cable and satellite television have soared."

Such issues were routinely ignored by the sports media until about the 1970s. Until that time, sports media outlets viewed themselves more as cheerleaders for local teams and athletes, and often protected players from negative publicity. No one was a bigger American hero than Babe Ruth, who more than anyone typified the decade of the 1920s—strong and powerful, yet seemingly carefree with huge personal appetites. The press well knew of Ruth's weaknesses, especially his fondness for liquor and prostitutes, but never reported any of it because it would tarnish his heroic image. There is a well-documented story about writers traveling on the team train late one night. First, a naked Ruth ran through the car, followed by a woman wielding a knife. One reporter looked at another and said, "It's a good thing we didn't see that, otherwise we'd have to report it."

Changing cultural conditions, especially the cynicism of Watergate and the Vietnam War, helped shift the focus of sports media. Faced with more competition from a growing number of outlets, sports media became more investigative, more personal, and some would say more entertainment oriented. A pivotal moment came with the publication of *Ball Four* in 1970. Major league pitcher Jim Bouton wrote the book, which became a controversial sensation for its honest depiction of players, including their sexual adventures and psychological hang-ups. The book horrified baseball executives, who saw it as a "threat to the game," and baseball purists, who did not know who to handle such truthful reporting of sports figures. Bouton later wrote, "I think the overreaction to the book boiled down to this: people were simply not used to reading the truth about professional sports. By establishing new boundaries, *Ball Four* changed sports reporting . . . it was no longer possible to sell the milk and cookies image again."

Many would argue that today's sports media aren't necessarily more "serious," just more intrusive. With more media outlets, there's more coverage of sports than ever before, but very little of it takes a serious approach. Some outlets, like ESPN's *Outside the Lines* series, make a credible attempt to look at the important issues associated with sports in today's society. But most of today's sports media focuses on

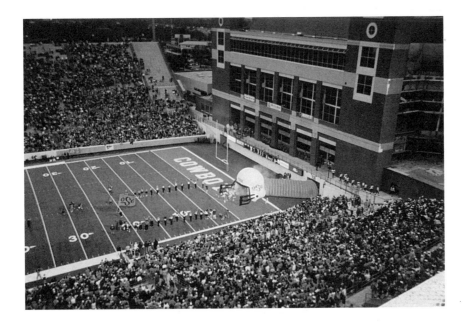

Figure 2-1

Given the tremendous
money, fan attendance,
and interest involved in
sports, should the games
be covered seriously or
simply as pastimes?
Courtesy: Mary Lou Sheffer.

the games, the personal lives of the athletes or their sensational behavior, on and off
the field.

This provides a lot of ammunition for those who think that the media should
treat sports as entertainment. Their position is when you get to the bottom line,
most sports are about games. They are not life-and-death matters, but simply a
matter of who wins or loses a particular contest. To them, sports are essentially just
another diversion or pastime for most people and should be covered with that in mind
(Figure 2-1).

Several sports journalists, including local television sportscasters Fred Roggin,
George Michael, and Ted Leitner, have made successful careers simply by refusing
to take sports seriously. Roggin uses videotape and sound effects, whereas Leitner
prefers creative stories, such as hockey fights with no highlights and a segment called
"Deep Thoughts with Charles Barkley." Many sports hosts and reporters on radio
have done the same thing. "I have to be interesting more than anything," said radio
sports talk show host Mike Gastineau of KJR-AM in Seattle. "People ask me is it
journalism or entertainment? Well, it's a hybrid, but it's got to be interesting. For
example, how many preset buttons do you have on you car radio? Ten or 15? It takes
two seconds for you to be driving along and say this is boring and go to another
station."

The tension between serious and nonserious approaches was clearly illustrated
in a 1999 interview between former baseball great Pete Rose and NBC reporter

Jim Gray, who has since moved to ESPN. During ceremonies at the World Series to honor baseball's "All-Century' team," Gray managed to get a live, on-field interview with Rose, who was still officially banned from baseball for allegedly betting on games. Gray repeatedly asked Rose about his involvement and whether it was an appropriate time to admit his guilt; a line of questioning that offended Rose. Rose obviously believed the interview would be little more than the usual entertaining fluff, while Gray wanted to use the opportunity to ask Rose some very serious questions. The following is a transcript of the interview between Pete Rose and Jim Gray:

JIM GRAY: Pete, the overwhelming evidence that's in that report . . . why not make that step tonight?

PETE ROSE: This is too festive a night to worry about that, because I don't know what evidence you're talking about. I mean, show it to me.

GRAY: We don't want to debate that Pete.

ROSE: Well, why not? Why do we want to believe everything he says?

GRAY: You signed a paper acknowledging the ban. Why did you sign it if you didn't agree?

ROSE: But it also says I can apply for reinstatement after one year. If you remember correctly in the press conference . . . as a matter of fact, my statement was I can't wait for my little girl to be a year old so I can apply for reinstatement. So you forgot to add that in there.

GRAY: You applied for reinstatement in 1997. Have you heard back from commissioner Selig?

ROSE: No. That kind of surprised me. It's only been two years. He has a lot on his mind. I hope to someday.

GRAY: Pete, it's been ten years since you've been allowed on the field. Obviously, the approach you've taken has not worked. Why not take a different approach?

ROSE: You say it hasn't worked . . . what do you exactly mean?

GRAY: You're not allowed in baseball, not allowed to earn a living in the game you love and you're not allowed to be in the Hall of Fame.

ROSE: That's why I applied for reinstatement and I hope Bud Selig considers that and gives me an opportunity. I won't need a third chance; all I need is a second chance.

GRAY: Pete, those who will hear this tonight will say you've been your own worst enemy and continue to be. How do you respond to that?

ROSE: In what way are you talking about?

GRAY: By not acknowledging what seems to be overwhelming evidence.

ROSE: You know, I'm surprised you're bombarding me like this. I mean, I'm doing the interview with you on a great night, a great occasion, a great ovation, everybody seems to be in great mood and you're bringing up something that happened ten years ago.

GRAY: I'm bringing it up because I think people would like to see . . . Pete, we've got to go; we've got a game.

ROSE: This is a prosecutor's brief, it isn't an interview and I'm very surprised at you. I am, really.

GRAY: Some would be surprised you didn't take the opportunity. Let's go upstairs to Hannah. Congratulations, Pete.

Source: Courtesy NBC/MLB

The interview created a firestorm of controversy and public reaction, with most people believing that Gray had gone too far. Letters to NBC and much of the reaction across the country criticized Gray for his timing and his persistence. Typical of the reaction was Rob Neyer of ESPN, who wrote that the incident "sickened, repulsed and disgusted" him.

One of the few who stuck up for Gray was Michael Shapiro, who has written sports for the *New York Times* and *Sports Illustrated.* "What if Gray had not pushed Rose?" he asked. "What if he had reduced himself, as so many of his colleagues have, to the role of asking, 'So, big fella, heckuva night, huh?' Reporting is neither about deference nor is it always about asking nicely. It is about finding out. We need, we want to know, be it profane or sacred." Gray later apologized for perhaps "spoiling the moment," but not for his line of questioning. He was later vindicated for his approach when in 2004 Rose publicly admitted that he had bet on baseball, after denying it to reporters for more than a dozen years.

What Determines Approach?

What approach media outlets ultimately decide upon depends on several factors. Obviously, one is the nature or tone of the story. Certain stories must be presented as "hard" because they are more serious or deal with serious issues. No one would suggest that a story like the Olympic massacre of 1972 should be presented in anything but a serious, straightforward manner. But there are many stories, like the Rose–Gray interview, which seem to blur the line between serious and nonserious.

The media outlet that presents the story also determines the approach. Some outlets, such as the *New York Times,* build their reputation on a no-nonsense, straightforward presentation. At the same time, there are media outlets that present sports in a more entertaining way. Deservedly or not, ESPN is gaining a reputation of frivolity and fluff, primarily because of the personalities of some of its on-air talent.

Personality is a key component in deciding on an approach. Simply put, the personality of the sports journalist will often determine which road to follow. The best sports journalists have always created and presented content as a reflection of their own personal style—Howard Cosell was acerbic and bombastic, whereas Dick Vitale is flamboyant and excitable. Cosell would never succeed as Vitale, and vice versa. The problem is when young sports journalists try to copy or imitate someone else in

Figure 2-2

Basketball commentator Dick Vitale has his own distinct personality, which dictates his approach and style. *Courtesy: ESPN/Ray Martin.*

the business. "Too many sportscasters look and sound alike or try to mimic national sportscasters," says television news director Ron Lombard. "We like to see people who are natural communicators and can do it with their own style" (Figure 2-2).

Finally, the audience is an important factor in deciding on a sports media approach. If one considers the number of specialty sports magazine and cable channels now available, it's obvious that audiences are becoming increasingly segmented and specialized. Audiences are differentiated in many ways—by interest in a particular sport or team, by level of interest, or especially by the time of day and type of media consumed. If someone goes to the Internet to get details of a game, that person generally wants the information presented in straightforward, no-nonsense way. The next day, that same person might enjoy reading a more opinionated commentary about the game or tuning into an entertaining sports talk show on cable television. Part of the negative reaction to the Rose–Gray interview may have been the fact that a World Series audience includes a lot of casual sports fans, who might be tuning in more for the entertainment than the actual game.

Meanwhile, the debate continues, and there is no definitive answer as to which approach to sports media works best. The best approach is the one that is most effective given the type of story, the personality of the reporter, his or her audience, and the media outlet involved.

Style

The nonserious approach is by far the most common in sports media today for a variety of reasons. With so much competition, sports media outlets must look for ways to make themselves unique. The financial pressures of making money have also forced many outlets to look at nontraditional audiences. There's always going to be the hard-core fan who reads the sports section or watches the sports on local television, but that group is shrinking. "Sports is extremely polarizing," said Brent Magid, president of Frank Magid Associates, a television consulting firm. "Avid sports viewers are a distinct minority. The majority can either take it or leave it, or despise it."

Different Styles

Opinion

There are several styles of presentation currently in use, some of which have been in use for several years. Opinion journalism has become very popular for both print and broadcast, especially with the advent of the Internet. The idea is for the sports media journalist to give opinions about a certain topic in the hopes of provoking a reaction among audience members. This is extremely common in sports talk radio, and for newspaper sports columnists. "I hear all the time about people who say, 'I don't care about sports, but I tune in to you all the time,'" says Leitner, who worked for several years at KFMB-TV in San Diego. "That's exactly what I'm trying to do. People will tune in because they just want to hear what this jerk has to say . . . or because they think it's interesting or funny or whatever."

Several legendary sportswriters built their careers on sharp opinion writing; men like Red Smith, Jimmy Cannon, and Dick Young. "In the era of television and radio," said veteran baseball writer Roger Kahn, "you don't say, 'The Dodgers beat the Giants, 6 to 2,' you say, 'Yesterday, in the Dodgers 6–2 win over the Giants, the most interesting thing that happened was . . .' That's the best definition of what a morning story of a ballgame ought to be. (Baseball writer Dick Young) worked that out by himself, and that was the New Journalism."

Young covered the Brooklyn Dodgers for the *New York Daily News* and according to Kahn, "If a player had a weakness, Young would write about it, explain it, describe it, analyze it . . . and certain players began to distrust him." Shapiro said, "It's hard to imagine today's (sports talk) callers—let alone the mercifully silent listeners—being satisfied with the sort of sportswriting of the era before 1950, before Dick Young made his way from the comfort of the press box down to the clubhouse, shoved his mug in a ballplayer's face and asked, 'What were you doing trying to steal third with two men out?' "

While Young represented the best of opinion writing, today's airwaves and newspaper columns are often filled with the worst. With more media outlets there is a growing demand for content, and opinion has rushed to fill the void. Unfortunately, much of it comes from loudmouths who like to hear themselves talk or see their names in print. There are no standards or rules as to what qualify as "valid" sports media opinions. Validity is usually measured by ratings or circulation, not quality. Who can define a quality opinion anyway? Oftentimes, it's simply who has the biggest audience. "There is an element to these shows of 'You top this,' " says Mike Lupica of the *New York Daily News* and a contributor to ESPN talk shows. "People expect you to say something strong," says Mike Greenberg, co-host of ESPN Radio's *Mike and Mike in the Morning* with Mike Golic. "You have to know where the line is and go right up to it but not cross it."

Aside from its ability to attract audiences, the use of opinion should be carefully considered. Primarily, it violates many of the journalistic standards of fairness, objectivity, and impartiality.

But there's also the issue of whether opinion actually adds anything to sports media or whether it's just a lot of noise coming from empty barrels. ESPN programs *Around the Horn* and *Pardon the Interruption* are extremely popular with viewers, but are those opinions any more valid than anyone else's?

The "Homer"

An extreme form of opinion is the "homer," who is constantly playing up to local audiences by supporting local teams and athletes. The hallmark of the homer is a noncritical attitude and a willingness to shamelessly root for the home team. A good example is the late Harry Caray, who was the leader of what baseball author Curt Smith calls "the Midwest cheering school." In the post–World War II era, baseball announcers in the Midwest developed huge followings by promoting the fortunes of the home team. Several other announcers and sportswriters had successful careers as homers, including Bob Prince in Pittsburgh, Russ Hodges in New York, and Byrum Saam in Philadelphia.

The number of homer announcers seems to have dwindled in recent years. For one thing, technology has eliminated the regional boundaries that created the "us against them" mentality. Superstations such as WGN in Chicago and WTBS in Atlanta promote their teams to a national audience, and it hardly makes sense to alienate potential viewers. In fact, much of these audiences watch to root for their home teams against the Cubs and Braves. In 2003, Turner Sports "demoted" Braves announcers Skip Caray and Pete Van Wieren from TBS television and assigned them to WSB radio. Turner executive producer Mike Pearl said the move was made to give the larger national audience for the television games, "unbiased editorial content," even though it drew strong criticism from Braves fans. (So strong, in fact, that Turner executives reversed their decision after only a few weeks.) Even so, a national stage demands an unbiased announcer. Networks and other outlets can't take a chance on a homer who doesn't have national appeal.

Criticism

The opposite side of homerism is criticism, or the sports journalist as provocateur. While homers try to sympathize with the audience, critics are purposively negative. Again, the idea is to increase audience by provoking reaction, even if it's negative. One of the best examples was sportswriter Dave Egan, who covered Ted Williams and the Boston Red Sox in the 1940s and 1950s. While the other sports media celebrated Williams and his achievements, Egan was constantly critical, even in the face of overwhelming evidence of Williams's ability. One time a rival asked Egan why he was so hard on Williams. "How many letters do you get a week?" answered Egan. The rival replied that he got maybe a dozen or so. "I get thousands," said Egan. "Maybe they're all calling me a bastard, but I'm the bastard they're writing to."

Criticism has its obvious drawbacks, including the strain it puts on the relationship among sports media members, players, coaches, and even audiences. There are so many media outlets today that the audience may respond to overt criticism by simply going to another outlet. It certainly makes it more difficult for media members to do their jobs, in that many times coaches and players will cut off access when they feel they've been treated unjustly. "We feel like targets," said former major league pitcher David Cone. "A lot of times [the media are] looking for a reason to get on you. Negativity sells." Long-time sportswriter Bill Plaschke noted that outfielder Raul Mondesi once threatened to beat him up after a critical column, a situation that is not uncommon given the growing hostility between media and players.

Part of the strain comes from the fact that many players and coaches don't feel the media are qualified to offer any meaningful or substantive criticism. Former NFL coach Jim Mora spent much of a memorable press conference answering criticism by telling the media, "You don't know (what you're talking about). You just don't know." At another press conference, former Purdue football coach Jim Colletto told a reporter he didn't know "his butt from a hot rock." The First Amendment guarantees the rights of media members to be as critical as they want, but it doesn't make their jobs any easier.

First Person

Criticism and homerism upset a lot of traditionalists because the styles violate the sacred journalistic notions of fairness and impartiality. To a certain degree, so does the concept of first-person reporting. This is simply the journalist putting himself or herself into the sports story, whether as a commentator or as a participant. As a participant, the reporter takes part in the story to some degree, like the sportswriter who practices with a local basketball team. In 2004, Damien Pierce of the *Ft. Worth-Star Telegram* wrote about his practice experience with the TCU Lady Horned Frogs basketball team. "Sure, I knew I wasn't quite in the shape of some of these women, but nothing a few weeks on the treadmill can't fix, right?" wrote Pierce. "I'd blend into the crowd and maybe embarrass a few Lady Frogs with my killer crossover." The point of the story and Pierce's sarcasm was to show how physically demanding it was to play women's basketball.

Even when the sports reporter doesn't actively participate in the story, he or she can still take a first-person approach. Dan Jenkins, who wrote for *Sports Illustrated* for many years and has written several sports books, was famous for including his perspective within the context of a story. In his coverage of the 1960 U.S. Open golf tournament, Jenkins wrote a story that focused on his following the leaders around the course and his reaction to their play. "As we (Jenkins and fellow sportswriter Bob Drum) arrived at the green, (Arnold) Palmer was in the process of drilling an 18-foot birdie putt into the cup. We stooped under the ropes at the fifth tee, and awaited Arnold's entrance. He came in hitching up the pants and gazed down the fairway. Spotting us, he strolled over. 'Fancy seeing you here,' he said with a touch of slyness."

First-person or participatory sports journalism is becoming more common, but something that should be carefully considered. Again, it violates many traditional notions of journalism. Perhaps more important, it's very difficult to do it well. Experienced journalists such as Jenkins can weave themselves in and out of stories, but still keep the focus on the main event. It's very easy to let the reporter become the main point of the story, which takes away from what's really interesting. Finally, this type of style has a certain "so-what?" factor. Is it really relevant or important to the audience to see the sports reporter swing a golf club, kick a football, or take part in a basketball practice? Consider whether there are alternative ways of telling the same story.

Social Commentary

Social commentary is another dangerous area for sports journalists. Such commentary usually goes beyond opinion and frames the story within the context of some important social issue, such as discrimination, race, or gender. For example, a social commentary on the (alleged) use of steroids by major league baseball players might not focus so much on what players are taking them, but rather on the larger issue of whether such enhancements are good for the game. Social commentary usually focuses on a specific problem, why it's happening, and what should be done to fix it.

There is certainly nothing wrong with interjecting social commentary in sports reporting. In the early 1990s, both Arthur Ashe and Magic Johnson admitted their exposure to AIDS/HIV, and the coverage of those events significantly helped to increase awareness across the country of the epidemic. But commentary of Johnson's situation also focused on his admission of sexual promiscuity and whether he "deserved" his status as a role model and sports hero.

Any issue that involves moral behavior is extremely difficult to report because the audience has so many different definitions of morality. People generally do not like to be told what to think or believe, especially when it comes to sensitive issues involving personal habits or values. This is especially problematic in sports, which as we have seen is often characterized as less important than what's going on in the rest of society. There is a large segment of the audience that attaches no social significance to sports and simply wants to know who won, who lost, and what happened in the game.

Even so, social commentary is becoming more popular in the sports media, primarily because controversy sells in today's competitive environment. With so many outlets needing content, commentary is an easy and inexpensive way to fill the void. Finally, and maybe most importantly, many journalists are convinced they can use the sports media to make a difference. They see sports as a microcosm of society and use their media outlets as a platform to expose social ills. Commenting on the 2004 Super Bowl in which Janet Jackson bared herself during the halftime show, Mike Lupica of the *New York Daily News* wrote, "She was just peddling herself the way everybody is peddling something at the Super Bowl, from sex pills to beer to faster Internet service. This is how things go in a Paris Hilton, Madonna-kissing-Britney world."

Even more than approach, style depends on the personality and experience of the sports journalist. It is generally not done by young or inexperienced reporters, although there are exceptions. Social commentators must also have an accommodating media outlet and managers and editors who are willing to take the heat for controversial content. Most of all, it takes someone with passion who sees sports journalism as a way to make things better, not just as a way to report scores and statistics.

Techniques

Print, broadcast, and the Internet are all different types of sports media, but they all rely on the same reporting techniques. Most importantly, all these different media require planning and preparation on the part of the sports reporter.

Planning Ahead

No matter what the medium, a sports reporter must consider certain factors before heading out to cover a story. Many of these are logistical—where is the event? How do I get there? Do we have proper credentials? Where do we want to set up for a live shot? What is my deadline and when do I need to have my story finished? Such logistical details must be determined beforehand and are usually done so in consultation with other staff at the media outlet. Assignment editors, producers, copy editors, engineers, and others will work with reporters in these areas. Reporters usually have a great deal of input in these decisions, but that is not always the case.

The first decision is how to present the story. For a newspaper, will it be a quick game recap or a more developed game story (see Chapter 3)? For broadcast, will it be a live report, a package, a voice-over, or maybe a combination of all three (see Chapter 4)? Producers and editors usually help determine how a reporter is to cover a particular story, and a variety of determining factors are taken into account.

Deadline

Probably the most important of those factors is deadline, because it will directly affect the way the story is presented and reported. If a reporter is covering a night game that starts late or runs long, that obviously impacts the type of story he or she can prepare. From a broadcast perspective, instead of a longer treatment such as a package, the reporter might have to go with a quick live report. Rick Cleveland, sportswriter for the *Jackson Clarion-Ledger*, remembers the long night in 2001 he spent covering an Arkansas–Ole Miss football game that went seven overtimes. As the game approached and then passed his deadline, Cleveland had two stories prepared and ready to send back to the paper—one in which Ole Miss won and the other in which Arkansas won.

Because Cleveland was able to keep in contact with staffers back at the newsroom, he was able to head off a potentially difficult situation. The story points out the need for better communication between all parties. As much as possible beforehand, know the exact lines of communication and keep channels open as the story continues to unfold. The very nature of sports coverage means the story will often keep changing. Bad weather, lengthy games, and technical breakdowns are just some of the problems reporters can experience in covering a story.

By communicating directly and quickly with others in the newsroom, the reporter can get important input in determining the next course of action.

Communication

It's also important to plan out and communicate with others who will be with you covering the story at the scene. If two or more newspaper reporters are covering the same event, it's important that each understands and clearly defines his or her

Possible Video or Still Pictures	Possible Interviews	Possible Natural Sound	Possible Outside Elements	Table 2-1
Gymnast practicing	Gymnast, coach, parents	Coach during practice	Music	Planning Ahead
Shots of ribbons, medals, etc.	Other gymnasts	Gymnast during practice	Video of famous gymnasts competing	
Olympic video file		Previous competitions		
Video of her competing locally				

own role. In a broadcast sense, many reporting problems are simply a lack of communicating what shot or angle to get for a story and can be eliminated by talking with the photographer beforehand. Make sure the shooter knows what exactly you want from the story—the story angle, what shots you have in mind, and any specific shots that would require extra effort to get. Certainly, some photographers will balk at being "told what to do." But ideally the reporter and photographer should work together to report as a team, and most photographers will not object to anything that makes them and the final product look better.

This involves more than just bossing around the photographer; it means having an idea for your story before you get to the scene. Plan the story out in your mind, including pictures, natural sound, and interviews. Often, this process doesn't occur until you get to the scene and get a feel for the story. Many times the final product won't look anything like what you had mapped out. But preparation is one of the key elements in sports reporting. If you get back to the newsroom without the material you need, it's too late.

For example, say you have been assigned to do a feature story for the evening newscast on a local gymnast training for the Olympics. You have most of the facts and information you need for the story, but what other information should you consider before you begin working? It's helpful to sketch out what elements you'll need to put the story together (Table 2-1).

Keep in mind that all of this could change, depending on what you find when you get to the story. You might not have any access to file video of her performances or technical problems could ruin some of your audio elements. A lot of reporting has to be done "on the fly" once the reporter and photographer assess what's available to them at the scene. But it's never appropriate to go into a story blind, and many times stories will work out just as you planned them out ahead of time. For broadcast reporters, we'll discuss such techniques as "natural sound" (the sound that occurs naturally at a story) in Chapter 4.

Research and Background

Aside from logistical decisions, a sports reporter must often do research and background work. Some of this information can be provided by sports information outlets (see Chapter 10) and much of the rest is accessible on the Internet. In some cases, phone calls and other traditional "leg work" will have to be done, especially in the case of athletes and events that aren't very well known. The bottom line is that sports reporters should make every effort to understand about the people and events they're going to report on, before the event takes place.

Interviewing

Interviews are a crucial component of sports reporting, whether for print, broadcast, or the Internet. If a batter strikes out in a key situation in the ninth inning, you interview the batter, the pitcher, and the managers after the game. Given the demands of the public and the shortening of deadlines, there's probably no better alternative for most of the sports media. And that's why it's even more important to know the key elements involved in interviewing. Some interviews you can't do anything about, such as trying to wedge a microphone in a pack of two dozen reporters surrounding a player after the game. In those situations you take what you get and move on. But much of sports reporting involves interviewing where you have time to plan a strategy beforehand to get the best possible responses.

Objective

The first element in a strategy is determining the objective of the interview. Most sports interviews are designed to inform, such as "what happened in the first quarter?" or "who's your backup goaltender this year?" There's another segment of interviews that is purely for entertainment. When Shaquille O'Neal goes on a late-night talk show, the host does not ask about his groin injury or his rebounding average. He asks about something interesting or funny O'Neal has done lately that will entertain the audience.

Another type of objective is the confrontational interview. Not many sports reporters want to intentionally provoke an athlete or coach, although sports talk show host Jim Rome might be an exception. Rome has built a national reputation on his willingness to prod and push interview subjects until they respond. (In the case of former NFL quarterback Jim Everett, the response was to physically attack Rome during the show.) Provoking an athlete is physically risky and doesn't do much to help you get further interviews. But in some situations, the reporter must be aware of the potential for a confrontational interview. If a horde of reporters are waiting outside a courthouse to get a comment from an athlete who has just testified about his own drug use, they should expect that the athlete will be reluctant and be prepared for a possible confrontation.

Many of the problems today involving interviews occur when athletes and reporters have different understandings of the objectives involved. Most likely, Pete Rose thought that when Jim Gray wanted to interview him the conversation would center on his inclusion in the "All-Century" team. Gray's objective was seemingly much different, in that he wanted to question Rose about the latter's involvement with gambling and his attempts to have his baseball suspension lifted. It's not known if Gray made his objectives clear to Rose when he asked for the interview, but it's always a good idea to let subjects know exactly what you want from the interview and not to "ambush" them, if possible.

You should never go into an interview without planning out a strategy beforehand. At the very least, this means getting all the pertinent background and information on the subject. But it also improves the interview to consider elements such as objective and audience. For example, consider how a reporter might handle the following situations.

Situation #1. The reporter is assigned to interview a person who has just been named head coach of a popular and highly successful college basketball program. The interview will appear in the sports segment of the noon news.

   Objective: Entertainment/informational

   Audience: Expects positive, "feel-good" story

   Tone: Light-hearted; nonconfrontational

In this situation, the audience probably has high hopes for the new coach and only wants to hear good things about him. The danger for the reporter is falling into a trap of "hero-worship" and losing a sense of journalistic integrity.

Situation #2. The reporter is assigned to interview a person who has just been fired as head coach of a popular and highly successful college basketball program.

   Objective: Informational/possibly confrontational

   Audience: Expects anger, conflict, possible confrontation

   Tone: Deadly serious

Here's the complete opposite of the first situation. In this example, if the reporter does manage to get an interview, he can expect a completely different tone and atmosphere. The coach may feel he was fired unjustly and have an "axe to grind" with his former employers. Even if there's nothing sinister at work, the occasion is very tense and serious, and that's what the audience expects. The concerns for the reporter here are remaining objective and not taking sides in the dispute.

It was also obvious during the interview with Rose that Gray had done his homework. He knew the specific details about Rose's situation, the agreement Rose signed when he was banned from baseball, and about his application for reinstatement. Rose could not argue with the facts, only Gray's assessment of them and the forum in which he chose to debate them. There is no substitute for preparation before conducting an interview. Athletes, coaches, and especially the audience can tell if a reporter doesn't have the facts straight.

Such cases are not only embarrassing for the reporter, but also lessen his or her credibility; a critical mistake could cause considerable problems in getting future interviews. ESPN's Roy Firestone was reminded of this lesson when he interviewed Indiana basketball coach Bobby Knight in the spring of 2000. Knight had come under tremendous pressure amidst allegations that he once choked a former player during practice. A videotape of the incident had circulated in the general media for quite some time, but Firestone never bothered to view the tape and could not question Knight about it. As a result, Firestone came under criticism for not approaching the subject and being too "soft" on the coach (Figure 2-3).

Figure 2-3

Roy Firestone has a reputation as a great interviewer, but took some criticism for his questioning of Bobby Knight. *Courtesy: ESPN.*

Audience

Another important aspect of interviewing is considering the audience for the interview. In other words, the reporter should always keep audience expectation in mind when conducting the interview. In what forum will the interview appear? Going back to the late-night talk show, the audience does not expect to hear any "exclusives" or "serious journalism" when a sports guest appears on the show and it would be foolish for the host to ask such questions. But the audience for a radio sports talk show or for ESPN expects something quite different.

Again, this may have played a role in the problems between Rose and Gray. The World Series attracts a national audience, not entirely composed of "hard core" sports fans. Many in the audience were people with just a cursory knowledge of Rose or even baseball in general. Given the setting, people did not tune in to see verbal combat, which may account for the negative reaction to Gray's questioning. Did that mean Gray should not have asked what he did? There's nothing wrong with asking tough questions, but in this particular situation the audience may have felt as ambushed as Rose. Certainly, a sit-down, one-on-one interview would have been more appropriate, but perhaps Gray felt this might be his only shot with Rose and he had to take it.

Much of the negative reaction from viewers came from people who admired Rose as a ballplayer. To them, Gray had crossed the line because he had tried to bring down a man who had once been a public hero. Many of the interviewing problems sports reporters face come from the fact that most of their subjects are considered heroes and somehow above ordinary people. It's difficult to report on the playing brilliance of Kobe Bryant the mega-superstar basketball player and then turn around and report on his involvement with a rape charge.

In many cases, reporters spend most of their time building up a player and then later having to tear him down. Former sportswriter Gene Collier wrote, "Sports journalism biblicizes Michael Jordan ... while simultaneously building databases on the anecdotal idiocies of Dennis Rodman and Lawrence Taylor, and then sells it to a sports-addled public eager for violence or competitive validation or some definitive moral scorecard." The challenge for the sports reporter is to cut through the hero worship and resist the temptation to deify the modern athlete. This is especially difficult regarding professional athletes, who make millions of dollars and have become larger-than-life celebrities. But to treat them as such prevents the sports reporter from asking serious questions. And according to Collier, it also "produces a creature that expects its strengths will be celebrated and even embellished while its weaknesses will be tolerated, and that the culture exists merely to extend privileges and ignore flaring evidence of arrested development."

Respect

Between hero-worship on one end and open antagonism on the other exists a middle ground where the sports reporter should strive to respect his interview subject. Sometimes this means nothing more than respecting the athlete's right not to talk. Some athletes and coaches, notably former baseball players Albert Belle and Steve Carlton, simply cut off relations with the media and refused to talk except on their own terms. In some cases, athletes will have a friendly relationship with the media and then cut off access when they feel they have been treated unfairly. Respect the right not to talk and work around it. Trying to circumvent this situation only leads to more problems and further antagonizes everyone involved.

It also is important to develop respect for the subject, which means to a relationship of trust between the reporter and the athlete. Athletes and coaches will often feel more comfortable and open up when they believe they can trust the reporter. Sports reporter Tim Cowlishaw covered the Dallas Cowboys in 1986 and 1987 and remembers the first time he had a private interview with then-coach Tom Landry. "The man whose answers seemed so predictable in the daily group interviews—although probably no more predictable than our questions—suddenly became expansive as he relaxed on his sofa."

This does not necessarily mean the reporter and the athlete have to develop a friendship; in fact, a friendship can be detrimental to the process if the reporter finds out some damaging information about a close friend. Athletes and reporters rarely become "friends" in the current atmosphere of sports reporting, but the reporter can still cultivate a trustful relationship. This is usually accomplished over time, as the athlete gradually understands the reporter acts fairly and isn't out to "get him." As part of this process, it's important for the reporter to adhere to some reasonable limits imposed by the athlete. Reporters should try to honor an athlete's requests concerning when or where the interview takes place, such as if the athlete doesn't want to be contacted at home or wants to wait a reasonable amount of time after a game to grant an interview.

Reporters can use such tactics if they have time to develop a trustful relationship with a subject. But much of sports reporting is "hit and run." Consider the on-court interview basketball star Shaquille O'Neal gave to a Los Angeles television station after a game in 2004. During the course of the live interview, O'Neal used several expletives that the station did not have the chance to bleep out. O'Neal later apologized, but the incident raised questions about the value of such on-field, on-court interviews when athletes are fresh from the heat of competition and don't have time to compose themselves (Figure 2-4).

In such situations, or in the case of interviews conducted in a locker room or in a news conference, there is little reporters can do to build trust. There are usually dozens of reporters present, all of them looking for a "scoop" or fresh angle to the story, and

Figure 2-4

On-field interviews have more raw emotion and honesty, but are also more unpredictable. *Courtesy: The Daily Mississippian.*

there's no way the interview subject can be completely open. In fact, quite the opposite happens, and athletes and coaches are more likely to be defensive, evasive, and give incomplete answers. News conferences and locker room interviews are notorious for failing to provide interviews of any real value. The only exception is when players or coaches let their emotions get the better of them after a game, and in that case the resulting interview is noteworthy mainly for its sensationalism. But even considering all these drawbacks, interviews done on the field, in the locker room, or in a news conference remain an important part of sports reporting, if for no other reason than because that's where reporters can get access to the people essential to their stories (Figure 2-5).

If the reporter has the time for an in-depth interview, there are some things he or she can do to put the subject at ease. One thing is to engage the athlete in idle conversation before the cameras or tape recorders start rolling. Such "preinterviews" involve topics like family, common interests, the weather—anything to make the subject a little more relaxed. Sometimes, athletes get so caught up in these harmless conversations that they don't even realize the camera or tape recorder has started rolling (and yes, it's imperative that you always make sure the subject knows the interview has begun).

Another way of putting someone at ease in a hit-and-run interview is to save the tough questions for the end. Starting with harmless and innocuous questions

Figure 2-5

With so many cameras and reporters around, it's hard to get a compelling interview at a news conference. *Courtesy: Mary Lou Sheffer.*

automatically puts the subject at ease and lessens his fears that you're out to get him or her. When you eventually get to the tough question, your chances of getting a willing and thoughtful response increase. Plaschke recalls the game he covered in which a player hit a home run, but later committed an error that cost the game. In the locker room afterwards, Plaschke asked first about the home run and says that the player was then "relaxed (enough) to be revealing and insightful when answering my next question about the error."

There's also a very practical reason for this tactic: starting with a difficult or embarrassing question opens the possibility that the subject will terminate the interview and leave you with nothing. If the same thing happens when the question comes at the end of the interview, at least you've got something you can use. In some cases, a reporter who has only one question to ask will start with a series of softball questions anyway to improve the chances of getting a good answer to the only question he or she really wants to ask.

But don't use this strategy in a "hit-and-run" situation. For example, if an athlete is walking from the locker room to his car, you might have time only for one or two questions. Don't waste time trying to build up trust—ask what you need and keep moving.

Specific Questions

There are all kinds of theories about what kinds of questions to ask in an interview. Obviously, no one wants a player or coach to glare at him after a game and ask, "Where did you come up with that?" But that simply comes with the territory of being a sports reporter and it will happen to anyone who does enough interviews. We're really not talking about dumb questions, but rather "obvious" questions. Athletes get most upset at having to hear questions they feel the reporters should be able to answer themselves. Former major league pitcher Jim Bouton once described a situation in which a teammate made a crucial error that lost a ballgame. As writers converged on the player after the game for an interview, other teammates came to his defense. "What the hell do they need quotes for?" asked Tommy Harper, "They all saw the play."

Even the most experienced sports reporters occasionally ask "dumb" questions, if that's the right term for them. Maybe it's better to say that just as athletes and coaches get tired of answering the same old questions, reporters get tired of asking them. Sometimes you just run out of ideas, especially at mega-events such as the Super Bowl. Table 2-2 is a sampling of some of the questions asked over the years at Super Bowl media day. Author Jeff Merron admits that while some questions are asked in jest, these seemed to be genuine.

The essence of good interviewing is to find the things that aren't so obvious. There are few things as redundant, as boring, and unfortunately as commonplace as the quick on-field interview after a game in which the reporter asks the hero to

Question	Response
To Raiders quarterback Jim Plunkett: "Lemme get this straight, Jim. Is it blind mother, deaf father or the other way around?"	Plunkett patiently explained that both his parents were blind and that his father had passed away several years earlier.
To Broncos running back Bobby Humphrey: "Why do you take your earring off for the game?"	Humphrey replied that he preferred not to have a diamond "to be pushed through my ear to the middle of my brain."
To Bills running back Thurman Thomas: "How do you get psyched up for big games?"	Thomas said that he "reads the newspaper and looks at the stupid questions you all ask."
To Cowboys quarterback Troy Aikman in Dodger Stadium: "Troy, does it seem a little strange answering football questions in a baseball stadium?"	"No."
To Bills linebacker Cornelius Bennett: "Do you believe you can win?"	"What kind of question is that? What kind of question is that? What kind of question is that? That's a (expletive) stupid question. I'm (expletive) you asked me that question. I didn't come anywhere to lose."
To Rams quarterback Kurt Warner: "Kurt, two questions: Do you believe in voodoo, and can I have a lock of your hair?"	"No."

Table 2-2

Asking Dumb Questions
Source: espn.com.

Table 2-3	Poor Approach	Better Approach
Interviewing Approaches	(First question) "What about that key mistake you made that lost the game?"	"You really seemed to play well in the early going. Talk a little about that."
	"On that 3rd-and-10 play in the 2nd quarter, you seemed to be in the wrong defense."	"That 3rd-and-10 play in the 2nd quarter really seemed like a big play . . . how important was it?"
	"What happened here . . . describe this play . . . etc."	"How does it feel . . . what does it mean . . . what happens now?"

describe the technical points of a dramatic moment; the same moment just witnessed or heard by millions of people. Interviewers should strive to get responses that tell us something we don't know or something that adds a level of depth to the scene. Instead of asking the player what kind of pitch he hit for the game-winning homer, ask him about what it was like to play after he sprained his knee in the third inning.

Make no mistake; sometimes you have to ask the obvious question anyway. "How does it feel?" "What were you thinking?" "What was it like?" Remember that it's not the question that counts anyway. Sports reporters don't win awards for asking the most penetrating questions. All you're trying to do is elicit the best possible response from the subject, and if it takes a dumb question to do it, so be it (Table 2-3).

Too often, reporters get bogged down in the strategy and technical details of a game. Print and Internet reporters naturally focus on this because they have so much space to fill and their readers have time to carefully analyze complicated ideas. But broadcast viewers or listeners have no such luxury, and most of them probably don't care anyway. Don't lose the forest for the trees; most people want to see the big picture.

A broadcast interview can get too caught up in analyzing plays. Remember, a television audience can see what happened, and except in extraordinary circumstances, the pictures don't need further embellishment. Concentrate more on the motivations and explanations behind the action that provide the viewer or listener with an emotional connection. With some notable exceptions, most details about a game are soon forgotten.

One of the best techniques in interviewing is called the "Golden Moment." That's where the interviewer simply stops talking or asking questions and gives the subject time to respond. It may seem awkward to have long moments of silence after a response, but it indicates to the subject that you expect him or her to keep going. Oftentimes, responses become better and more thoughtful after such pauses.

Story Outline

One of the last things you should do before you go out to cover a story is create an outline, which is simply a sketch of what you think the finished story will look like. This forces you to think about such things as what elements you will include, how

Broadcast Outline	Print Outline	Table 2-4
Planning 10 p.m. live shot, which will include a taped package. Package will include natural sound of Knight on sidelines, video of Knight, important plays of game, and some postgame comments from Knight. If possible, we want a live interview with Knight, but may have to settle for a live interview with an Indiana player or fan. If he is agreeable, it might also be possible to put a live microphone on Knight and use that sound in the package. If the game runs long, we'll do a live report with a few highlights that focus on Knight.	The story will center on Knight, including interviews with him, his players, and Indiana fans. A good visual image would help illustrate the story, such as before tip-off when Knight is introduced and is sure to receive a great ovation from the Indiana crowd. We might want to consider sidebar stories (see Chapter 3) on the Indiana fans reaction or reaction from Indiana players.	Typical Story Outline

they will appear, and what order you'll put them in. Basically, you're trying to visualize how you want the finished product to look.

It's important to remember that you're not writing the story ahead of time, which you obviously shouldn't do. You're mainly planning and organizing how you want to present the story, and many of these decisions can be made ahead of time. For example, if the Texas Tech basketball team plays a game at Indiana University, you know the main focus of the story is going to be coach Bob Knight's return to his old school. Working from that perspective can help you map out whom to interview and how to present the material.

Assume that we're covering the Texas Tech–Indiana game, which has a tip-off time of 7:30 p.m. Given a 10 p.m. broadcast deadline and a 2 a.m. newspaper deadline, a reporter in Indiana might create the outlines given in Table 2-4.

Creating an outline allows you to plan ahead of time for certain elements, such as the photograph you want of Knight receiving his ovation. Things like that have to be worked out ahead of time or you don't get them. In this case, the photographer has to be ready and in the proper position for the best shot. Your outline also should include back-up plans in case something falls through. For example, the broadcast reporter knows a live interview with Knight would be ideal, but not necessarily feasible. The game might run late or Knight might simply refuse to take part.

This points out the fact that an outline is just a blueprint and can quickly change. A different issue might become the focus of the game, such as if it runs several overtimes or if a fight breaks out between the two teams. It could be that Knight is sick and won't even be at the game, which changes your approach drastically. It's important to remember that the final product hardly ever resembles the outline.

At the Scene

The changing nature of a sports story demands that reporters be flexible, stay in constant communication, and keep their eyes and ears open for possible new angles.

Figure 2-6

Reporting at the scene
of the story requires
flexibility and
communication.

There are dozens of ways in which a story can change in just a few seconds, and thus change your story and its presentation. The computer on which you've spent the last few hours composing the game story could crash, forcing you to think of alternatives. The same thing could happen to a broadcast reporter if the station's live truck goes down. In addition to equipment problems, there are issues of interview access, deadlines, and logistics (Figure 2-6).

As much as possible, reporters need to have back-up plans in place for such situations. The broadcast reporter might have to "piggy back" with another station, or maybe the print reporter had been saving the story on a floppy disk. The ability to make critical decisions in the face of difficult and changing circumstances is essential to today's sports reporter.

That also means that the reporter should keep in constant communication with others back in the newsroom. If something occurs that necessitates change in the story or the way it's presented, producers and editors need to know immediately. This wouldn't necessarily involve such things as how the reporter covers the story, but it certainly includes any significant changes to presentation and delivery.

In some rare cases, the story will change so drastically that reporters will have to forget all the plans they made in advance in favor of completely new approaches. If a power failure in the middle of game causes it to be postponed or cancelled, that obviously becomes the new focus on the story. Such situations are rare for sports reporters, but they do happen, and the media should know how to handle them. In some extreme cases, no amount of planning will help reporters, but for the most part, good preparation is the starting point for all sports reporting.

References

Bouton, Jim. (1981). *Ball four plus ball five*. New York: Stein & Day.

Cowlishaw, Tim. (2000, February 13). Writers remember. *Dallas Morning News*.

Collier, Gene. (2000, January-February). The ex-sportswriter: 'I was looking for heroes in all the wrong places.' *Columbia Journalism Review*.

Getz, Jim. (2004, August 17). Arlington council to vote on stadium. *Dallas Morning-News*. http://www.dallasnews.com/sharedcontent/dws/news/localnews/cowboysstadium/stories/081704dnmetarlcowboys.82fe4676.html

Golenbock, Peter. (1984). *Bums*. New York: Pocket Books.

Greppi, Michelle. (2002, August 19). Time out for sports? Local stations debate how much coverage viewers really want. *Electronic Media*, p. 9.

Halberstam, David. (1989). *The summer of '49*. New York: Avon.

Jenkins, Dan. (1986). *You call it sports, but I say it's a jungle out there*. New York: Simon and Schuster.

Laurence, Robert P. (1999, March 22). Leitner's light touch. *Electronic Media*.

Lupica, Mike. (2004, February 3). Jackson's stunt exposes league. *New York Daily News*. http://www.nydailynews.com/sports/story/160869p-141111c.html

Martzke, Rudy. (2003, May 9). Talk shows' tendencies make crossing line inevitable. *USA Today*. http://www.usatoday.com/sports/columnist/martzke/2003-05-09-martzke_x.htm

McGraw, Dan. (1998, July 13). Big league troubles. *U.S News & World Report*.

Merron, Jeff. (2003, January 21). Now that's a stupid question. *ESPN*. http://espn.go.com/page2/s/merron/media.html

Not-so-great moments in sports. (1985). [Home video]. HBO Video: New York.

Pierce, Damien. (2004, March 1). Beat writer. *Ft. Worth Star-Telegram*. http://www.dfw.com/mld/dfw/sports/8076500.htm

Plaschke, Bill. (2000, January-February). The reporter: 'that's twice you get me. I'm gonna hit you right now, right now!' *Columbia Journalism Review*.

Raissman, Bob. (2003, March 28). TBS homers, going, going, gone. *New York Post*. http://www.nydailynews.com/sports/story/70734p-65761c.html

Rosenthal, Phil. (1999, March 22). Everybody's a comedian. *Electronic Media*.

Serby, Steve. (2004, February 5). Las Vegas sets $uper record. *New York Post*. http://www.nypost.com/sports/15317.htm

Shapiro, Michael. (2000, January-February). The fan: 'sports journalism is about myths and transcendent moments.' *Columbia Journalism Review*.

Print

Print sports media obviously have a much longer history than their counterparts in broadcast, holding a monopoly on sports coverage from the mid-to-late 1800s to the 1920s. We have already discussed in Chapter 1 how the sports media incorporated cultural values in coverage, which was especially true in the early days of print and magazine reporting. Consider the following excerpt from coverage of the 1892 Harvard–Yale football game in the *New York World:*

> An Aetna of humanity, bellowing with the combined thunder of a dozen tornadoes. A huge quadrangular crater filled to the brim with the hoarse tumult of human passions and blazing with blue and crimson fires. In this crater great black drifts, that heaved and swayed and rolled like earthquake-shaken hills, and under all the deep diapason of voices, the thousand inarticulate cries of grief and joy and quick, sharp shrieks of rage. A battery of 40,000 feverish eyes focused with the intensity of burning glasses on a bare plot of withered turf, where twenty-two gladiators were fighting the fag end of a royal battle.

While that style may have worked in the 1890s, it would certainly not go over well with audiences today, a fact that points to the need to adapt writing style and presentation to changing situations.

An Overall Framework

We can begin with a big picture—look at what a sports story should try to do and then get into more specifics. When we step back and look at sports reporting from a distance, we learn that it's really not correct to call it sports writing, but rather sports communication. Writing implies a one-way process in which a reporter creates something and then the audience consumes it. The term communication implies a two-way process in which dialogue and feedback are important and where the audience has a more direct and active role in the process. Communication also suggests engaging the interest and attention of the audience, which is essential in a fragmented media environment.

The sports communication process can be visualized in three parts. Initially, you should start with a simple idea, theme, or message that the audience can easily understand. "This team played well and won" or "this player had a great game despite playing in pain" are themes audiences can readily identify and understand. Too often, sports communicators try to make stories complicated and incorporate several different ideas and angles, which often confuses and overwhelms the audience. A helpful suggestion for finding a theme is to reduce the story to one sentence. All stories, no matter how complicated, can be reduced to one sentence. That's the starting point for the rest of the story.

The next step is using the available elements you have to communicate the story in the most effective way. Many writers, especially young ones, have the tendency to overwrite, thinking that the more explanation the better. But powerful visuals, whether still photographs or video, can be much more effective in communicating a story than words (see Chapter 6). If you have strong pictures, use them to tell the story. If not, you have to work harder with your writing to support the theme of the story. The same goes for interviews and quotations. Sometimes, it's better to tell the story in the subject's own words, especially if your writing would not add anything to the story.

A first-person account is an excellent example of how to support your theme in different ways. Personal accounts and diaries have become very popular in recent years, both in written and in broadcast forms. John Feinstein spent an entire year with the Indiana University basketball team to create *A Season on the Brink*. The landmark book was a chronological account of the 1985–1986 season, and a compelling look at big-time college basketball. It's highly likely that Feinstein would have written the book much differently if he did not have almost unlimited access to players, coaches, and administrators.

H.G. Bissinger did much the same thing with his work *Friday Night Lights*, which focused on high school football in west Texas. ESPN has created a popular series called *The Season*, which is a detailed look at one team from the start to finish of its season. Much of the show is simply putting a microphone on players and coaches and letting them tell the story in their own words.

The point is not that you have to go into depth and detail of these stories, but rather that there are many ways to communicate a main idea. Pictures, sounds, interviews, and words contribute to the final product and all can be used in different ways. Find out what are your strongest elements and emphasize those in your story.

A final point is to make sure that the audience understands what you're trying to communicate. At the end of the story, someone who has read it or heard it should be able to say, "I get the point." There are many ways in which the point can become lost or confused. Maybe your message was too complicated and overwhelmed the audience, or maybe there were technical problems that prevented a clear understanding. Work to minimize these problems so that your message gets through clearly. The audience doesn't necessarily have to agree with the message, but it should have no problems understanding it.

Specific Types of Reporting

Game Stories

There are several different types of stories related to a single sports event or even an individual athlete. One of the most common is the game story, or the reporting of details of a game just finished. In writing the game story it's important to understand what audiences are looking for, which depends greatly on what type of audience will be reading or consuming the story.

In the immediate aftermath of a game, say the first hour or so after it ends, audiences mainly want a version of the traditional journalism "five Ws": who won, who played well (or poorly), what were the important plays, and what other important things came out of the game. This would be a "quick hit" type of story, and more of a bare-bones, essential account of what happened. It would include the important details of the action, but not the depth that comes with interviews or other information. In today's media marketplace, such stories would be especially appropriate for wire service reports, reporting for games that go late into the night or beyond deadline, and stories about games in out-of-town markets where there isn't much local interest. Table 3-1 shows a typical "quick hit" hockey story written for publication or broadcast immediately after the game.

Developed Game Story

The developed game story is an extension of the abbreviated story, with more detail and depth added. This type of story is generally for audiences who already have the

---

Table 3-1

Abbreviated Game Story

(Tulsa)—Jim Simpson scored three goals, and Ron Duchette had three assists as the Tulsa Wolfpack beat the Kansas City Rangers 5–3 Tuesday night.

Simpson's third goal of the night at 1:54 of the third period gave him his 20th career hat trick. He now has 13 goals on the season, and has scored five in the last two games. Earlier in the third period, Simpson assisted on a goal by Park Hatfield that broke a 3–3 tie and proved to be the game winner.

Clint Stoner, Rick LaFleur, and Pete Connor scored for Kansas City, which dropped to 9–12–2 on the season. Dale Balon also scored for Tulsa, which climbed to the .500 level for the first time since October 19. The Wolfpack are now 12–12–4.

Wolfpack defenseman Steve Richter left the game with a bruised foot after blocking a shot in the first period. He did not return and is listed as day-to-day.

basic information from the game and are interested in filling in some of the details. A good example is a story that runs in the morning newspaper about a game of local interest from the previous night.

The developed story should give the audience a sense of not just what happened, but how it happened and why. This can be done by focusing on strategy, analysis, key plays in the game, and the like. It's also important to try to add some emotion and feeling to the story to give the audience the sense that it was at the game. Interviews and reaction from players and coaches are good ways to communicate the emotion of a game. Finally, the reporter should try to put the game into some type of perspective or context. Why was this game important? What does it mean? Is there anything from the game that will have a long-term impact on the players or coaches? Table 3-2 shows a more developed game story using the same basic information from our hockey game.

Beat Game Story

The beat game story goes beyond the developed game story in terms of details, analysis, and reaction. This type of story assumes that the audience has some sort of continuing interest in the subject and a certain level of knowledge and sophistication. It's usually a day-after story of a game or team that has strong local interest and a solid audience base. These are the types of stories usually reserved for "beat" writers who cover teams on a continuing basis.

Beat coverage is very common in newspaper reporting, and a paper usually assigns one or two reporters to cover a team on a day-by-day basis. The reporters are responsible for any and all information related to the team, including any breaking stories or "scoops." Because beat writers spend so much time with the team, they develop close relationships with players and coaches and have access to information not normally available. Beat coverage is obviously time-consuming in that a reporter has to travel with the team and is on the road for long periods of time (Figure 3-1). Table 3-3 shows our hockey story in beat form.

Beat Reporting with Michael Wallace

Michael Wallace grew up in the Washington, D.C., area and has worked for the *Washington Post*. For the past several years he has been the University of Mississippi beat writer for the *Jackson Clarion-Ledger*. Although he writes for a paper in Jackson, he lives full time in Oxford to give him better proximity to the Ole Miss athletic teams. His stories also appear in other outlets, such as *USA Today*.

Q: *Describe a little what a typical week might be for a beat writer covering a team. How many stories do you do?*

(Tulsa)—Jim Simpson scored three goals, but it was his hustle on another play that impressed his coach the most.

Simpson assisted on Park Hatfield's game-winner Tuesday night to lead the Tulsa Wolfpack to a 5–3 victory over the Kansas City Rangers.

Simpson's hustle led to Hatfield's goal when his backcheck prevented an icing call. Simpson then worked the puck out of the corner and drove to the net. Marc Robard stopped his shot but left the rebound for Hatfield, who flipped it over the goaltender for his sixth goal of the season at 10:47 of the third period to make it 4–3.

"Without a doubt that was the play of the game," Wolfpack coach Brian Jones said. "I thought Jim had a lot of energy all night long."

Simpson recorded his 20th career hat trick when he scored his third goal of the night at with 1:54 remaining on a 2-on-1 break with Ron Duchette. He now has five goals in the last two games.

"You can score a bunch of goals in a few games," Simpson said. "And sometimes you go without a goal. It's part of the game. The most important thing is that we win."

Scott Dale gave the Rangers a 1–0 lead 6:10 into the game with his third goal of the season. Dale took a wrist shot from the top of the left faceoff circle that glanced off the glove of Robard and into the net.

Kansas City knotted the score at 1 just 33 seconds later when two Wolfpack defenders got their skates entangled and fell, giving Clint Stoner a breakaway. Stoner beat Ian Laperriere for his sixth goal of the season.

Simpson put Hartford ahead 2–1 with his 12th of the season at 9:17, converting a backhand shot from just outside the crease as he swooped in on Robard.

Simpson's 13th goal of the season gave the Wolfpack a 3–1 lead at 19:37. Duchette won a faceoff in the Kansas City end and Steve Smith sent the puck back to Simpson behind the left faceoff circle and Simpson ripped a rising slap shot that beat Robard high to the glove side. "They scored late on that faceoff in the first period and that put us squarely behind the eight ball," Rangers coach Matt Davidson said.

Rick LaFleur's third goal of the season pulled Kansas City to within 3–2 at 3:08 of the second period. LaFleur took a pass from Pete Connor on a 2-on-1 break and backhanded the puck past Laperriere from close range. Connor tied the score at 3 with his seventh of the season on a power play at 3:27 of the third period.

"We fought back and made it 3–3," Davidson said. "Then they scored that fourth goal and that was probably the turning point in the game. With any kind of a better effort we might have had a chance to win this hockey game.'"

Wolfpack defenseman Steve Richter left the game with a bruised left foot when blocking a shot during the first period and did not return.

"The tendon that runs over the plate and screws that I have in my ankle just got hit right on that," Richter said. "Putting weight on it and moving my foot right now is really sore but there isn't a break. It's not a broken bone so I'll just take an anti-inflammatory and see how it feels from day-to-day.'"

Table 3-2

Developed Game Story

A: A typical week for me in my current position as an SEC college sports reporter consists of pretty much a 7-day work week that ranges anywhere, realistically, from 40 to 60 hours. I attend practice 2 to 3 days a week, travel on Fridays for road games, and return on Sundays. I generally write four stories during the week and three stories on game day (if it's a day game; two if it's a night game). On Sunday, we do a preview write-up of the next opponent. Stories range from player/coach features, injury or breaking news, and analyzing matchups at key areas.

Figure 3-1

Michael Wallace. Sports beat writer, *Jackson Clarion-Ledger* Courtesy: Adam Chapman.

Q: What are the important skills or assets a beat writer needs? It would seem that good relationships and access are pretty important.

A: It is very important to be persistent and hungry on these kinds of beats. Competition can be fierce, especially with the explosion of the Internet and talk radio. Above anything else, you have to be able to effectively gather accurate information. You have to be a reporter first and writer second. That calls for the ability to maintain professional sources and contacts within and around the team you cover. If it means buying a source lunch one day in exchange for a very pertinent piece of insight or information, then cough up the lunch money. But it's also important not to get into any habit of "buying a scoop." If you work hard enough, there's always someone else you can get tips from. Relationships with coaches and players often run hot and cold, depending on how the season is going, so it's important to keep an even keel and remain as fair, accurate, and balanced as possible with all stories.

Q: When you have to get so close to players and coaches can that cause some problems?

A: Absolutely, which is why you have to treat it as a professional relationship and not a personal one. It's hard not to sometimes want to pull for a guy to do well, especially as you get to know that player and some of the things he or she goes through just to be on the field or court. As close as reporters are to the scene and subjects, we can never imagine what it's like to have to perform at your best in front of live crowds in excess of 100,000 folks at times. I write for a 100,000-plus circulation paper and have stories running every day, but the feeling is not the same. It has to be a clear line between the media and subjects, where both sides know there's a point that can't be crossed in terms of expectations and emotions.

Q: How do you balance honest and sometimes critical reporting with the need to keep access with players and coaches?

A: The quick and easy answer is to pray that coaches and players don't have subscriptions to your newspaper. But with staffers and assistants always in search of bulletin-board material to motivate players, it's highly likely that someone will run into a critical article or two written about them. This goes back to a previous point. Reporters have to maintain a distance physically and emotionally from subjects they cover. If you're fair as a reporter and do enough research, attend enough practices, and speak with enough coaches and players, you'll have a true feel of what you're writing about. The subject of a critical story can only respect what's written about him—or ignore it completely—if it's done the right way. Once a coach or player feels that a reporter has the old axe to grind, then what was supposed to be a professional relationship between reporter and coach/player can become personal and petty. That does not benefit anyone involved.

Q: A beat writer is someone the fans get to know very well. What is the relationship like with the people who read your stories?

A: Those relationships always run in cycles. Most times, you're better off as a reporter to not get into a debate or even a modest conversation about the team of interest with a fan. One side sees things logically, or as much as possible. The other side has tunnel vision. There are two constants in this business for me: Fans rip newspapers and reporters in their towns even when things are going well for the team. And they ignore them when things are going bad. I do have several polite, meaningful, and insightful conversations with fans, but the overwhelming majority who respond—which I don't consider to represent the entire fan base—are generally unhappy or not satisfied with something. When you write something that can be viewed as flattering or positive about the team, you hear little or nothing.

Q: Beat writing is very demanding in terms of the number of stories you have to do and all the travel. How do you maintain your focus throughout a long season?

A: You take a moment to be thankful that you get to do something you love, something any hard-core sports fan would quickly trade places with you to do. I got into sports reporting because I lived and loved sports. I'm an ex-athlete and was lower-level Division I basketball recruit. When it was time to move on to real life and a real job, I was blessed to be able to stay in the field I loved anyway. The practical answer to this question is to take it all in stride. Seasons can drag on you, especially if the team you're covering is struggling. The job and the people you deal with can become a pain in those times. But you wake up and realize there's another story out there that needs to be done. You realize that there are thousands of readers who begin their day reading what you write and end their day looking forward to the next story that will be thrown in their driveways or pulled up on their computer screens.

Beat reporters often write their stories in "serial" format, assuming that their audience has a strong interest in the subject and has kept up with previous stories written about the team. That's why these stories don't give a lot of basic explanation found in other writing. The writer assumes the audience knows the important points of reference. Such stories are also more conversational and free-flowing and are not restricted as much by the traditional journalistic conventions like the inverted pyramid, which dictates that the most important information in the story goes first. As with the developed game story, beat stories also make an effort to provide perspective and context.

Table 3-3	The following is another type of story using information from our fictional hockey game. Notice how much of the information, such as Hatfield's penalties and Simpson's slump, is not explained but assumed as already known.
Beat Game Story	(Tulsa)—All those silly penalties that Park Hatfield has suffered this season? Consider him even now. That goal-scoring slump Jim Simpson was in? Consider it over.
	The Wolfpack's hulking center just about dislocated Slava Karenko's left shoulder with what looked like a textbook interference penalty midway through last night's third period. That unpenalized pancake block freed Simpson for a dash to the net that produced the rebound Hatfield flipped home for a tiebreaking goal in a 5–3 Wolfpack win over Kansas City.
	When Simpson completed his first hat trick of the season by converting a gorgeous pass from Ron Duchette with 1:54 left to seal the victory, the Wolfpack were back at the .500 mark for the first time since October 19. However, the night was not without its frightening downside for the Wolfpack: a defenseman left the arena walking with a cane after suffering a bruised tendon in his previously broken left ankle.
	"I don't think .500 is our goal, so I don't think we can be too proud of that," Wolfpack captain Wayne Trottier said. "I think what we are happy about is that we are playing better."
	Simpson in particular.
	Simpson has taken off in the two games since Brian Jones declared: "Jim has to pick it up."
	Asked if that was a coincidence, the smiling Simpson did not hesitate: "Yeah. I didn't change anything."
	Of course, the entire Rangers team remains quite uncomfortable holding third-period leads. And when Pete Connor scored a power-play goal 3:27 into the third, Kansas City had erased what once had been a 3–1 deficit, marking the fifth time in eight games the Wolfpack had blown a lead in the final 20 minutes.
	That's when Simpson, Hatfield and Ron Duchette went back to work.
	Hatfield's moving, resounding, unpenalized pick came moments after Simpson outraced Karenko to a puck in the right corner to nullify what would have been a Wolfpack icing.
	Simpson, who has five goals in his last two games after scoring just two in his previous 15, then held the puck long enough for his linemates Duchette and Steve Smith to head to the bench, allowing Hatfield to come on and join the tiebreaking play.

"Without a doubt, that was the play of the game," Jones said. "I thought Jim had just a lot of energy all night long."

Simpson also had a whopping nine shots on goal, and the ninth was as gorgeous a goal as you'll see—a flying conversion of a two-on-one rush with Duchette that caused a trickle and then a rain of hats to fall to the ice.

Table 3-3

Cont'd.

Game Day Sidebars

Sidebars are additional feature stories that accompany or complement the main game story. They are often done by the beat writer, but can also be written by a columnist or someone else who is writing to add more perspective and depth.

A sidebar can be on any number of issues related to the game, such as player profiles or fan interest. In some cases, these side issues are important enough to become the focus of the main story and push details of the game to the background. Consider someone who coached a particular team for more than 20 years before leaving to coach that team's main rival. When the coach returns to face his former team, it will likely become the most important theme of the game coverage. What happens in the game itself becomes secondary, unless the play is especially outstanding or unusual. There are other examples when side issues can become more important than the game, including instances where an important record is about to be broken. When Emmitt Smith of the Cowboys broke the all-time NFL rushing record in a game against Seattle, almost all the coverage focused on Smith, and not the fact that his team actually lost the game.

Sidebar stories are usually written and communicated more like features (see later in this chapter). They generally try to personalize sports issues and present them in a little softer light. Again, such stories are not limited to athletes and events, but can be about any number of things (Table 3-4).

Feature Reporting

When he passed away in 2002, Roone Arledge was eulogized as a man who revolutionized television sports. Arledge created *Monday Night Football*, worked on 10 Olympics, and won 36 Emmy Awards, but he also changed the way networks presented sports to the American public. His *Wide World of Sports* series, which started back in 1961, was the first attempt to move away from reporting results and focus more on the human element. Series host Jim McKay said Arledge pioneered the concept of "putting the focus on the human being involved in sports." More than any other person, Arledge pushed the sports media into a more feature-oriented presentation.

Table 3-4	The following is a typical sidebar story, this one related to our fictional hockey game.
Game Sidebar Story	(Tulsa)—Randy Thomas knew he would bring good luck to the Wolfpack and winger Jim Simpson, if only he could get to a game. After last night, Thomas might be in for season tickets.
	Thomas, a 9 year old from Tulsa, is a huge Simpson fan who wanted nothing more than to see the Wolfpack play in person. But between school, soccer practice and some family misfortune, Thomas had never been able to go. Somehow, word got back to Simpson, who provided tickets for Thomas and his family to last night's game. And coincidence or not, Simpson had his best game of the season, breaking out of a year-long slump by scoring a hat trick.
	"I may have to make sure he gets tickets to every game," Simpson joked afterwards. "I want to make sure my good-luck charm is here as much as possible."
	Thomas, who watched the game from a luxury box with his mother, father, and older brother, was obviously thrilled—not only to be at his first hockey game, but to know that he had helped his hero. After the third goal, it seemed he was going to jump right out of the box and down onto the ice.
	"I knew Jim would play great," he said, grinning from behind blue and silver face paint. "He's the best."
	The Wolfpack have a section called "Simpson's Seats," which lets thousands of underprivileged kids attend games. But apparently this was a special case, and a very special stroke of good fortune.
	"I happened to hear about Randy and thought maybe I could do something nice for him," said Simpson. "I guess it kind of worked out nice for me too."

Feature reporting is extremely essential in today's sports media environment. For one thing, sports media outlets are using good feature reporting to expand their audiences. People who don't have a "hard core" interest in sports and usually don't bother with the sports media may become consumers if they are presented with interesting stories. In addition, more sports reporters are realizing that good sports reporting is about people, not necessarily about games or scores.

Context

More than any other type of sports reporting, the feature relies heavily on context. Context is the way the story is framed and is what makes the story interesting, relevant, or important to the audience. Some stories can be framed around a human context, or in terms of individual emotions, actions, or ideals. Audiences respond to stories that have an interesting human context or, in other words, stories that focus on human qualities everyone can relate to and understand. In this way, the audience can identify with the story or the person in the story, even if there's no immediate or direct connection.

Olympic skater Dan Janssen became a national icon, not because of his skill or achievements on the ice, but because of his persistence in the face of seemingly insurmountable frustration. Audiences everywhere could identify with Janssen overcoming his sister's death and repeated on-ice stumbles to finally win a gold medal. It's should be noted that these common qualities do not always have to be admirable. Baseball great Ty Cobb was and is a fascinating story, even though he has universally been characterized as contemptible, mean-spirited, and abusive. Cobb becomes a much more sympathetic figure when told from the perspective of tragedy, that his father's accidental death pushed Cobb to greatness and, despite all his athletic success, Cobb was essentially friendless and died a lonely figure.

There are several qualities or contexts that can make sports stories more interesting. Tragedy, redemption, inspiration, and vindication are emotional qualities with which everyone can identify. Audiences can always identify with tragedy, often because they see so much of it in their everyday lives, and they can empathize with others in the same position, especially if it is undeserved. In his poignant account of how several black basketball players were unjustly shot by New Jersey police, Doug Most concludes with a quote from one of the players that all readers can understand: "I try to live my life as if it never happened, but then I see my friends playing ball, and I know I can't play, and it hits me. We went on this trip with high hopes and high dreams. You go to sleep in paradise and wake up in hell."

Redemption is also a powerful human context, one that is both easily understandable and universally shared. Audiences like to read about someone who has overcome repeated failure or tragedy—like Dan Janssen—because that person represents the triumph of the human spirit under difficult conditions. Woody Woodburn wrote a story about former Olympian Lou Zamperini called *The Toughest Miler Ever*. The story wasn't about Zamperini's Olympic experience, but rather his time in a Japanese labor camp during World War II. The appeal of the story is what Zamperini survived in life, not on the track.

Nostalgia is also very popular in today's culture, especially as the baby boomers grow older and move toward retirement. A nostalgic context can take many forms, including the reexamination of a specific event, game, or player. Sportswriter Roger Kahn's bestseller *The Boys of Summer* was a look back at the Brooklyn Dodgers of the 1950s and an update of their lives since that time. Dave Anderson did a similar treatment in *The Greatest Game Ever Played*, a revisiting of the 1958 NFL Championship between the Colts and the Giants. Anniversary stories are also quite common, especially on the 5th, 10th, 20th, or 25th anniversary of a particular game or event.

Nostalgia stories can also center on a particularly memorable individual or personality. One of the most popular pieces ever written by sportswriter Frank Deford was on "Bull" Sullivan, who coached junior college football in southern Mississippi. "What I had in mind was an anecdotal story about a very tough football coach—this huge ex-Marine, brutal, foul-mouthed, demanding, rough—almost a cliché," said Deford. "But when I began talking to people who knew him, I found out far more than I ever dreamed I would." Deford's story, which ran in *Sports Illustrated*, was not only a nostalgic recount of football in the old days, but it also showed a more sympathetic side of Sullivan.

Personalization

Deford's approach demonstrates the need of personalizing stories. Because good sports stories are essentially about people, write in a way to humanize the story and get away from focusing on the score. Focusing on people makes the story more appealing to the audience, which might not have any initial interest in the subject. From a strictly American perspective, very few people care about Olympic badminton, but they would be much more interested if a U.S. athlete was successful or had an interesting story to tell.

When photographer Brian Lanker was assigned to Deford's story on Bull Sullivan, he initially had reservations. After all, Sullivan didn't seem like a very appealing character. "When I started reading the story I didn't think I'd like Sullivan," Lanker said. "But I was pulled in by Frank's writing, and then I couldn't put the story down. I've read it six times now, and every time I finish it I have tears in my eyes."

Sometimes, stories have more of a social context than a human one, which is a way of saying that the people in the story aren't as important as the issue or situation they face. Good writers still tell stories through people, but if the social context has importance or significance, the people in the story are used to illustrate that fact. Even a story about a relatively famous athlete can still focus on the social context.

Stephen Rodrick's *Can Riddick Bowe Answer the Bell?* is a compelling account of the former heavyweight boxing champion. Rodrick calls Bowe a "lost soul," who has trouble finding himself after winning and then losing the heavyweight title. According to Rodrick, "He sluggishly shadowboxes in front of the television. 'I mean I've never done anything else. What else am I gonna do? Get a job?'" The story certainly makes Bowe into a sympathetic figure, but in a larger sense Rodrick could have written the story about any number of former fighters. The point is the social context, of getting too much too fast, and about how the promise of big money sports chews up and spits out so many athletes who don't prepare themselves to compete in life.

The wide variety of social issues attached to sports can provide social contexts for stories. Race, gender, and discrimination are certainly the most common, but there are many others. In *The Blessed Fisherman of Prosper, Texas*, Charles Pierce writes about Deion Sanders, one of the most magnetic sports personalities of recent times. But the story centers not on Sanders' "Prime Time" persona, but rather his conversion to fundamental Christianity. Pierce raises the issue of spiritual conversion in today's society and whether the much-publicized stories of changed lives are actually true. "This might be an act," he writes. "Might just be the Prime Time shuck again, the gold covered up now in choir robes. But watch him walk his land, and there is a peace, an ease, a kind of steady grace that might be theological and might not be."

One could argue that it's difficult to differentiate between a human and social context. Is Most's story an account of personal tragedy of young basketball players, is it an indictment of a legal system that unfairly discriminates based on race, or is it both? Pegging a story into one particular hole is not what's important, but rather providing that overall framework of personalization and context that draws the reader into the story. Some will look at Most's story as a personal tragedy, whereas others will view it as social injustice. The story compels on both levels.

Magazines

Sports magazines in the United States have almost as long a history as their newspaper counterparts. The first edition of *The Sporting News* was published by Alfred H. Spink and his brother Charles on March 17, 1886, in St. Louis. A total of 4986 issues of the weekly appeared with the Spink name at the top. The eight-page paper sold for five cents, or $2.50 per year, and featured news of baseball, cycling, hunting, boxing, and the stage.

Baseball dominated the printed sports media in the early years of the 20th century, and *The Sporting News* eventually became a baseball-only paper. It was also challenged by other competitors, including F.C. Lane's *Baseball Magazine.* Writing in 1915, editor F.C. Lane sounded much like today's writers when he addressed the situation of baseball economics, "It is a system which is universally inefficient and unsatisfactory, and costs an annual fortune."

Most sports magazines of the time focused on baseball or some similarly narrow field. The first attempts at a general-appeal sports magazine took place in the 1930s and 40s, but failed. Finally in 1954, *Time* editor Henry Luce believed the time was right for *Sports Illustrated*, which he claimed was "not *a* sports magazine, but *the* sports magazine." *Sports Illustrated* premiered on August 16, 1954, and capitalized on an explosion of interest in sports across the country.

At first, the magazine had more of an appeal to upscale audiences by focusing on such events as yachting and polo. But eventually SI found a large audience through a combination of large, color photographs and in-depth writing. Writers such as Roger Kahn, Robert Creamer, and Dan Jenkins gave the magazine a unique identity that helped legitimize sports journalism. Today, *Sports Illustrated* has more than 23 million readers and 3 million subscribers, making it the third-highest circulation magazine in the United States. It has also spawned several media ventures, including *Sports Illustrated for Kids* and *Sports Illustrated on Campus*. Its annual swimsuit issue is presented across several media, including magazine, television, and home video.

Despite the historical success of *Sports Illustrated*, there are troubling signs for national, mass audience sports magazines. *Sport* magazine competed with *Sports Illustrated* for awhile in the 1970s, but eventually was shut down. *The National Sports Daily* lasted a very short time in the early 1990s, despite having as its editor Frank Deford, one of the most respected sports magazine writers in the country. National sports magazines have a slim shot at survival because they buck the two biggest trends in today's magazine industry—media integration and niche publishing.

Sports Magazines: Past, Present, and Future

Angela Renkoski (Figure 3-2) worked at Meredith Corporation for nearly 10 years with a variety of magazines and continues to do freelance magazine work. She teaches

Figure 3-2

Angela Renkoski, Drake University.

magazine editing and production at Drake University and heads that school's magazine internship program with Meredith.

Q: *Have sports magazines changed drastically in the last 15–20 years or so, and, if so, how?*

A: Yes, because society has changed drastically in that time period and those changes are reflected in the pages of our sports magazines. They center on the dramatic increase in sports viewing (and, it must be said, sports betting), especially for the major sports; society's altered perception of sports as entertainment; and our nation's rampant love affair with celebrities. These show up in certain modifications in formula and content. However, two big developments for the sports magazine industry are worth noting.

One remarkable change is having more than one strong national sports magazine— three, in fact, that appear to have the staying power to succeed long-term (*Sports Illustrated, The Sporting News,* and *ESPN: The Magazine*).

Conversely, the other notable development is the proliferation of niche titles. In addition to the magazines focusing on the individual major sports we might naturally think of are plenty of magazines touting the joys of participation in other sporting activities. The largest categories are hunting and fishing with 157 magazines and outdoor recreation with 91 titles. Skiing and winter sports lists 61 titles, field sports has 51, water sports has 37, and contact sports, 20. There are 72 titles under golf, 29 titles under guns and shooting, and 24 for bicycling. Specialty sports boasts 28 titles, including ones on bowling, paragliding, and professional bull riding.

The circulation for these magazines ranges from the tens of thousands to the millions, with most in the less-than-100,000 category and many less than 50,000. They blossom due to devoted readers willing to pay premium subscription rates and with advertising related to the particular sport or activity. Niche publications also flourish because new sports are created or gain a following or some technological advance in equipment all the time, so there's always a need for a magazine to fit a new need.

Q: *Do sports magazines today have a specific "philosophy?" Do they emphasize visuals, written content, etc.?*

A: For the general interest titles, the philosophy is visual format and entertainment (lists, polls, tidbits), with an emphasis on the individual over the team. The emphasis on the visual comes at the expense of copy. Stories across the board have gotten shorter and more compartmentalized and are more likely to be accompanied with large visuals. In the extreme, all the information is conveyed in a caption placed on one large photo, with perhaps an inset close-up photo. The emphasis on entertaining the reader and presenting sports as entertainment in magazines are in part functions of the reduced attention span in younger readers and the ubiquitous nature of television, sports talk radio, and the Internet.

For the niche magazines, the philosophy centers on gear and reader participation. New products, product reviews, and any type of gear associated with a sport or activity are the bread and butter of most niche publications. At the very least they're a staple part of the formula. Another of the traditional functions of magazines is to form a community of like interests. This is especially true of niche publications, which is why you can find your true golf soul mates in one of the 72 titles covering your exact interest and feel for the game. As part of the community feel, the niche publications are selling and conveying not just the sport but a whole lifestyle associated with the activity.

Q: How important are these "niche" audiences to sports magazines? Are general interest magazines like SI on the road to extinction?

A: Niche audiences appear to supplement the general interest sports magazines, not directly compete with them. People who are passionate about a sport are passionate about reading about that sport and the people in it. They want tips on how to do it better, how to get in better shape to participate, and how to buy the best and newest gear, and they want inspiration and knowledge from the people excelling at it. So niche and general interest titles are not mutually exclusive.

Niche publications are so different from the general interest titles and serve such a different purpose that they are not sounding the death knell for the general interest magazines but may represent a more symbiotic relationship.

Q: Are sports magazines facing the same pressures (profit emphasis, move toward entertainment) as other media?

A: One of the big pressures is to hook young (20- to 34-year-old) readers and keep them. Another big pressure, especially for the general interest titles, is to increase return on investment (ROI) and return on equity (ROE), so the magazines produce bigger dividends for their corporate owners' shareholders. As larger corporations buy up more magazines, this becomes more of a concern. Even niche titles, such as *Bicycling* and *Backpacker*, which are owned by Rodale, and *Boating*, which is owned by Hachette Filipacchi Media U.S., fall into this category.

Similarly, this pressure calls for increases in revenue from advertising. *SI*'s circulation revenue in 2003 was nearly half (45%) the amount of its advertising revenue. For *ESPN*, the discrepancy is wider: Its advertising revenue for the same year was more than four times its circulation revenue. *TSN* makes more money from circulation, so its advertising revenue was only two-thirds the amount of its ad revenue. With that much financial influence, the pressure on editorial has to be great.

This pressure translates into a blurring of the line between advertising and editorial, to the point where most sports magazines demonstrate a disquieting coziness with their advertisers. Despite the proliferation of these ad-edit conflicts, sports magazines don't appear to be in danger of harming their credibility. Perhaps readers have gotten so used to seeing ads all over stadiums and arenas, noting ads on uniforms, having bowl games and replays and key stats and other segments on TV "sponsored" by a company, that reading ads plastered all over the pages of their sports magazines no longer fazes them. It seems likely this slope, now that it's slippery, is not likely to dry up or flatten out soon.

Niche Magazines

A publication like *Sports Illustrated* has survived because of its presence across media platforms. SI no longer exists as solely a magazine, but also as a producer of home videos and television shows, a sports marketer, and through its own Web site. Teaming up with cable giant CNN, *cnnsi.com* has more than tripled its audience to 10 million per month, racking up 230 million page views in September 2003. In a similar fashion, *ESPN: The Magazine* is but one part of the growing ESPN empire. Launched in 1998, the magazine claims a readership of nearly two million. But it's also connected to ESPN's 32 broadcast entities, a radio network, and numerous other media enterprises (see Chapter 1).

In today's media environment, ESPN and *Sports Illustrated* use their magazines in a coordinated effort to increase audiences for all their media outlets. *ESPN: The Magazine* includes writing and analysis from many of the broadcast network's highly visible anchors, such as Dan Patrick and Stuart Scott. The content in the magazine interconnects with ESPN's other media platforms, encouraging readers to watch ESPN networks, listen to ESPN radio, eat at ESPN restaurants, and buy ESPN clothes. Thus, while the content in the magazine is "original," it is also clearly branded with the corporate identity.

While more and more sports magazines have some sort of Internet presence, it is not necessarily a requirement for success. Many have carved out a successful niche by catering to specialized groups, which is almost essential given the growth in media options and the fragmentation of today's audiences. The general interest sports magazine has given way to a highly specialized and specifically targeted publication, usually based on the type of sports or interest involved (Table 3-5).

Table 3-5 is by no means comprehensive—there are more categories and probably dozens more entries in each category. But it does give you some idea of how today's sports magazines target very specific audiences. Sometimes, there are niches within niches, as witnessed by the number of fishing magazines. *Bassin', Fly Tyer,* and *Marlin* all appeal to different groups of fisherman trying to catch very different kinds of fish.

Content

In terms of creating content for today's sports magazines, the stories are usually long and very detailed, given the nature of the audiences. Niche audiences have an understanding of their sport that allows the writer to go into much greater depth than someone writing for the sports section of the daily newspaper. The writer assumes that the reader will understand the technical jargon and strategic nuances associated with the activity. Consider the list of articles from the May 2003 issue of *Bowling Center Management*: "Do It Yourself: Lighting Layout," "Financing Basics: Know Thy

Table 3-5	**Sport or Interest Group**	**Magazine Titles**
Targeted Sports Magazines	Fishing	*American Angler, Bassin', Fly Fisherman, Fly Tyer, Marlin, Sport Fishing*
	Off-road racing	*ATV Magazine, ATV Sport, Dirt Rider, Mountain Biking, Ride BMX*
	Guns and shooting	*American Handgunner, Guns Magazine, Gun Ammunition Magazine, Sporting Gun*
	Hunting	*Field & Stream, Bowhunter, Bowhunting, Gun Dog, Hunting*
	Bowling	*Bowling Digest, Bowling This Month, Bowling World, Bowling Center Management*
	Extreme outdoor sports	*Crossfire Paintball Digest, Action Pursuit Games, Paintball 2 Xtremes, Shark Diver, Skydiving, Windsurfing*
	Golf	*Golf, Golf Digest, Golf for Women, Travel & Leisure Golf, Golf World, Golf Tips*
	Martial arts	*Inside Kung-Fu, Filipino Martial Arts, Martial Arts Magazine, Martial Arts World*
	Automobiles and racing	*Muscle Mustangs and Fast Fords, American Thunder, Speedway Illustrated, Grassroots Motorsports, National Speed Sport News*
	Other outdoor sports	*Boating, Bicycling, Canoe & Kayak, Climbing Runner's World, Sailing World, Salt Water Sportsman, Powder, Shooting Sportsman, Skateboarding, Snowboarder, Surfing, Trapper & Predator Caller, Waterski*

Banker," and "Equipment Leasing Techniques" all assume a certain level of knowledge and sophistication on the part of the reader.

In cases where magazine articles introduce readers to new subjects or characters, there is still much more depth of reporting and story development. The very nature of the magazine format allows writers to create longer pieces and to go into greater detail in terms of personalization and character development. Deford's story on Bull Sullivan is a good example, and it ran for 16 pages. Otherwise, the development and writing of feature stories for magazines are not that much different than other print forms, in that it relies heavily on human and social context.

The role of the sports magazine continues to evolve in today's changing media environment, but while it can certainly carve out a profitable niche, it's likely that the sports magazine will never again have the level of prominence it did during the heyday of *Sports Illustrated*. Even the mighty *SI* has taken on its share of critics in recent years, including Michael MacCambridge, who wrote a definitive history of the magazine in 1997. According to MacCambridge, *SI* lost its editorial edge, moving away from important stories on drugs and violence and focusing more on entertainment and commercial opportunism. Where *SI* once featured groundbreaking stories such as the role of the black athlete, it now puts more emphasis on its swimsuit issue or giving away free trinkets for buying a subscription. The change lays not so much with *Sports Illustrated*, or sports magazines in general, but with the economic and technological realities of the modern media industry (Figures 3-3 and 3-4).

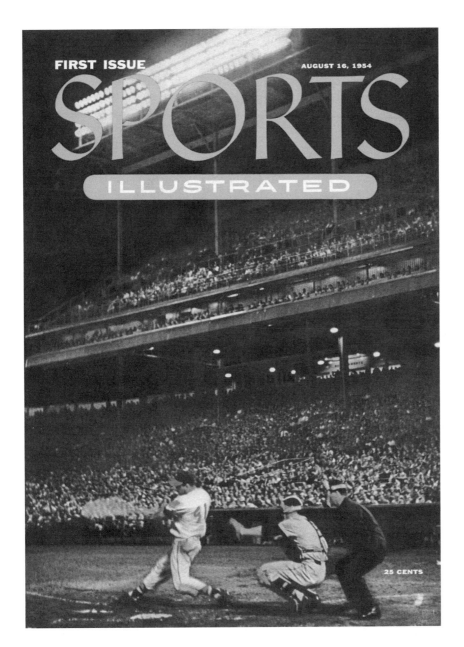

Figure 3.3 and 3.4

Then and now; the very
first issue of *Sports
Illustrated* from 1954
and a 2004 version.

Figure 3.3 and 3.4

Cont'd.

Sports Magazines with *Sports Illustrated*

Sports Illustrated recently celebrated its 50th anniversary and is probably the most widely read and influential sports magazine in U.S. history. David Bauer, *SI*'s deputy managing editor, is responsible for issue planning, story topics, and page layouts. Jeff Price is vice president and chief marketing officer and has complete responsibility for all of the magazine's marketing functions.

Q: Sports Illustrated has been the gold standard for sports magazines over the years. What has made it so successful, and why has it continued to flourish while so many others have failed?

BAUER: First of all, I think *SI* has a very clear understanding of its readers; we know who they are and what they expect of us, but at the same time we know how to surprise them and challenge them. I think the strength of that two-way relationship is the core of our ongoing success. Second, we are always willing to report the truth about sports, warts and all, and that forms an important and lasting part of our reputation; *SI* has often been described as "the conscience of sport" and I think that's an apt description. Third, we have always been and continue to be a well-written magazine and our readers know it and appreciate it; *SI* is in the business of telling stories, and with a staff of writers that is the best in that business, we think we do it better than anyone.

Q: We've seen stylistic changes to the magazine in the past several years. What other significant changes has SI made in terms of approach, audience, management, and the like?

BAUER: With the evolution of sports media, especially television, and the 24/7 sports information overload, the magazine has had to become less retrospective about the week in sports, and more anticipatory. We've had to be sure that our stories analyze more deeply or expound more expansively or interpret more surprisingly than other media. And to some degree we have broadened our own horizons as to what constitutes an *SI* story. Can a chess match make a sports story? We would say yes.

PRICE: On the business side, we've done a great job at maintaining our overall audience and growing our key demographic—young men. We continue to deliver more young men than virtually any other media vehicle. We're strengthening those demos and extending our brand through vibrant outlets like SI.com and SI on Campus.

Q: It seems like the trend today is more toward specific-interest sports magazine rather than general-interest magazines. Is that a concern for SI and what, if anything, is the magazine doing about it?

BAUER: It's not a concern at all. *SI* is a weekly sports newsmagazine, and as such it remains unique, with its own very large niche. Most sports fans have, and have always had, multiple sports interests and *SI* is the only magazine that services that fan on a weekly basis. At the same time, we recognize areas of special interest within our readership, which has led to the creations of special sections. SI Golf Plus, for example, carries the best weekly coverage in the industry, is published 40 times per year, and is sent to 500,000 subscribers who are avid golfers. *SI* Adventure is a monthly section that profiles adventure and outdoor sports for 450,000 *SI* subscribers that participate in multiple outdoor sports.

Q: We hear a lot about "convergence" in today's media. How important is that to SI? What is the magazine's role in terms of its relationship with the Web site, the home video department, etc.

PRICE: As we continue to build the overall *SI* brand, elements such as SI.com and our TV relationships are key. SI.com's editorial operations were moved to New York from Atlanta to more closely align that coverage and commentary with the magazine. TV partnerships that we have developed around properties such as sportsman of the year, the swimsuit issue, and major preview issues such as the NFL, college football, and baseball all contribute to bringing this well-known magazine brand to life in other media.

Q: Michael MacCambridge wrote a history of the magazine in 1997 and said that it had lost its editorial edge, and now focuses more on commercialism and entertainment. How do you respond to that?

BAUER: If commercialism in this context means "what sells," then, yes, of course *Sports Illustrated* is guilty of commercialism. No successful magazine can ignore its market. But I would suggest that our editorial decisions are based much less on "what sells" than on "what will impact our readers." As for the notion that *SI* is more focused on entertainment, I don't see that as a negative. Sports in 2004 is entertainment. Moreover, our readers expect to be entertained by our unique coverage of sports. This is not to suggest that sports is only entertainment; *SI*, we think, continues to set the agenda for debate on the significant social and ethical issues facing the sports world. As one example (and not an isolated one), our groundbreaking report on steroids in baseball led to public outcry, Congressional hearings, and changes regarding drug testing in major league baseball's current collective bargaining agreement. *SI* consistently publishes stories that challenge conventional thinking and misguided behavior in the world of sports. As mentioned before, we consider that an important part of our reputation and our readers consider it an important part of what they pay for.

Because sports is by definition meant to be playful, *Sports Illustrated* also seeks to entertain. *SI*'s writers long ago mastered the use of humor, irony, and passion in their stories. That continues today in the varied talents of writers such as Rick Reilly, Gary Smith, Steve Rushin, and Frank Deford.

The Print Experience

This chapter has focused more on specific types and styles of writing, whereas Chapter 2 concentrated more on an overall approach to sports reporting. Taken together, they should give you a general idea of how to create content for a print sports outlet.

While these things are important, there's so much more that goes into sports reporting. A good print reporter is an investigator, a researcher, a craftsman, and, yes, even a performer. Today's print reporter is also well read on a variety of subjects beyond sports, including the law, politics, and culture. All of these things come into play when writing a story or creating sports media content.

Print Reporting with Howard Schlossberg

Howard Schlossberg (Figure 3-5) is on the faculty of the journalism department at Columbia College in Chicago, where he coordinates the sports reporting sequence of courses within the news reporting and writing track and also coordinates print internships. He is also a sports correspondent for the *Daily Herald* newspapers, where he covers prep sports. Schlossberg is the author of the book *Sports Marketing*, published in 1996.

Q: What does it take to be a good print sports reporter?
A: Young reporters must go to an event prepared: know the players, the coaches, the records, the impact of the game upon the standings, the history of the rivalry, and the intangibles, the things that can't be measured. For instance, the impact of a player returning from injury or acquired in a trade, or at the prep or college level, coming back from a suspension or just having transferred in. In other words, as a prepared reporter, you should have some of your postgame questions ready even before the game.

All games are different, but have the same elements, from hero to goat, from winner to loser, to the big play that turned the game. Your job is being able to observe them and sort them in order of importance and to be able to report them to the fans who otherwise might not have noticed them at the game or on TV. People who wanted to know what happened went to the game or watched it on TV. Your job is to tell the people who didn't go or watch what they missed while still telling the people who did go or watched why they saw what they did and how it happened.

There really isn't much difference in reporting on the Super Bowl or a high school game. OK, the audience is larger. But the basics of reporting apply. Who did what, why, and how. Always remember the six Ws and H: who, what, where, when, why, how, and what's next. The latter is critical, especially in sports, because every game, every event, has a shakeout that will impact the team and the fans down the road.

Figure 3-5

Howard Schlossberg.

OK, the Super Bowl will have more stories, more "sidebars" featuring materials you can't fit in at length in your game story, but even a high school championship game will have those.

Q: *What does convergence mean to print reporters?*

A: The medium has evolved over the years and so has the role of the reporter. The basic reportorial skills and news judgments are still paramount, as is superior writing ability. These days though, you still have to keep in mind the business end of the deal—that your writing has to help sell papers—and that the outlet you work for just may have a business relationship or even a common ownership with broadcast outlets for which your reporting skills may be called upon. Some days you have to decide if you're a cheerleader or a reporter, or if you're a gossip columnist or a reporter. And the way things are heading, you'll have to decide what you're going to write in print and what you're going to say on the air.

Many writers today flip back and forth between broadcast and print. You only need look to ESPN to see that so many of the reporters and anchors who show up regularly on its programming also have gigs as newspaper columnists and reporters around the country, if not on espn.com or in *ESPN: The Magazine* at the most-visible levels, where sports reporters are as much celebrities sometimes as the athletes.

These can be delicate situations though. Many print outlets enjoy having their reporters on the air for the exposure and awareness they bring, but will often restrict them to not breaking news on the air that they otherwise would've published in one of their stories or columns. And you have to remember broadcast is live. You can edit your copy in print, but once said into the microphone, it's "out there." Just ask Bob Ryan of the *Boston Globe*, whose disparaging comment about New Jersey Nets star Jason Kidd's wife on a local Boston talk show got him a suspension from the paper and a temporary disappearing act on the ESPN programming he often graced with his sharp, biting humor.

Clearly though, sports writers are becoming broadcast stars on an increasing basis, so knowing broadcast style is starting to become paramount, even for writers who think they'll never do TV and don't want to. They could wake up tomorrow morning finding out their newspaper is now owned by a broadcast conglomerate that wants them to contribute on the air whether they want to or not. The ever increasing rate of media consolidation via mergers and acquisitions and the Federal Communication Commission's increasing slant toward favoring such speaks to this decision falling in your lap sooner than later.

Print reporting hasn't changed just because there's an Internet now that allows instant access to information. Instant access only means the ability to make "instant mistakes." You still have to check out everything. If your mother tells you she loves you, get corroboration. If she tells you over the Internet, get it checked twice. Be a good reporter and the technology will take care of itself. The technology is just a way to transmit or gather information more quickly. Your writing style is your writing style. Develop it, hone it, and then let the technology take it for a ride. Don't make it your goal to be a sports "blogger," free of editing and free to write whatever you want. Being a good reporter is the first qualification of being a good "blogger."

You will be expected to contribute to more than one platform as you go through your career, so be sure to be familiar with them. Just because you want to be a print reporter so bad nothing else matters, you'll wake up one morning and find out your paper is now part of a conglomerate that wants your contributions to its web sites, magazines and broadcast outlets, not just its newspaper. Take that extra broadcast writing class. It'll pay off by the time you get to ESPN.

Q: Why is it important for a sports reporter to go "outside the lines" and know more than just sports?

67

A: Let's say you're sitting in the press box at what is now U.S. Cellular Field in Chicago and out on the field runs a man and his son, and they mug the Kansas City Royals first base coach.

It's the eighth inning of a meaningless late-season game. And now you're not a sports reporter anymore. You are a crime reporter, dealing with the police, ballpark and Major League Baseball security and eyewitnesses ranging from fans in the stands to the players themselves. Hopefully, you paid attention in basic journalism class when crime reporting was covered because there's no time to refer to the textbook now.

While that situation really occurred in Chicago, real crime reporting for sports writers is fast becoming a reality. Which athlete got arrested today? For what? Drug possession? Illegal weapons possession? Drug trafficking? Drunk driving? Heavens forbid, murder? And don't think it's only on the professional side. College and high school sports increasingly cross these boundaries. You'd better know the law because you're going to be reporting about it, working with it. And you'd better know contract and labor law. The next strike or lockout, or player holdout, is always just around the corner.

Media relations? No, not the kind where you ask the team publicity agent to arrange an interview for you, but the kind where you talk about how the media rights' fees impact player salaries and owner revenues. Construction? Yeah, that too. The number of new stadiums that have been built or are being built around the country is staggering and so is the amount of both private and public money being spent on them. You'd better know how to discuss their impact on the finances of the games and the teams' relationships with their communities.

What's outside the lines today is as increasingly important to sports writing as the games are themselves. You'll find that out the first time you're interviewing a police detective instead of a ballplayer, a politician instead of a coach, or an attorney instead of a manager. It's why as a sports writer, your byline is likely to show up in the news or business section sometimes and why the line between sports and mainstream news is graying.

References

Arledge brought modern innovations to TV sports. (2002, December 2). *ESPN.* http://espn.go.com/classic/obit/NEWarledgeobit.html

Bowling Center Management. (2003, May). http://www.bcmmag.com/insidebcm/

Corporate fact sheet. (2004). *ESPN.* http://sports.espn.go.com/espn/news/story?page=corporatefactsheet

Lane, F.C. (1915, February). Baseball management that costs a fortune. *Baseball Magazine.* http://www.geocities.com/redsoxfan_02269/1915.2baseballmanagement.htm

MacCambridge, Michael. (1997). *The franchise: a history of Sports Illustrated magazine.* New York: Hyperion.

Miller, Robert L. (1984, April 30). Letter from the publisher. *Sports Illustrated,* p. 4.

Most, Doug. (2001). *Shot through the heart.* The Best American Sports Writing. Boston: Houghton-Mifflin.

Pierce, Charles F. (2001). *The blessed fisherman of Prosper, Texas.* The Best American Sports Writing. Boston: Houghton-Mifflin.

Rodrick, Stephen. (2001). *Can Riddick Bowe answer the bell?* The Best American Sports Writing. Boston: Houghton-Mifflin.

Sports Illustrated. (2004, July 29). *Wikipedia Encyclopedia.* http://en.wikipedia.org/wiki/Sports_Illustrated

Sports Illustrated. (2004). *Sports Illustrated.* http://sportsillustrated.cnn.com/adinfo/

The Sporting News. (2004). *Baseballlibrary.com.* http://www.baseballlibrary.com/baseballlibrary/ballplayers/T/The_Sporting_News.stm

Turano, Cara. (2001). *The rise of intercollegiate football and its portrayal in American popular literature.* Paper presented at the Center for Undergraduate Research Opportunities Symposium, Athens, GA.

Woodburn, Woody. (2001). *The toughest miler ever.* The Best American Sports Writing. Boston: Houghton-Mifflin.

4 Broadcast

In many respects, writing for sports broadcasting is the same as writing for print because most of the same basics apply. Broadcasters cover game stories with the same things in mind—giving audiences the important details about who won and who played well. In terms of feature reporting, broadcasters should also look for important human or social contexts around which to build their stories. The same guidelines of interviewing discussed in Chapter 2 apply to broadcasters as well.

However, there are some obvious stylistic differences between print and broadcast. While print reporters mainly concern themselves with words, broadcasters must take into consideration words, video, and sound. The effort of combining these elements into a coherent whole makes the broadcast story a different animal. It also requires that the sports reporter use some unique approaches. When creating broadcast content, reporters should consider the following strategies.

Writing Strategies

Active Voice

This is one of the basic commandments of broadcast writing, but one of the most ignored. Basically, beware of the verb "to be," which typically indicates the passive voice, because it suggests that something is being done to the subject, rather than the subject doing something. You should always try to write that the "player caught the ball," rather than "the ball *was* caught by the player." Active voice is shorter, more conversational, and more ideally suited to writing about sports action (think of the impact of such words as "slammed," "knocked," or "flattened"). Writing in active voice is easy, but is often ignored because it takes a little more time and creativity. The easiest way to convert to active voice is simply to turn around the sentence:

Passive: The game was over by halftime.

Active: The Lakers ended the game by halftime.

In situations where you can't turn the sentence around, you can change the verb:

Passive: LeBron James was in Chicago today.

Active: LeBron James visited Chicago today.

In such situations, remember that changing the verb should not change the meaning of the sentence. It's also permissible in broadcasting writing to simply drop the verb:

Passive: The Cowboys were busy in the draft today.

Active: The Cowboys busy in the draft today.

In some rare situations, it's simpler and easier to leave the passive alone, especially when trying to change it to active convolutes and confuses the meaning. But in most situations, using active voice makes for better, more memorable, and more conversational writing.

Grammar

With a few minor exceptions, such as the ones noted earlier, writing for sports broadcasting should follow the rules of basic grammar. That means proper sentence structure, style, and word usage. Some of the more common mistakes made by sports broadcasters include:

- Pronoun agreement. The pronoun must agree with the subject, which can cause a lot of confusion.

  Wrong: Pittsburgh has the ball on their 20-yard line.

  Right: Pittsburgh has the ball on *its* 20-yard line.

  Always remember that a team, group, or city referred to as a singular is an "it." More than one player, team, or group is a "their or they" ("The Steelers have the ball on *their* 20-yard line").

- Attribution. Attribution always goes first in broadcast writing, while newspaper writing puts it second. Since the listener or viewer only gets one chance to hear the information, it's important to know who's saying it.

  Wrong: The Rangers need a complete overhaul in the off-season, according to general manager Glen Sather.

  Right: General manager Glen Sather says the Rangers need a complete overhaul in the off-season.

  In the first sentence, the listener can't immediately tell who has the opinion and might attribute it to the sports anchor.

Words and Numbers

Keep in mind that you're trying to communicate a story or idea. Using words the audience doesn't know or understand slows down and impedes the communication process. This isn't a call for simplistic or monosyllabic words, but merely a reminder that your writing will really hit home when the audience knows exactly what you're trying to say.

Wrong: Experts say Ravens linebacker Ray Lewis prevaricated to police.

Right: Experts say Ravens linebacker Ray Lewis lied to police.

Wrong: Greg Maddux will make $11,555,432 this season.

Right: Greg Maddux will make more than eleven and a half million dollars this season.

Is it really important to know exactly how much money Greg Maddux makes or is it more likely that too many numbers and figures will simply confuse the audience? Is it better to say that Howard Cosell was erudite or that he was well educated and well spoken? Ironically, Cosell's use of big, complicated words may have been a factor in why so many viewers disliked him. And while it may have been part of Cosell's act, in general, talking down to an audience is disrespectful and ineffective.

Simplicity

It's not just a matter of simple words, but using them in the right way. Too many writers try to get too complicated, with the result that the viewer suffers from information overload. Baseball author Bob Marshall points out the difference between fellow baseball writers Roger Angell and Roger Kahn. "Angell's stock-in-trade is the five-comma sentence. There is usually a clause of explanation and a clause of history that is more important than the verb. Where Angell's sentences are languid and lazy, Kahn's are short, choppy and dripping with drama."

Angell: "The umpires, who were on strike for higher wages last spring, worked the spring games as usual this year, but some of them appeared to be feeling a mite irritable for the preseason, when games are conducted in a lighthearted, almost offhand fashion."

Khan: "On a warm August night, in a southern Ontario town called Guelph, a dozen Americans are playing hockey. There are no commercial interruptions. There is no crowd. We begin, George and I, to define sport."

While Roger Angell is a delight to read, his style does not translate well to broadcasting because it would overwhelm the audience. Instead, sports broadcasters should strive for Roger Kahn's sense of economy and simplicity.

Solid Reporting

Good writing starts with good reporting and often a poor final product is simply a lack of basic reporting skills. "(You need) to have an idea of how to write, how to write quickly and how to write succinctly on deadline," says the NFL Network's Rich Eisen. "It also promotes attention to detail, and gives you a basic repertoire and background—how to seek out sources, checking sources."

In 1993, the University of Miami (Florida) conducted a survey of daily newspaper sports editors. While the survey did not specifically include sports broadcasters, its findings certainly apply to the overall sports media industry. Respondents strongly encouraged the importance of the "five W's" associated with basic newswriting. "Kids are coming out of school who don't learn the language," said Paul Anger, executive sports editor of the *Miami Herald*. "I think that journalism schools need to emphasize that (we) need people who are willing to get news no matter what" (Figure 4-1).

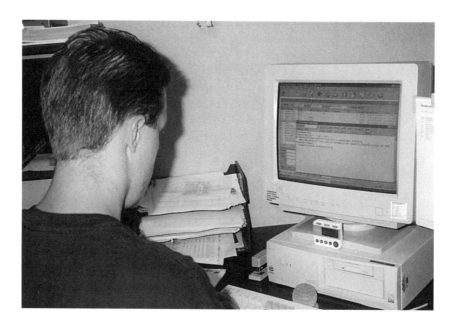

Figure 4-1

Technology has made the broadcast writing process easier, but not necessarily better.

Broad Education

A typical college student interested in sports media probably has a tremendous knowledge of sports. He or she probably became a fan at a very young age, and perhaps played sports as well. But too many students make the mistake of thinking that a tremendous knowledge of sports will translate into good sports broadcasting. Without a doubt, sports broadcasters have to know about the sports they cover. But the sports media now encompass a wide variety of topics, including drugs, crime, race, politics, law, and religion. Simply put, sports broadcasters can't write effectively if they don't know anything about these other areas. "Every year, sports reporters become more diversified," says Anger. "They have to be more well-rounded than any other journalist. They must be critics, reporters, and feature writers."

Men such as Cosell, Jack Whitaker, and Jim McKay succeeded as sports journalists because of their interest and background in other areas. Such interests add an important depth and knowledge to your sports writing.

Creativity and Originality

Many of today's problems with writing are due to a lack of effort on the part of the writer. It's much simpler and faster (especially when facing a deadline) to recycle old material than to come up with something new. That's why the audience hears so many sports cliches (Table 4-1).

Creativity does not necessarily mean going over the top. Some simple creative ideas include doing a story in rhyme, using more alliteration, or remembering the "rule of threes." Which of the following sounds more appealing?

"The Cougars showed a lot of poise in their win over Central."
"The calm and collected Cougars showed a lot of poise."

There are literally hundreds of ways to make your writing more exciting and interesting. Just make sure that whatever you do fits in with the general mood and tone of the story. Certain types of writing are inappropriate for certain types of stories, such as taking a light-hearted approach to a very serious story. But in general, don't be afraid to experiment. Creative writing isn't limited to feature stories.

Personalization

We will make the point throughout this book that all stories are essentially about people. Sports stories are not so much about games, championships, or records as

Table 4-1	Cliché	Comments
Sports Cliches to Avoid[a]	1. "Shock the world"	Note to players, broadcasters, and sportswriters: Most of the world isn't aware, and doesn't care.
	2. "He's got to step up now"	We've been keeping track of "step up," or trying to—its use is so common that we stopped counting at, about, a zillion.
	3. "He's got a great work ethic"	An insult to factory workers, farmers, coal miners, small businessmen, and millions of others who bust their butts every day just to make ends meet.
	4. "You can feel the electricity . . ."	
	5. "They have to generate some offense"	Here's a question: Can you "generate some defense"?
	6. "Statistics can be misleading"	Real meaning: "It doesn't make sense that this team is winning (or losing). But I can't tell you why."
	7. "They know how to win"	It means, simply, they've won in the past. Also: Is it ever possible for a team to "know how to win," but still be losers, simply because they don't have the talent?
	8. "They have to come together as a team"	Usually uttered, sans real analysis, when a team isn't playing well for many different reasons.
	9. "They've got great team chemistry"	No evidence whatsoever that, if such a thing exists, it makes much of a difference.
	10. "You can't say enough about him"	Real meaning: "I've already said as much as I know about him, and repeated it many times over. Now my producer is telling me to shut up."

[a]This list comes straight from ESPN (*espn.com*), which is probably guilty of creating (or at least overusing) many of them.

they are about the people involved. Your writing should not only focus on the people involved, but it should connect to the people in the audience. Why should the people sitting at home care about this story? What does it mean to them? Write *about* the people behind the events, and write *for* the people watching at home.

Using Sound

One of the most common mistakes young sports broadcasters make is to write too much. They feel like they have to analyze every play, describe every piece of video, and explain every sound bite. Remember, in television and radio the words are only one component of the overall presentation. Think of your story as a recipe, with the words as one of the ingredients, along with sound, pictures, and graphics. Sometimes, you need to use more words and other times, hardly any at all.

In general, pictures and sounds have more impact than words. So when you have very strong video and audio, keep your writing to a minimum and let the other elements tell the story. When your sound and pictures are poor, you'll have to write more to compensate.

Consider a story on a local high school soccer game. If there is an especially dramatic game-winning goal followed by a celebration, you really don't need to write a lot of description; let the video tell the story. But if the game is more mundane and the video unexciting, it may need more help from your writing. If the sound and pictures are especially good, you might consider a natural sound piece and eliminate the narration. It proves very effective to let the subjects tell the story in their own words.

Natural sound is the sound that occurs "naturally" at the scene of any story. For a football game it could be the roaring crowds or marching bands. At a golf match, it's the long periods of silence followed by cheers or groans. Natural sound (or "nat sound") has become much more important over the years in electronic sports reporting. Up until a few years ago, most sports reporters ignored nat sound and instead used canned music or just plain silence. But later generations of reporters and news directors realized that natural sound could make or break a story. The cheers of a crowd, the smash of a hockey player hitting the boards, or the sound of the water splashing when a diver hits a perfect dive all contribute to the scene and the mood of the story. Modern-day reporting involves taking occasional pauses to let the nat sound come up to full volume. Just as good play-by-play men pause after a dramatic moment so listeners can hear the crowd, so too can the sports reporter use nat sound in putting together the daily story.

Occasionally, the broadcast reporter has such dramatic video and natural sound that he or she decides to use them exclusively and without any narration. Such pieces can be more effective than the run-of-the-mill story, but the reporter should take caution in such situations. If you have good video and good nat sound, there's no harm in emphasizing them. But such stories are very difficult and shouldn't be done often without a lot of experience in the basics of reporting and editing. There's nothing better than a dramatic "sound and pictures" piece when it's done right, but there's also nothing worse when it's done wrong. As with any reporting or editing technique, nat sound should usually be used in moderation or it distracts from the message the reporter wants to communicate. Never forget you're trying to communicate a story or idea to the audience, and you shouldn't use any technique that takes away from that (Figure 4-2).

Outside Elements

Things such as music, graphics, and standups can really help your writing, but should be used with caution. Any of these outside elements should only be considered if they add something to the story. For example, many sportscasters have gotten in the habit

Figure 4-2

The challenge of broadcasting writing is properly incorporating and editing together all elements, including video, sound bites, and natural sound.

of putting a music track under highlights or in feature stories. Many times, music can add a lot to the story, but more often than not, it becomes a distraction. But by far the biggest offender is the standup.

A standup is a short video segment where the reporter appears on camera at the scene of a story. Too many sports reporters fall into the trap of putting a standup into every story. There can be a variety of reasons for this—it could be a matter of station policy, the reporter is too lazy do the extra writing, or he or she simply wants more television "face time." Standups should be used sparingly and *only* when they add something to the story. There are valid reasons for using a standup in a story, such as when it's important to place the reporter at the scene, there's an extremely tight deadline, or there's a lack of quality video. When a standup is used, it presents extra challenges for the writer, who must have the story planned out in his or her mind at the time the standup is shot. Too many times, the reporter doesn't have a plan in mind, and later tries to fit an inappropriate standup into the story.

Never let a standup, or any other outside element, take the place of good writing. It may require more work, but doing the extra writing usually makes for a better final product.

Leads and Terminology

Writing for sports broadcasting can come in various forms. But before we go on, some explanation of terminology is important (the abbreviations are common broadcast shorthand):

Reader (RDR) – A written story with no video, audio, or graphic elements.

Voice over (VO) – A story in which the anchor reads a portion of the copy over video, usually in the form of highlights.

Voice over/Sound on tape (VO/SOT) – A voice over with the added element of a short interview on tape (sound bite).

Package (PKG) – A self-contained, taped story that includes some combination of video, audio, graphics, and natural sound. Usually done by a reporter and introduced by the anchor.

Full-screen graphics (FSCG) – Full-page graphic information that the anchor talks over during a story. It usually involves complicated numerical or statistical information that requires more explanation. The CG stands for "character generator" and refers to any written or printed material that appears on the screen. It's also commonly referred to as "chyron" or "supers." A common practice today is to CG the scores in a ticker format that runs at the bottom of the screen.

Natural sound (NATS) – The sound that occurs "naturally" at the scene of a story, such as crowd reaction, coaching yelling, or the sounds of the game.

No matter whether the broadcaster uses a reader, VO, VO/SOT, or package, all written stories start with a lead. The lead is the first few lines of the copy that set up the rest of the story. Most print journalists were taught to put some form of the 5 "W's" in the lead: who, what, when, where, or why, and that form is quite common in print writing. But in broadcasting, such writing would overwhelm the listener with too much information. Therefore, the main job of writing a sports broadcasting lead is to create interest and attention that compels the listener to stick with the story.

There are several different types of broadcast leads, each of which depends on the tone or style of the story involved. The hard lead is basically a summary of the story in a no-nonsense delivery and is usually reserved for the most serious or important stories.

Hard sports lead: "A jury in Atlanta today acquitted Ravens linebacker Ray Lewis of first degree murder charges."

In contrast, the soft lead is as its name implies and is used primarily for softer, more feature-oriented stories.

Soft sports lead: "Compared to his recent battles with cancer, Lance Armstrong must look at the Tour de France like a ride through the park."

You can see how foolish it would be to use a soft lead for the Lewis story, or even a hard lead for the Armstrong story. Similarly, you would not want to use a humorous lead for a serious sports story.

Humorous lead: "Who could have guessed before the tournament started that Tiger Woods could shoot a 15 on the final hole and still win the U.S. Open?"

Some leads lend themselves to different types of stories, such as the throwaway lead or umbrella lead. In the throwaway lead, an innocuous line is used before the real story begins. An umbrella lead combines several different points of the same story.

Throwaway lead: "More trouble tonight for Yankees third baseman Alex Rodriguez. He made three more errors to raise his league-leading total to 16."

Umbrella lead: "While the Lakers worry about Kobe Bryant's injured foot, they also have concerns about Karl Malone's advancing age."

There is one type of lead that should be used only in rare situations, if at all. The question lead is dangerous because it could ask a question that turns off or disinterests the audience.

Question lead: "Could anyone have played a better game tonight than Martin St. Louis?"

In this case, the audience could think, "Yes" or even worse, not have any interest in the answer. It's much better to rephrase the question as a statement:

New lead: "It seems impossible that anyone could have played a better game tonight than Martin St. Louis."

No matter what type of story involved, the lead should involve the hook of the story. The hook is simply the main or most interesting part of the story. Each story has several angles, but usually one sticks out as the central theme. It may be the human or social context discussed in Chapter 2. This is the one that should be emphasized in the lead, if possible.

> **Poor lead:** "More than 15,000 people watched the Maple Leafs beat Ottawa tonight."
> **Better lead:** "A hat trick from Brian Leetch keyed the Leafs big win tonight over Ottawa."

Unless the attendance figure is the central issue of the game, it doesn't belong up top. In some cases, extremely high or low attendance figures are important, but even then are rarely used in the lead.

As mentioned, the type of lead used should correspond to the tone and style of the story. Young sportscasters often fall into the trap of cramming too much information in a lead, which either overwhelms the listener or gives away too much of the story. Always remember that the lead exists mainly to compel attention and keep the audience tuned in. Save the details for the rest of the story.

> **Poor lead:** "Brandon Webb won his biggest ballgame of the season tonight, as he allowed only 1 run and struck out 13 in a 5–1 win over San Francisco."
> **Better lead:** "Brandon Webb may have won his biggest ballgame of the season tonight."

In the second example, the lead indicates that Webb pitched well and won, but saves the details for the rest of the story. Another pitfall for young sportscasters is the plain or boring lead. The facts and information may be correct, but the lead fails to generate any interest or excitement. Consider our Webb example:

> **Poor lead:** "Brandon Webb won his biggest ballgame of the season tonight, as he allowed only 1 run and struck out 13 in a 5–1 win over San Francisco."
> **Better lead:** "Brandon Webb may have won his biggest ballgame of the season tonight."
> **Even better:** "Brandon Webb's smoke could have started a brushfire in the desert tonight, as he won perhaps his biggest game of the season." (or) "That smoke in the desert tonight didn't come from any Arizona brushfire . . . but rather from the strong pitching of Brandon Webb."

The vivid images of "smoke," "brushfire," and "desert" all tie in with the theme (good pitching, game involving Arizona Diamondbacks, etc.) and compel much more attention than the vanilla version.

Packages, Voice Overs, and Voice Over/Sound on Tape

All forms of broadcast sports writing should have the same basic elements: beginning (lead), middle, and end. But writing for stories that include taped elements requires a little more effort and imagination than writing a reader.

Voice Over

The main focus of writing a VO is to make sure the script matches closely with the video. Ideally, the writer should find a middle ground between writing too specifically for video (the script exactly matches the pictures) and writing too generally (the words and pictures have no relationship at all). Remember, when the viewer can see exactly what's happening, too much description is overkill.

> **Poor writing:** "Here James takes the handoff from Manning ... dodges a tackle at the 15, stumbles for a bit ... then regains his balance and goes into the end zone for a touchdown" (too specific).

> **Poor writing:** "The Colts offense has looked great so far this year and they lead the league in scoring" (too general).

> **Better writing:** "The Colts lead the league in scoring this year and added to that total when Edgerrin James broke this nice run to make it 14–0."

The first example is more like play-by-play and gives us too much detail. The second example is a little better, but doesn't relate the information to what's happening in the video. It would be much better if it mentioned something about James or the score. The third example is the best of both worlds: not too specific and not too general, with some added information for more depth.

Voice Over/Sound on Tape

The VO/SOT requires the same writing to video as the VO and adds the element of a sound bite (taped interview). The main trick of writing for sound bites is the lead in, or the words that come right before the sound bite. In radio, sound bites (or actualities) have to be preceded by the name of the speaker for identification purposes.

> **Radio:** "The Lady Volunteers have a tough road ahead, according to coach Pat Summitt." (actuality) or "According to coach Pat Summitt, the Lady Volunteers have a rough road ahead." (actuality)

In such situations, it's important to identify the speaker because the audience has no way of knowing who it is. No such restrictions apply in television, where the speaker is clearly identified by chyron or CG. Thus, television sports writers can be a little more general in introducing a sound bite and can even omit reference to the name.

Television: "And the Lady Volunteers know they have a tough road ahead." (sound bite—Pat Summitt)

In the rare cases where the chyron malfunctions and no name appears on the screen, the sportscaster can simply tell the audience once the sound bite ends.

Television: "And the Lady Volunteers know they have a tough road ahead. (sound bite) "By the way, that was head coach Pat Summitt."

In either television or radio, it's important not to introduce the sound bite by repeating what's in the interview.

Poor writing: "The Lady Volunteers say they're fired up and ready for the NCAA tournament." (sound bite: "We're fired up and ready for the NCAA tournament. We think we can go a long way—even to the national title.")

In this case, the introduction to the sound bite simply duplicates what's on tape. Try to introduce the sound bite in a more general way by leading into the interview or by adding new information.

Better writing: "The Lady Volunteers seem excited as they head to their 16th straight postseason appearance." (sound bite: "We're fired up and ready for the NCAA tournament. We think we can go a long way—even to the national title.")

Packages

Because the package combines all the other elements of video, audio, and sound, it's the most difficult and time-consuming format to write. There are no hard-and-fast rules for writing packages, but it's good to keep in mind some of the things we've already mentioned:

- remember your leads
- write to video
- emphasize your best elements (video, interviews, nat sound, etc.)

- take time for nat sound breaks
- keep your writing short, choppy, and conversational

Young writers also worry about the length of a package, figuring that they better make it nice and long to impress their boss and the audience. As a result, they often put in way too much information and overload the audience. Most often, less is more—and better.

Scripting

Television

No matter what form of story you use, it has to be properly scripted. That is, it must be written in a way that the director can understand. Any story, no matter how brilliantly written, is useless if the technical director can't figure out how to get it on the air.

Each station has its own specific way of scripting, but as a whole, the television industry follows a general standard. Take a blank piece of paper and draw an imaginary vertical line down the center. Everything on the right side of the sheet is the copy written for broadcast. It's what will appear in the teleprompter and what the anchors will say on the air (Figure 4-3). Everything on the left side is technical information for the director. Each story comes with its own directions, but they usually include most of the following information (Tables 4-2 and 4-3).

Talent/Camera: This is indicated in the upper left hand corner of the script and indicates what anchor is reading the story and on what camera. The name of the anchor is usually indicated by initials.

When to roll tape: If there is a tape in the story, the director must know when to roll it. This can be indicated by the abbreviation VO (for a voice over) or PKG (for a package).

How long the tape runs: This is indicated by a block of time, such as [1:23] or [:14]. For a VO/SOT, the time indication tells how long the sound bite runs. In a package, it shows how long before the report ends and the anchor resumes talking.

How the tape ends: The outcue (or outq) tells the director the last few words of the report, so he or she knows when it ends. For a package, the outcue is often "standard" (or STD), which is the station's usual sign-off language ("for Channel 13 Sports, I'm Joe Jones"). For a VO/SOT, the outcue is simply the final few words of the sound bite.

Proper CGs: The director must also know what chyrons are needed in the story and where they must appear. Chyrons can be locators (where the story is

Figure 4-3

Proper scripting is important, in part to make sure the anchor will see the correct material in the teleprompter.

BES		
Cam-1		A tremendous effort today by the Central High track team led to a surprising—and emotional—win at the state track meet. Joe Jones has the story.
PKG		
[1:31]		
outq: STD		
CG: Springfield		
CG: Jim Smith/Wins Pole Vault		
CG: John Johnson/Central Coach		

Table 4-2

Example of Scripted Television Package

Table 4-3	BES	
Example of VO/SOT Scripted for Television	Cam-1	When Jim Smith soared more than 15 feet in the pole vault today, it wiped away more than 75 years of frustration for Central High at the state track meet.
	VO	
	CG: Springfield	Smith's vault not only won him the gold medal in the event ... but it clinched the overall track title for Central—the first state track title in school history.
	SOT	
	[:20]	
	outq: "it's unbelievable"	
	CG: Jim Smith/Wins Pole Vault	
	VO	Smith was Central's only gold medal winner, but his win helped the Cougars edge Little Springs for the overall title ... 121 points to 119.

taking place), proper names or full-screen graphics. Most newsrooms now have computer software that automatically formats the script in the proper format. But care must be taken to load the correct information into the computer, to avoid embarrassing technical errors. Nothing is more frustrating than working all day on an important story, only to see the report fouled up in the control room. And in probably 90% of such situations, the reporter is more at fault than the director.

Radio

The technical requirements of a radio script are a little less demanding than television, simply because radio has fewer elements to deal with. The radio director or producer doesn't have to worry about chyrons or how something looks on camera. Thus, the radio script focuses mainly on when to roll tape, the length of the package or actuality, and its outcue. There are different script formats for different stations, but a typical example might look like Table 4-4.

Table 4-4	Talent	Controversy at the Olympics today over the gold medal awarded in men's gymnastics. Tim Johnson reports that a scoring error may force American Paul Hamm to give back his gold medal.
Radio Script for Technical Direction	Take Tape	
	Length: 1:19	
	Outcue: STD	

The radio script should be clean and easy to understand, no matter how it's formatted. The bottom line is simplicity and for the radio director or board operator to easily know the technical elements of the story.

References

Careers in sports: TV sports anchor. (1999, September 7). *ESPN.* www.espn.go.com/special/s/careers/anchor.html.

Marshall, Bob. (1981). *Diary of a Yankee-hater.* New York: Franklin Watts.

Salwen, Michael and Garrison, Bruce. (1994, January 15). Survey examines extent of professionalism in sports journalism. *Editor & Publisher, 27 (3).*

The list: sports clichés that must go. (2003, January 21). *ESPN.* http://www.espn.go.com/page2/s/list/cliches.html.

The Internet

By the Numbers

There's no doubt that the Internet has had an incredible impact on sports media, especially in terms of the way content is created, distributed, and consumed. And its influence is growing. According to a Harris Poll, more than 137 million American adults are now online, which is 66% of the adult population. In 1995, only 9% of all adults were online. Today's average user spends more than 3 hours per week on the Internet.

Much of that time spent is with some form of sports media. When people are asked what they use the Internet for, the two most common responses are looking up information (92%) and communicating or interacting with others (85%). These are exactly the reasons why Internet sports media are so popular and pervasive. Millions of pieces of sports data, statistics, and artifacts can be compressed and stored for easy and instant retrieval. Information on players, coaches, and events that used to take days or weeks to find can now be accessed in seconds.

The element of interaction may be even more important. The Internet allows an ongoing, virtually live conversation between sports media providers and consumers. Literally millions of fans who had been shut out of the sports communication process can now take part in a variety of ways, including such things as feedback with sports media sites, the purchase of sports merchandise, participation in sports-related games online, or live conversations with other fans in sports "web blogs."

As a result, the use and popularity of Internet sports media have exploded. The Pew Center reports that the number of Americans using the Internet for sports-related purposes has grown significantly in just the past few years. Nearly half of all Internet users check for sports scores or information, which represents a growth rate of 73% (Table 5-1).

Table 5-1

Sports-Related Internet
Use in the United States

Percentage of Internet users who have checked for sports scores or information online	44%
Actual number of Internet users who have checked for sports scores or information	52 million
Growth rate in number of Internet users checking for sports scores or information	73%
Number of users who check sports scores or information on a daily basis	14 million
Growth rate in Internet users who check scores or information on a daily basis	50+%
Demographics of sports-related Internet use	Typically male and younger (18–29)

Source: Pewinternet.org

Table 5-2

Fastest Growing Web
Sites, August 2004[a]

Site	Unique Visitors (in Millions)	Change from Previous Month
U.S. Olympic team sites	2958	N/A
Athens2004.com	3027	+1121%
NFL Internet Group	10,907	+86%
Sportsline.com sites	4881	+34%

[a] Figures are for U.S. audiences. The total number of people accessing sports Internet sites increased 11% from June 2004 to August 2004.
Source: comscore.com

A snapshot of Internet usage from 1 month in 2004 shows how popular sports sites have become. In August 2004, the fastest growing sites were related to the Olympics, which were then taking place in Athens, Greece. But the NFL and Sportsline.com sites also enjoyed steady growth. This would seem to suggest that seasonality plays an important part in the usage of growth of sports sites. When it's football season, football sites get more hits, while basketball and hockey drop. The reverse happens during the winter and spring (see Table 5-2).

In addition, consumers are increasingly turning to the Internet for sports fantasy games. Seven million Americans visited, on average, 200 fantasy sports web pages per person every month from October 2003 through May 2004. The industry took in $3 billion in 2002, or 1.5% of the $298 billion spent on sports that year, according to a study commissioned by the Fantasy Sports Trade Association. *CBS SportsLine.com* earned $14.4 million from fantasy football and baseball in 2003, up 40% from the year before. "The Internet allows you to compete not just against your peers like you used to do, but everybody across the world," said Greg Ambrosius, president of the FTSA. "This is like the ideal niche industry or hobby, if you will, for the Internet."

One of the most popular, and controversial, uses for online sports media is gambling, with gross wagering now estimated somewhere in the vicinity of $70 billion. Just since 1995, roughly 1400 gambling sites run by 300 companies have launched on the Internet. Despite the fact that online sports gambling is clearly

Year	Profit Estimates (in Billions)	Table 5-3
2000	$2.2	Growth of Online
2001	$3.0	Gambling
2002	$4.1	
2003	$6.0	
2004	$8.3	
2005	$10.2 estimated	

Source: *USA Today*, March 29, 2004, p. 1B

illegal in the United States, "You're seeing some hugely profitable businesses," says Sebastian Sinclair, CEO of a New York consulting firm that studies the gaming industry (Table 5-3).

Expect online gambling to grow, despite efforts to shut it down. Technology allows online gambling sites to get around current law by simply hosting the site outside the United States. Efforts to enact tougher legislation have bogged down in Congress. "One of the things that frustrates government is that the medium transcends borders," says gaming attorney Anthony Cabot. "How effective is the prohibition (against online gambling)?" asks Sinclair. "Not very."

One area of Internet use that has lagged behind is showing live or taped sports events. Growth in this area has been somewhat slow, for both technical and economic reasons. "Streaming" video on the Internet has been around for several years, but has often suffered from poor video quality due to the enormous amount of bandwidth required. There's also the crucial issue of how content provided can make money from video streaming. For now, most providers are going with a pay-per-use model, such as College Sports Television. In 2005, CSTV announced a 2-year agreement with the NCAA and CBS to stream college basketball tournament games during "March Madness." CSTV paid $3 million for the rights and will charge consumers between $10 and $20 for the service. Company president Brian Bedol expects the package to make money in the first year. "We could have subscription buys of several hundred thousand," he said, "in addition to millions of viewers through free two-minute highlight clips following each game."

The CSTV deal suggests that streaming will eventually have a tremendous impact on sports media, especially as technology becomes even more sophisticated and new revenue models become available. For example, major league baseball boasts nearly 100,000 subscribers to its service that streams live audio of all its games. Fans pay $30 for access to games, which suggests a fairly healthy revenue stream. The NFL offers "Field Pass," in which all league games are streamed at a cost of $34 for the entire season. "We've been testing the waters, exploring the marketplace," says Peter Brickman, senior director of broadcast operations and technology for the NFL. "Traditional modes of distribution still work very well. We always want to be ready if there's a shift."

Content Considerations

Understanding audience demographics and habits is a big part of figuring out how to create content for Internet sports sites. We have a picture that sports sites users are generally younger, male, and that their numbers are growing every day. We also know some of the things these users want to do when they access Internet sports sites, which leads to some of the basic questions we must answer in order to reach these audiences effectively.

Functionality

The media outlet has to decide what function the site will have. Should it be simply a content provider? Should it incorporate some sort of feedback mechanism in which users can communicate to the media outlet or with each other? How important are graphics, presentation, and the "look" of the site?

The answers to these questions are often determined by the amount of money and other resources the media outlet has available. Obviously, the smaller the outlet and the fewer the resources, the less sophisticated the site. This might be the case for a radio or television station that is also trying to maintain an Internet site. In such situations, many stations have simply taken their broadcast material and put it on their Internet site, a process known as "shovelware." Using shovelware is usually simple, inexpensive, and an efficient use of resources in that stories are typically copied or "shoveled" from the newscast computer right into the Web site, which can be as simple as moving computer files.

However, most broadcast outlets use their Internet sites as a promotional tool and not necessarily as a stand-alone medium. Such sites can generate traffic, but have limited appeal in that the content is often not original and local audiences are much smaller. To get around this problem, it has become quite common for stations to combine with other media outlets in the creation of an Internet news site. For example, a newspaper and television station in the same community might host a combined site that offers users the combined resources of both organizations. This is a very effective method that is also used in many larger markets.

In addition, several companies now specialize in creating Web sites for broadcast outlets. Such services usually include things such as hardware and software, training, and technical support. One way smaller stations can give their web pages a professional look is to contract it out to a professional site service, which will handle most of the details of running the site, except for providing local content. These services don't necessarily cost much money (in some cases networks will allow their affiliates use of a standardized site design), but they aren't very personalized or unique. If you surf the Internet, you'll notice that the Web sites of many stations affiliated with the same network look virtually identical.

Versatility

Assuming a content provider has enough resources, most media outlets use their sites as a combination of information, interactivity, and merchandising.

We've already noted the importance of the information function. One of the most basic types of information would be considered "breaking news": updated scores of games in progress or just finished, any important sports news that is happening at that moment, or sports news that is unavailable from other media in the market. Many of the hits that take place on Internet sports sites are for updated game scores, something that is especially important to people who are working or don't have access to other media. One of the primary values of the Internet is that it can quickly disseminate breaking news to the public, although at present most people still turn to television or radio in such situations.

Internet sports sites still have informational value beyond scores. Even when television and radio provide the score of a game, the Internet site can be accessed for greater depth and detail, including statistics, reaction, and visuals. The amount of information that can be processed, stored, and retransmitted is staggering. In this way, the site functions like a newspaper—providing the depth and analysis that broadcast stations avoid because of time restrictions.

In a very real sense, the Internet is a hybrid, combining the speed and reach of broadcasting with the detail and depth of print. But there are drawbacks. Again, not everyone has Internet access. Those that do use the Web don't necessarily spend a lot of time there—the average time spent viewing per page in the United States is about 55 seconds. The nature of the medium also demands constant updating, which can be a tremendous drain on resources. Scores, articles, and pictures must be refreshed around the clock, which means a lot more work for Web technicians and sports content providers.

One of the great advantages of the Internet is interactivity—the ability for the sports media consumer to take an active role in the communication process. Traditional media have focused on one-way communication; the writer or reporter created and presented the content, and the audience consumed it. Today, technology has created several ways in which the audience can participate.

The most obvious is direct feedback. The single greatest use of the Internet is the sending and reading of electronic mail, which allows people to comment directly to media outlets. Some outlets will use this information to improve their products, whereas others simply ignore it. The important part is that audience members now have a direct line of communication with sports content providers, in which they can voice their opinions, complain, or make suggestions. From a practical standpoint, e-mail can help the outlet sort, classify, and file audience feedback, a practice that has traditionally been done somewhat haphazardly. What the outlet does with the feedback is its own business, but in the name of good audience relations, some attempt to contact audience members is usually made, even if it's the electronic version of a form letter.

But audience members not only use the Internet to talk to the media outlet, they use it to talk to each other. Sports billboards and chat rooms continue to grow in popularity. According to the Pew Report, about a third of all online users engage in some sort of chat room, which represents almost 30 million people. The sports media don't directly benefit from these activities, but sports billboards and chats do increase and promote interest in sports, which can drive up media consumption. There's also the sense that just using the billboard indicates that people are accessing the site, and that gives the media outlet a captive audience.

Most media sites have to be very careful about what goes in their billboards and chat rooms, as many sports conversations can get ugly or even profane. Typically, a billboard user has to agree to a set of conditions set forth by the media outlet on issues such as copyright, hacking, libel, and a variety of other illegal activities. For example, the billboard run by the *Austin American-Statesman* out of Austin, Texas, has a lengthy list of legal "dos and don'ts" and ends with the disclaimer that the site is used, "at your own risk. You understand that you are solely responsible for any damage or loss you may incur that results from your use of any communications server or any material and/or data downloaded from or otherwise provided through our sites." Many fans get around this issue by creating their own "web blogs" independent of any media. These "bloggers" have become a major force in sports media.

Polling and audience surveys have also become popular forms of Web interactivity. Almost every sports site has some version of an online poll that asks the audience to vote. ESPN *SportsCenter* runs its "Question of the Night" in conjunction with *espn.com* and can get up to 100,000 votes per question. To ESPN, the results of the poll are not as important as the audience measurement and cross-promotion. The idea is to get people watching *SportsCenter* to also access the *espn.com* site, and viceversa.

Don't expect any meaningful information to come out of Internet sports polls because such polls are completely unscientific. Audience members can vote as many times as they want and not everyone has access to the polls. But for media outlets, online surveys are a terrific way to engage audience members and promote other media within the corporate family. It also gives content providers a snapshot of some of the "hot button" issues on the minds of audience members, which could help in determining what stories and angles to cover.

The third major source of content on Internet sports sites is merchandising. According to recent studies, 8 out of 10 people online use the Internet to research a product or service. The number of people purchasing online has grown 63% since 2000, making it the fastest growing segment of the online experience.

Sports media sites have embraced the revenue potential of Internet merchandising. The "dot-com" bust of the early 2000s showed that there was far more potential than actual profit in the Internet, and content providers began scrambling for extra ways of making money. Given the somewhat iffy efficiency of advertising on the Web, sports has become an especially lucrative field for merchandisers, given the tremendous demand for apparel, equipment, and memorabilia.

The sports media site can also sell itself, meaning the products and services it creates. For example, when you click on the front page of the ESPN site there are generally two or three pitches for ESPN products, such as the college football pay-per-view package or ESPN's "Insider" subscription service. The *CNN/Sports Illustrated* site allows you to subscribe to SI or purchase the popular swimsuit issue. Some content is restricted to those who already have a magazine subscription.

Uniqueness

Regardless of whether it's print, broadcast, or online, sports content providers should determine who's in their audience and what that audience wants. And research clearly shows that in these areas there are important differences between the Internet and other media.

Research indicates that typical Internet users are younger, more educated, and less racially diverse than the general population. More specifically, the average Internet user is between 18 and 29 years old, college educated, and white. Even though these differences are slowly disappearing, there is still a significant "digital divide" that should be taken into account.

The younger Internet audience has grown up with computers, but not necessarily with traditional media formats. Print material is typically presented in an inverted pyramid format, where the most important information comes first, followed by less important information. Broadcast content is usually delivered in a straightforward, chronological style. But Internet users like the freedom they have to jump in and out of different stories at the same time. Internet sports content should be structured in this nonlinear style and not focus so much on conventional presentation formats.

Among other things, this means that the site should have many hyperlinks. Hyperlinks are the underlined portions of Internet text that allow users to jump to another part of the story or even to a completely different story. If the story is about a specific game, hyperlinks should allow the user to investigate other information related to the story, such as pictures, interview segments, or expert analysis.

The emphasis on video and audio should also be a major consideration in producing Internet sports content. In effect, the Internet combines both print and broadcast news. The text looks very much like a newspaper story, but it can also be supported with pictures and sounds. In our game story example, the user should ideally have the ability to look at video of the game or hear an interview segment with the star player. Most sports outlets incorporate these features into their Web sites, assuming they have the resources and technical capability. If not, the Internet version will be much simpler and more scaled down.

The written material of an Internet news story should be simple, straightforward, and much like an inverted pyramid newspaper story, where the facts are presented in descending order of importance. Internet users are notoriously impatient—remember, the average user spends only about 55 seconds at a particular site before moving on—and they don't want to wait for the important details. There should be an emphasis on headlines and news briefs, with an opportunity for users to explore stories in greater detail if they want.

In many ways, an Internet sports site should be produced much like a video game—high intensity, visually engaging, and easy to understand and access. Many of the people who use the Internet regularly are very comfortable with video games and can understand news much better when it is presented in a friendly format.

Resources

All of these things we've discussed—interactivity, merchandising, chat rooms, and the like—assume a certain level of technical sophistication. Some media sites just don't have the resources, either human or technical, to provide all these amenities. As a result, many sports sites, especially those run by smaller companies or stations, are very simple and bare-boned. When sports sites have to take a minimalist approach, they usually focus most of their efforts on informational content. This appeals to a large segment of the online population that uses the site simply to get scores and game details.

Resource availability is the most obvious factor that determines content for an Internet sports site. The more money and resources an outlet has, the more it can provide in the way of Internet content, interactivity, and merchandising. ESPN is 80% owned by the Walt Disney Company and is on the cutting edge of Internet technology. It introduced its "ESPN Motion" technology in 2003, which "puts the power of video selection in your own hands. No longer are you force fed clips —you decide what you want to watch. The Motion Showcase page previews all the current Motion video available to you and organizes it by sport so that you can easily navigate to find all the clips that are most important to you." The product has generated nearly 3 million installations and has attracted more than 25 advertisers.

ESPN has hundreds of full-time employees working on its Internet site, as either technicians or content providers. Contrast that to a sports Web site run by a small radio or television station, which might have only a handful of staffers. More and more stations are recognizing the importance of a Web presence and are hiring people for that express purpose. But there are still lots of places, mainly in smaller markets and towns, that simply can't afford a complex Internet site. Oftentimes, smaller stations will outsource the work to professional media companies.

Even when a media outlet has the resources to create and maintain an Internet presence, it might regard the site as little more than an afterthought. Much of this thinking is due to unfamiliarity with the technology, a lack of successful economic models associated with the Internet, and uncertainty about the media environment. There's still a great deal of mystery about how to use the Internet and how to make money from it. These types of stations grudgingly create an Internet site, but usually only fill it with "shovelware" and content that has already run on the broadcast station.

However, the mindset of today's media owners is changing with the realization that the Internet is not some fad that's going away. The day where an Internet site is a poor stepchild to traditional print and broadcast media is fast disappearing and media owners are exploring new ways of using their sports sites in an integrated and converged fashion.

Internet Sports Sites with Gary Kicinski

Gary Kicinski (Figure 5-1) has been sports editor at USATODAY.com since June of 2000. Prior to that he spent 9 years at *USA Today Baseball Weekly* as a production editor and deputy editor. From 1979 to 1990 he worked for Gannett newspapers in Burlington, Vermont; Fort Myers, Florida; and Cincinnati, Ohio, in positions ranging from reporter to editor to page designer.

Q: What should a sports Internet site look like and what should it do? Are the considerations of content, layout, and presentation drastically different than on the newspaper side?

A: There is no blueprint for what a successful sports Internet site should look like. Each site has to consider its own audience and goals, weigh that against its resources, and come up with a design that best suits its needs. ESPN.com, for example, is trying to capitalize on its television audience and devotes a lot of space to cross-promotion. ESPN also tries to emphasize video and features that will give its Web users a TV-like experience so its design is tailored to its specific strengths and audience. USATODAY.com's sports section is one piece of a general news site. We emphasize breaking sports news and the brand expertise that *USA Today* has established over the past 20-some years. We try to emphasize the newspaper's reporting to help set us apart from other sites that rely on wire copy. We try to present it in an orderly, almost newspaper-like fashion, with a clearly defined top story and others of less importance positioned lower on the page. Complementary features such as audio, chats, surveys, and photo galleries are integrated into the presentation.

Presentation considerations are significantly different from the newspaper side. There are limitations to text size and font. There are limitations to how big you can play

Figure 5-1

Gary Kicinski. Sports editor, *USA Today* Web site.

art because large photos and graphics will slow down the page load time and frustrate users. And you don't have the opportunity to direct the reader's eye in any direction but down. A 35-inch story in the newspaper can be attractively displayed in a rectangular fashion with art and type treatment that makes it easy for the eye to follow the flow. The same story on the Web has no direction to go but down. You can break it up periodically with subheads or inset photos, but the impact is less effective because your perspective is limited to just the 5 or 6 inches that can fit on your computer monitor at any one time.

On the other hand, there are many things you can do on the Web that you can't do in print. Print has space limitations; the Web generally does not. Print cannot offer sortable tables, interactive graphics, live scores, or audio-photo galleries. So our presentation goal is to be able to add features that complement the printed story and give the reader an extra dimension of coverage.

Q: We hear so much talk about convergence today. How does an Internet sports site work together with a newspaper, radio, or television station?

A: Convergence is constantly evolving. At *USA Today* it has become a larger point of emphasis in the last 4 years. Here, the dot-com and print sections are located in different parts of the building. In sports, we attend the newspaper's daily and weekly planning meetings to identify news and features that merit additional packaging on the Web. We construct promotional "refers" for our content and provide them to the newspaper's editors for publication so that readers are aware of our enhanced coverage.

Over the years, reporters have grown more comfortable working for the Web. Many of them now do weekly chats with readers. Some will offer audio analysis for breaking news or to accompany graphics. Some have become proficient at taking digital recorders with them on interviews, which allows us to post audio from the news subject. Every day another brick is removed from the wall. In the beginning many print reporters viewed work for the Web as an intrusion upon their "real" duties. Over time most of them have come to see the Web as part of the brand. The growth of the Internet audience gives exposure to their work.

Q: How important is the idea of interactivity and getting feedback from users? What do you do with the feedback?

A: I would say only mildly important. Our feedback is limited to a dozen or so e-mails per day for the most part. Most of those are corrections or requests for coverage. Corrections are acted upon by directing them to the appropriate editor for verification. Requests for coverage are responded to or forwarded to an appropriate editor depending on merit.

We do have reporting tools that tell us the relative popularity of different aspects of our coverage, such as how many page views a story received. From this we learn things such as photo galleries are very popular, so we would be more inclined to devote an hour to building a photo gallery to complement coverage than to building a graphic, for example.

We try to provide interactivity to our users through chats, surveys, message boards, and write-in opportunities. We also try to make our graphics and photo galleries interactive, allowing the user to choose the kind of information he or she would like to access.

Q: Do you have an idea of how many people are accessing the site and what they are primarily using it for?

A: Yes, we can tell many things about our site usage. We can tell number of visitors, sessions, page views, and page duration. We can tell what time of day we reach peak usage (typically 9 a.m. to noon ET). We can also record usage patterns, such as where do users go next from the homefront? We can tell what kind of stories or features receive the most interest. We pass these numbers along to our counterparts at the newspaper in daily meetings, which they often find interesting because they have no way to similarly gauge the interest in their various features on a daily basis. They only have a single circulation figure.

Q: How many people does it take to run the site in terms of creating content, layout/design, updating information, and maintenance?

A: Our site currently employs 13 staffers in sports. There are 78 positions in editorial on the whole, including management. Almost all of those positions are involved in some manner of creating content and building story pages, section fronts, or other packaging aspects, including photos and graphics. If maintenance means technical support, we have about 20 dot-com technical support staffers, and are also supported at a system level by *USA Today's* tech support staff.

Q: How does the site make money? Is it profitable? Is there a concern that you're giving away free content that people who read the newspaper have to pay for?

A: The site makes money primarily through advertising, sponsorships, and partnerships. It has been a long, slow climb back from the dot-com bust of 3 to 4 years ago.

We do not charge for our news coverage. Our view is that people consume news in a variety of ways now and that the paper and the Web site can coexist. The newspaper heavily targets the mobile consumer—the subway rider, the frequent flyer—and for that kind of reader, the print version is more convenient and portable. Hopefully they will refer to expanded coverage online and when they reach their desk computer they will be inclined to visit our site.

Q: What are the new breakthroughs or developments that will influence the Internet sports sites of the future?

A: As broadband access becomes more prevalent for home use, expect to see more and more video, audio, and flash graphic technology. Also expect to see increased examples of database journalism as companies become more comfortable with transferring databases to a Web environment. Specifically in sports, there will be a continued push for real-time data from events, but it remains to be seen whether the leagues that control that data will tighten their grip on this information or loosen it up for the benefit of all. Fantasy sports will continue to grow in popularity and coverage will become mainstreamed into traditional sports content. Sports sites will increasingly repurpose their content to other platforms—cell phones, PDAs—as consumers will demand news and information while away from their computer.

References

88% of Americans say internet plays a major role in their life. (2004). *ITfacts.biz.* http://www.itfacts.biz/index.php?id=C0_2_1

America's online pursuits. (2003, December 22). *Pew Internet and American life Project.* http://www.pewinternet.org/pdfs/PIP_Online_Pursuits_Final.PDF

FAQ. (2004). *ESPN.* http://espn.go.com/motion/faq.html

Hu, Jim. (2004, July 19). Study: fantasy sports sites addictive. *CNET News*. http://news.com.com/ Study%3A+Fantasy+sports+sites+addictive/2110-1026_3-5275663.html?tag=nefd.hed

Lindemann, Carl. (2001, June 18). Stream 2. *Broadcasting & Cable*. http://www.tvinsite.com/ broadcastingcable/index.asp?layout=story_stocks&articleid=CA89604&doc_id=31165&pubdate= 6/18/01&display=features

Martzke, Rudy. (2005, January 27). 'March madness on demand' could take byte out of network. *USA Today*. http://www.usatoday.com/sports/columnist/martzke/2005-01-27-martzke-hoops_x.htm

McCoy, Kevin. (2002, March 29). Online gambling pays off for Internet sports books. *USA Today*, p. 1–2B.

Online Activity Paints a Rich Picture of the Minds, Hearts and Interests of World Citizens in February. (2002, March 11). *comScore Networks*. http://http://www.comscore.com/ press/release.asp?id=67

Sullivan, Andy. (2004, September 1). Livewire: fantasy sports thrive online. *Yahoo! News*. http://news.yahoo.com/news?tmpl=story&u=/nm/20040901 /wr_nm/column_livewire_dc_1

Taylor, Humphrey. (2002, April 17). Internet penetration at 66% of adults nationwide. *Harris Poll*. http://www.harrisinteractive.com/harris_poll/ index.asp?PID=295

Visitor agreement. (2004). *Austin American-Statesman*. http://www.austin360.com/lifestyles/content/shared/ help/agreement.html

6 Video and Visuals

Think of the most memorable moments in sports history and you'll probably think of some unforgettable visual image. Some events seem to stick in our memories because of the power of the pictures, such as Babe Ruth's farewell appearance at Yankee Stadium, the 1967 Ice Bowl in Green Bay, or Carlton Fisk madly waving his arms to help his home run stay fair in the 1975 World Series.

All of these images came from the cameras of sports photographers. Granted, they usually had the help of highly sophisticated equipment, which is not readily available in smaller markets. But whether you're shooting the Super Bowl for the networks or simply covering the local high school basketball game, the basics of sports photography remain pretty much the same.

Event Photography

Much of sports photography (or "videography" for television) includes covering events or games for the local high school or college. Basketball, football, baseball, and all the other sports each have their own unique challenges, but there are some general rules of sports photography that apply to them all.

1. Always keep the action in front of you. This is common sense—you want the viewer to see the action coming at him or her, rather than going the other way. There are always exceptions because of the unpredictable nature of the event. You may be in perfect position to get the game-winning touchdown, only to have someone make an interception and run 99 yards in the opposite direction. But for the most part, position yourself so you can see the action unfold in front of you (Figure 6-1).

Figure 6-1

A sports photographer should always have the action coming in his or her direction.

2. Just like real estate, in sports photography it's location, location, location. Positioning yourself in the right place is more than half the battle in getting good pictures, and every event demands that you be in the right place at the right time. We'll talk more about positioning in a minute.

3. Anticipate what's coming next. If you're covering a football game and it's 3rd and 10, what's likely to happen next? Probably a pass, which means you want to stay a little looser in your shooting and get ready for the ball to come downfield. If it's the last few seconds of a quarter in a basketball game, be ready for that long shot at the buzzer or possible fan reaction. Be aware of special situations like these and where you need to be.

4. Be prepared for anything. That includes the ball coming right at you and, more importantly, large players coming right at you. A photographer getting run over looks hilarious on the sports bloopers, but in reality it's painful and often dangerous for you and the equipment. Sports photographers often joke that news directors are less concerned about them than the equipment. While something of an overstatement, it does have some basis in fact. Today's equipment is extremely sensitive and easily broken, often at a cost of thousands of dollars. Some of the damage is unavoidable, but much of it is due to just

plain carelessness. Don't set your camera on the ground and leave it unattended, even if for just a few minutes, and the same goes for the tripod. Almost every station in the country has a story involving a wrecked camera that slipped off of an unattended tripod. As a side note, the tripod is used infrequently in sports photography. Still photographers can and do use some form of a tripod, and it's a necessity for television cameras shooting up top in a press box. But because most of the compelling sports photography involves good close-ups, most photographers prefer to shoot "off the shoulder" on field level.

5. Make sure you have the proper framing. Most sports photography involves a "happy medium" between too loose and too tight. If the framing is too loose, viewers can't identify the action or the players involved. Coaches love this wide angle when studying game footage, but for the people at home it's almost useless. There's also a recent trend to shoot everything ultratight, zooming in on faces, hands, or the ball. But this also frustrates the viewer because it doesn't give any depth or background, which adds important information to the picture. A close-up of a running back plowing into an unidentifiable pile of bodies ruins the drama of a game-winning touchdown. Better to pull back to catch other players and even fan reaction. It's fine to start tight, but then pull out so we can see what's going on. For example, you can start extremely tight on the quarterback calling plays at the line of scrimmage and then quickly pull out as the ball is snapped to catch the action. It's also acceptable to go the other way—start loose and zoom in. This works particularly well for events such as swimming and track meets, where you can start wide on the entire field and then slowly zoom in to focus on the leader. An exception to this might be print photography. Print photographers don't have enough rolls of film to shoot every play, and even if they could it wouldn't give a sense of the unfolding action. There are some instances when a still photographer can capture an important play, such as when one team is down at the opposing team's goal line. But print photography focuses more on reactions and emotions associated with the game, which can be conveyed by extreme close-ups of players, coaches and fans.

6. Don't cross the axis. This rule applies to videographers. The axis is an imaginary 180° line that runs in front of your shooting position (Figure 6-2). Crossing the axis would mean shooting from the other side of the field, looking back toward your original position. By doing this, you would see action going in both directions at the same time. Cutaways wouldn't make any sense because everyone would be looking in different directions. For continuity and easier editing, stay behind the axis, which simply means stay on the same side of the field and shoot in a consistent direction. Don't forget to factor the sun into the equation because you always want it behind you. Veteran photographers know this lesson well because shooting an old tube camera into the sun (or any bright

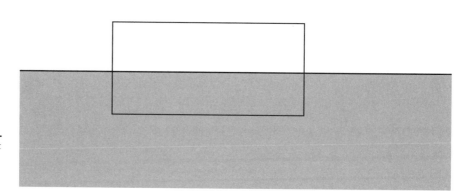

Figure 6-2

Don't cross the axis. Shoot in either the shaded area or white area, but not both.

light) would burn an image into the lens. While this doesn't present a problem for today's sophisticated chip cameras, shooting into the sun does darken the action and can turn the players into silhouettes.

7. Use cutaways. Cutaways are the short, nonaction shots used to add meaning or fill time between edited plays. A coach shouting at players, fans standing and cheering, and the scoreboard clock are all cutaways. Good cutaways can add some sense of drama and heighten the impact of the story. But make sure you get cutaways during the lulls in the action. Don't try to get a shot of the crowd when a golfer has a putt to win the tournament. Get reaction shots before and after the big play. Viewers are still more interested in the action on the field.

8. Save the experiments for later. In a game report, viewers want to see the nuts and bolts of the event. Fancy shots and strange camera angles don't answer their basic question—what happened? If you feel you have enough solid shots to tell the story, feel free to try something different. But keep the viewer, and the game, in mind.

Shooting on Location

Football

No sport, with the exception of golf, requires you to cover more ground than football. Unless you're shooting up top in the press box, you simply can't stay in one place and hope to get good pictures. You have to move and readjust your position constantly, usually between plays with only a few seconds to get to the next location.

There are three basic positions for shooting football (Figure 6-3). Position A is one of the most common at almost every level of football. With press box space at a premium, most photographers will have to shoot from the sidelines. Most shooters

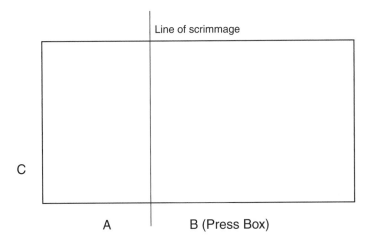

Line of scrimmage

C

A   B (Press Box)

Figure 6-3

Photographer positioning
for football.

try to position themselves about 10–15 yards in front of the line of scrimmage with the play coming toward them. This allows them to follow a runner or receiver into the end zone. Shooting from the sideline also makes for more close-up action and better natural sound, which helps place the viewer in the game and provides a better sense of the action.

The shifting depth of field makes this a difficult shooting position, as the photographer must change focus constantly as the action moves downfield. Changing focus is the most challenging aspect for young photographers, who find it difficult to keep one hand on the focus ring, while the other hand steadies the camera and operates the zoom knob. Be sure to know which way to turn the focus ring to keep the action in focus as it moves toward or away from you. In some cases, you can also get your focus during breaks in the action. For example, in a basketball game after a made basket at one end, photographers will quickly zoom to the other end and focus on the opposite basket. Many of today's newer cameras have an automatic focus feature, but it should probably be turned off (if possible) for sports photography. There's so much going on within the frame that the camera doesn't know what to focus on. Better to go manual and learn to use the focus ring.

There is also the possibility of players and coaches moving off the bench and getting in the way. Sometimes, the shooter may actually have to step out onto the field to follow the action. The NFL and most colleges have a 5-yard buffer zone around the sideline, which makes this very difficult, and sometimes photographers will "lose" the action for a few seconds or more.

Position B doesn't work well for print photographers, but is the recommended position for inexperienced videographers. Staying up top and as close as possible to the 50-yard line affords many advantages. The shooter can actually put the camera

Figure 6-4

Press box photographers
use tripods to follow the
action on the field below.

on a tripod (one of the few instances in sports photography where this is possible) to ensure a solid shot. Depending on the position, the shooter will not have to adjust the focus much, if at all. Most of the action will take place in the same depth of field and because the action is somewhat easy to follow, very seldom does the photographer get "faked out" or lose sight of the play.

One of the drawbacks of this position is that it doesn't allow for many good close-ups, which means it's not very practical for still photographers, who mainly shoot from down on the field. In many college and pro stadiums, the press boxes are hundreds of feet above the playing field. From this position, it's extremely difficult to capture the flavor or excitement of the event, so most of the footage shot from this location is used primarily for highlights (Figure 6-4).

Most large sports organizations routinely send two (or more) cameras to cover bigger games. For print and magazine, the photographers are placed at various locations and depths to get different perspectives of the game. For television, one camera is up top and the other is on the sideline. This certainly makes it easy to edit and helps avoid the problem of missing certain plays. If you've only got one camera, placement depends on the skill and experience of the photographer. If you're shooting for television, it's advisable to shoot every play in a game until the outcome has been decided.

Figure 6-5

Shooting from the back of the end zone works well when the ball gets close to the goal line.

Even then, if you put the camera down for just one play, you could miss something you'll never see again.

Position C is often used by photographers when the action gets close to the goal line. Standing at the back of the end zone ensures that the action has to come right at you, as opposed to the sideline where often the action goes far to the other side of the field. Remember to stand on the side of the end zone closest to your sideline position to avoid crossing the axis. Again, this position is not recommended for beginning shooters, as it is often hard to follow the action and tell exactly where the ball is going. And you still run the risk of missing the play, if there's a turnover and the ball heads downfield in the opposite direction (Figure 6-5).

Basketball

Shooting basketball is much like football, except on a smaller scale. And because of the continuous action, you won't have time to move around, but will have to find one spot and stay there. There are basically two positions from which to shoot (Figure 6-6).

Position A is on the floor, in one of the corners. Which corner depends on your axis and what side you start on, but generally the home team or the team of interest will move toward you. Depending on local rules, you may have to sit or kneel in

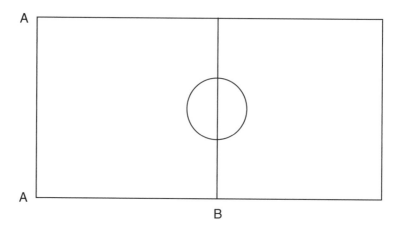

Figure 6-6

Basketball photography
positioning.

this position the entire game. In light of that, many experienced photographers will wear knee pads or some sort of brace so they won't get too uncomfortable. The lower position actually gives you a unique "looking-up" perspective on the game, making the players seem bigger and taller.

You want to use the corner instead of the center of the baseline for several reasons. Most obvious, the basket support makes it almost impossible to get any game action from a dead-center position. Because most of the action takes place inside the lane, the referees will also get in the way. Shooting from the corner also allows you better proximity to cutaways of the crowd and the bench.

Like football, shooting from the floor affords the audience a more intimate view of the game and brings it more into the action. The size and skill of the players become even more apparent when shooting from floor level. But the same dangers apply as in football concerning the possibility of contact with players. In fact, there are probably more camera–player collisions in basketball because the area is so much smaller and there's not any room to escape. The changes in the depth of field are even more drastic than football, and keeping good focus is a constant problem. As mentioned, one solution is a quick focus on the basket where the action is headed. Zoom in for a focus and then pull back out to the action.

Position B is probably the more desirable location; shooting from this position gives all the advantages mentioned for football, including steadiness and control. But again, availability may be a problem. Every high school and college gym is configured differently and space becomes a premium, especially when the place is packed. Be prepared to shoot anywhere—on staircases, from balconies, or even a catwalk above the playing court. In addition, print photographers will want to shoot as close to the floor as possible to get good close-ups.

Shooting basketball is not difficult, once you get used to it. It's fairly easy to follow the action by simply following the player with the ball. It's customary for the shooter to follow the player who has scored for a few seconds after the basket and then return to the action. Some videographers like a quick cutaway of the scoreboard after every basket, just for later help in identifying game situations during editing. Other times, the photographer will grab a quick cutaway after an important basket.

Shooting an entire game is impractical and seldom done. Usually, photographers will have to cover several games in one night, never spending more than a few minutes at each location. For the shooter, this means getting a few quick shots of each team making some baskets and some cutaways. Obviously, you're looking for the spectacular—the breakaway dunks, the long heaves at the buzzer, or something else out of the ordinary. But for the most part, the action will look the same.

Baseball

For print photographers, baseball is not that difficult. Because most of the action takes place in two places—on the mound or in the batter's box—photographers will spend much of their time focused in these areas. The action also moves slowly enough so that photographers can position themselves to get important action, such as an outfielder leaping over the wall to stop a home run.

From a television perspective, however, baseball is the hardest sport to shoot with one camera. While the action takes time to unfold, the ball usually moves too fast to follow—sometimes close to a hundred miles an hour. There are long periods of inactivity and then when the ball is in play, several things happen all at once and it's hard to figure out where to point the camera. And no matter what your position, you're in danger of getting clocked with a line drive or foul ball. But you can minimize your danger and improve your photography by shooting from the following locations (Figure 6-7).

Position A affords the safest location and the easiest to shoot. By positioning yourself above the action (the higher the better, within reason), you can follow the ball more easily. The phrase "within reason" means that you shouldn't be too high above the action. If you've ever sat on the top row of a big baseball stadium, you know how poor depth perception can make it difficult to follow the action. Ideally, you want to look up to see a high fly ball, not down. And again, this position may not be available, especially for games at local high schools and colleges. Especially at the higher elevation, you should start loose and slowly zoom in. If you stay too wide, it makes it much harder to tell what's going on, especially considering the size and speed of the ball. Again, this is not a good position for print photographers, who want to be as close to the action as possible.

Position B is also on a higher elevation, but on one of the baselines. Sometimes you have to shoot from this position, which creates certain problems. From dead

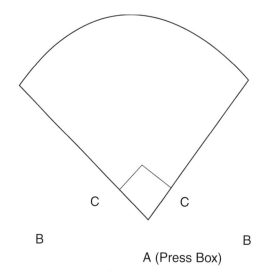

Figure 6-7

Baseball photograpy positioning.

center, it's much easier to follow the flight of the ball. From the sides, however, the ball will quickly travel out of your viewing frame, which means you have to guess or anticipate where it's going. One way is to pull out wider until you locate the ball. But you can also use your open eye (the eye not in the viewfinder) to peek at the position of the fielders. Using the open eye seems strange at first and takes lots of practice, but it can help in a variety of sports other than baseball.

In baseball, it's much easier to follow the fielders than the ball because they move so much slower. And fielders will always take you right where you need to be. Many shooters will find the correct fielder and then wait for the ball to arrive, especially if it's a long drive that appears headed out of the park. The photographer can stay focused on the fielder and then pull back to see the ball. It is extremely difficult to try and follow the ball with the camera and only the most experienced photographers should try it. Even when it can be done, it's probably still advisable to follow the fielders because they create all the action in the game.

Position C is the most dangerous place in the park—field level adjacent to the dugouts, but it's also the preferred position for most print photographers. If you ever get the chance, look at some old baseball action photos from the 1930s and 1940s. Sometimes you can see photographers on the field of play, just a few feet from the batters box—during the game! Today's photographers work from protected wells, but that does not completely eliminate the danger of getting hit by the ball or an onrushing player.

From a television perspective, following the action is very difficult from these positions, and it should only be tried by the most experienced videographers. The danger of getting hit by a stray ball increases, which requires maximum anticipation and awareness. This position also requires superior reflexes, as it's much more difficult to follow the action.

From whatever position, anticipation is the key to getting the good shot. It's important to know the situation so you can figure out what's going to happen next. If a batter singles to left with a man on second, follow the action until it's apparent what happened to the ball and then return to pick up the runner crossing the plate. As in basketball, stay with the runner for a few seconds after he's scored and then return to the batter standing on base. There are an infinite number of possible outcomes associated with each pitch, and more than any other sport, baseball photography requires anticipation, quick thinking, and knowledge of game strategy. In a first-and-third situation, the photographer has to be aware of a possible double steal, sacrifice bunt, suicide squeeze, or a pickoff move.

For videographers, it's also advisable to shoot everything possible, as time and resources allow. The two-out solo home run in the first inning could be the only run of the game. Because baseball has such long periods of inaction, cutaways become important. Tight shots of the pitcher delivering the ball, the batter swinging, or the managers in the dugout can really make the final product more memorable. Just be sure to pick the right spots for these cutaways. More than once, photographers have focused on a close-up of the pitcher, only to have the batter hit a home run. Those are the ones you can't get back.

Other Sports

There are no hard and fast rules for shooting other sports, but these suggestions might help the different situations you encounter. Again, print photographers will concentrate more on reaction and emotion, whereas videographers try to follow the action (Table 6-1).

Feature Photography

As sports reporting becomes more viewer friendly and personality oriented, feature reporting has become more essential. Sports departments now depend on these features to help attract newer and younger audiences, and feature photography can play a key role.

Shooting for features is entirely different than covering an event. In this situation, you're not trying to report hard, statistical information, but rather create a mood and draw the viewer into the story. You have to make the viewer care, and photography can go a long way in accomplishing that.

Table 6-1	Sport	Television Suggestions	Print Suggestions
Shooting Various Sports	Soccer	Follow the ball; it moves slowly and nothing important happens without it	Focus around the goal; that's where all the action is. The ball moves slowly enough to get good action close-ups.
	Golf	Focus on the putts—that's what wins tournament. Everything else is just a cutaway	There are many famous stories of golfers getting mad at photographers for taking shots during a swing and disrupting their concentration. You shouldn't shoot anything until the golfer has finished his or her swing, so mainly it's shots of follow-through and reaction. Reaction shots are especially compelling.
	Hockey	Like basketball, only much faster. Follow the players and keep it fairly wide	Like soccer, stay around the goal area. You'll also get good action shots of body checking in the corners. Also consider unique perspectives, such as placing a camera inside the goal.
	Boxing	Fairly easy because the action takes place in a small, enclosed area	The small area allows for good close-ups, especially of hands and faces.
	Volleyball	Follow the ball	This might be one sport to shoot from above or below, as both give a unique perspective; for close-ups, stay around the net area.
	Swimming	Start wide, then focus on the leader	Close-ups during the race, then focus on the finish
	Track	Same as swimming	Same as swimming
	Tennis	Easier to shoot from above because the action can fit in the frame. From ground level, position yourself in the corner to see both players. If you have to shoot from the sides, shoot long sequences of each player that you can later match edit together.	Close-ups of the players in action, concentrating on faces, hands, and feet; you can create interesting shots by shooting through the net and using interesting shadow perspectives.
	Auto racing	Put yourself somewhere where you won't get killed. There's no experience in the world like holding a camera in the front straightaway at Indy with cars coming at you at 200 miles an hour and only a 3-foot concrete wall between you. I'll never forget shooting a drag race from a certain position, then moving to a new location. Less than 2 minutes after I moved, a dragster went out of control and crashed right over the spot where I had been standing. Hopefully, the tape would have survived.	

General Rules

1. Emphasize close-ups. Close-ups can tell a story that other shots can't, such as players crying after a tough loss, the sweat and strain of a weightlifter, or the joy of a new state champion. In some cases, good close-ups can tell almost the entire story, with no narration. Some of the best sports reporting pieces are all photography and natural sound. Viewers care about stories because of good characters, and close-ups reveal character.

2. Don't be afraid to experiment. Here's a chance to do all that experimenting you had to put off at the game. Play with the camera; try different angles or different shots based on the mood you're trying to create. Lighting can be effective, especially sunlight, and things shot at dawn or dusk automatically have a different look and feel. One of the most famous football shots of all time is of former Dallas Cowboys coach Tom Landry. The photographer shot into the sun at Texas Stadium with Landry in the foreground, and the result was a classic silhouette of the coach in his trademark fedora hat. Angles can also change perspective, such as lowering the camera to ground level and shooting up at an athlete, which gives him or her a bigger and more intimidating presence. A popular angle now used in the NBA is a camera mounted on top of the backboard looking down on the players. Wayne Gretzky once said that he missed 100% of the shots he didn't take. The same can be said for feature photography—you don't know what you miss unless you shoot it.

3. Try first-person action. Ultimately, all sports are about people. What's it like to score the winning touchdown, hit a home run, or sink the winning putt? Use the camera to put the viewer in the place of the subject and give him a feel for what it's like down on the field. More and more sports leagues are emphasizing this as a dramatic way to attract new viewers. Some of the experiments include a "helmet cam" for football players, a "catcher cam" in baseball to let the viewer see what the batter sees, and the "goal cam" in hockey. On a local level, once a station ran a feature on a local athlete trying to make the U.S. Olympic bobsled team. He trained all summer by pushing a cart loaded with cinder blocks across the high school parking lot. It was one thing to show him pushing the cart, but something else to put the camera on the cart and let the viewers feel him push it.

4. Above all, still tell the story. No matter how fancy you get, how many great shots you take, or how much you experiment, it means nothing if you don't convey the basics of the story. Sometimes, photographers get so wrapped up in the technical aspects of their work that they forget the big picture. The raw tape may have some quality shots on it, but nothing that can be put together in a cohesive story. Good reporting and good photography are about

Figure 6-8

A good photograph should immediately communicate the main theme of the story.
Courtesy: J.D. Johnson/ The Daily Mississippian.

communicating and telling stories, and if you're shooting doesn't do that, you've failed your job (Figure 6-8).

Practicing

The only way to get better as a sports photographer is to practice, so take the camera out to live sports events as often as possible, keeping the following things in mind.

1. Respect and take care of the equipment. The best photographers treat their cameras like a member of the family, and not just because of the tremendous expense involved. Photographers know they can't produce good video without good equipment, and at most media outlets they are responsible for taking care of their cameras on a daily basis. Nothing will get you in trouble at a station faster than abusing the equipment, so take care to use the proper techniques in removing, using, and storing the camera. This also means using rain gear when the situation warrants.

2. Know what the camera can do. It's important to know about all the functions of the camera because it can help when you get in a difficult situation. First and foremost, this means being able to turn on the camera and prepare it for use. Learn about the power switches, F-stop, iris, gain, filter, zoom control, and white balancing because each camera is different. Other photographers can help, or you can simply read the manual. Getting the most out of the camera can save you in a difficult shooting situation, such as poor lighting. Countless

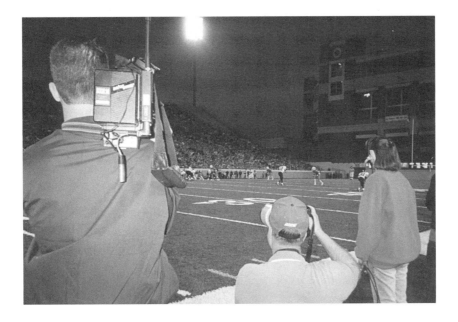

Figure 6-9

Before the action starts, sports photographers should concentrate on location, anticipation, and good positioning.

thousands of images have been ruined because someone forgot to white balance or shot on the wrong filter.

3. Concentrate on framing and focus. There are a million things for young photographers to worry about at a game, and many times they will not come back with perfect pictures. But there's a difference between good pictures and *usable* pictures, and as long as you have the proper focus and framing, the pictures are usable. Framing means keeping the action the proper distance away, which is accomplished most easily from an up-top position. The same goes for focus, which is why it's so advisable for inexperienced photographers to shoot from a higher position, where focus and framing remain fairly constant. With more practice you can go down to field level and develop stronger instincts (Figure 6-9).

4. Practice keeping your "other" eye open. This is mainly for television videographers. Cameras are built so the user puts his right eye in the viewfinder and keeps his other eye free. Work on using the left eye to expand your field of vision and keep you abreast of what's going on. This requires some extreme concentration, but can alert you to situations that need your attention.

5. Work on anticipation. Try to guess where the next play will occur and react accordingly. Each new play is a completely different situation, but with practice

you can prepare yourself for what will likely happen. Then it's simply a matter of putting yourself in the best position for the shot.

6. Be prepared. Shooting is hard work and involves heavy equipment. Dress accordingly for the camera and the weather. Plan ahead where you need to be and at what time, and give yourself enough time to get there.

The Photography of NFL Films

The people at NFL Films have the reputation as some of the finest sports photographers in the industry, and over the past 40 years they have built one of the best sports libraries in the world. NFL Films now has more than 250 employees processing 800 miles of film into more than 2000 hours of original programming every year.

A few years ago, several NFL Films photographers sat down in a roundtable discussion and talked about how they approach their jobs. NFL Films edited the discussion for its television series, *NFL Films Presents*, and the suggestions apply to anyone who wants to learn more about sports photography.

- Strive for perfection. Try to make every play the best it can possibly be.
- Look for emotion and reaction. Many times a frustration shot is more compelling than a celebration shot.
- Simple close-ups can tell you what the athletes are feeling.
- Respect the subject.
- Capture the moment. The best way to do this is to be in the right place at the right time.
- Try something different. Steve Sabol, who now runs NFL Films, gives a $1000 bonus to anyone who makes a really big mistake. "You wouldn't make that mistake unless you were trying to do something interesting," he says.

Editing

Editing is a much unappreciated part of the sports reporting process. You can have all the great shots in the world on your raw tape, but if you can't edit them together in the right way, you can't tell an effective story.

For print photographers, much of the editing decisions are out of their hands. The photographer may suggest one picture over another as being better or more appropriate, but the decision of what picture to run in the paper, how to crop or resize it, and its location and layout are often determined by editors or other newsroom personnel. The use of digital photography has drastically speeded up the transmission of photographs and the ease with which they can be cut, cropped, and arranged for layout.

From a broadcast standpoint, recent advances in technology have drastically improved the editing process. Not too long ago, all shooting and editing were done on film. The tape had to be physically cut and spliced together, which was an extremely time-consuming and difficult process that often made it impractical to get same-day highlights of events. The advent of videotape in the 1970s was a tremendous leap forward and helped speed up and simplify the editing process. Now, new digital technology promises to streamline the process even further. As stations begin the switch to digital equipment, the editing process will become more like home computing, with an emphasis on "cutting and pasting." The final product will not even exist on tape, but rather be sent in digital form to a central computer for playback (Figure 6-10).

Figure 6-10

One version of a digital editing system used in television sports departments.

In most large markets, editing (and photography) is a union job. That means you can't touch a camera or any editing equipment. But just about everywhere else, you'll be doing you own work. And whether you're working with videotape or digital equipment, there are some essentials to good editing for any broadcast sports story.

1. Don't let the highlights go too long or too short. So many times, because of time constraints, video is cut off just before the conclusion of a play. Nothing is more frustrating to the viewer than to hear, "Trust me folks . . . he eventually gets into the end zone." The average length for a single highlight play is between 10 and 15 seconds, so make sure you give yourself enough time. At the same time, don't give too much time to highlights. Remember, viewers can see the exact same thing on ESPN, CNN, and countless other outlets. Nothing is more boring than watching 2 minutes of highlights from a game you may have just watched on TV. Let the viewer see what's important, but save your real time for things that matter to the audience.

2. Don't be afraid of natural sound. The cheering crowd, the excited announcer, the coach yelling instructions to his players, all add something to the final presentation. Not too long ago, most sportscasters used either silence or canned music behind their stories. But natural sound adds something to the story that interests the viewer. Witness the popularity of "behind the scenes" sports films and putting a microphone on players during the game.

3. Cutaways can help, but don't overuse them. Some sportscasters (and especially news directors) fall in love with cutaways. Such shots always have a special place in sports stories, but remember what viewers want to see. Too many side shots lead to clutter and the story loses its momentum. In some cases, it's almost like the commercials between news stories.

4. Let the pictures tell the story. Truer words were never spoken. Good pictures can make or break a story much more so than narration or excessive writing. When the print picture is especially powerful, it is blown up on the front page of the sports section, signifying its importance in relation to the accompanying written material. For television videographers, if you have good pictures, editing becomes easy. But when a story doesn't have that knockout photography, then you have to get more creative. This could include things such as natural sound, graphics, music, and the like.

5. Get the story on the air. This really should be the first and great commandment. All the pretty pictures and narration in the world don't do any good if the tape is still sitting in editing at deadline or if the still picture doesn't get in the newspaper. Some sportscasters make the mistake of trying to be too perfect and do too much, especially with feature stories. Make sure you get a complete,

coherent story ready for air and then worry about the rest. Clean the suit first and then press the lapels.

6. Make sure the style of editing matches the tone of the story. Modern technology allows for all kinds of fancy edits, such as wipes, dissolves, and fades. But make sure you use these in accordance with the story. For example, dissolves and fades work better with slower or more serious feature stories. For highlights or game stories, it is better to stick with traditional hard edits.

7. When done correctly, the editing should complement the photography. Many shooters will "edit in the camera," which means they shoot certain sequences and shots with a specific idea of how it will look in the edit booth. Ideally, the photographer should have tremendous input in the editing process, and vice versa. Obviously, this becomes much easier when it's all done by the same person, but if not, it's important for the reporter to collaborate with the photographer during the shooting process.

References

Strauss, Robert. (2000, December 4). One on one: an empire built on the ballet of football. *Electronic Media*, p. 24.

7

Anchoring and Play-by-Play

Chronologically, anchoring is the very last thing a sports broadcaster does with his or her show. It comes after the research and legwork, after the planning and preparation, and after all the shooting, producing, and writing. However, anchoring is probably the single most important element of the entire process. Certainly, the other elements are important, but it takes good anchoring and good delivery to bring out the best in the writing and photography. A good sports anchor ties all the other elements together and communicates them in an interesting and entertaining way. It is five or so minutes that will make or break your sportscast and, in some cases, an entire career.

Play-by-play looks a lot like anchoring, but it is actually much different. In general, anchoring involves reading short segments of prepared material. Play-by-play is much longer and also has more of a live element. Although much more preparation usually goes into play-by-play, the actual presentation is spontaneous and unscripted.

Anchoring

From a technical standpoint, sports anchoring is not difficult. Thanks to modern conveniences such as the teleprompter, it involves nothing more than sitting in front of a camera and reading material you've already written. The real trick comes in the delivery, style, and presentation of the anchor. Most stations generally have the same stories, the same interviews, and the same hilights. The challenge is to present that material in a way that engages the audience and sets you apart from your competition.

Ask a hundred different people in the industry how to do this, and you'll probably get a hundred different answers. But most news directors, sports professionals, and television consultants agree that good sports anchoring includes some very basic elements.

Control

Perhaps the most important element is that the sports anchor be in control. Control includes several elements, including look, knowledge, and voice. Basically, it simply means that the audience sees the sports anchor as someone who knows what he or she is talking about and can communicate that information with confidence. That means the ability not only to communicate, but to handle anything that comes up, including technical problems, disruptions, and other almost daily occurrences.

Look and voice are a big part of control. Most news directors want a mature, established presence on the anchor desk, which is especially difficult for sports broadcasters just starting out. Television news director Joel Bernell says flatly, "I want someone who would fit in with the makeup of our anchor team, not somebody who looks like the news anchor's son." Obviously, there is very little you can do about how old you look, but you can certainly convey a more mature attitude in other things you do as an anchor.

One thing is to act more relaxed. This is also difficult for young sports broadcasters, who are bound to be nervous. It's also difficult to get relaxed after a long day of producing, writing, and editing, especially if you have to work against a tight deadline. But in one sense, relaxation is simply a matter of avoiding extremes. You're looking for the middle ground between hyperactive anchoring (a trap easy to fall into in sports) and low-energy anchoring. By definition, most sports anchoring requires a higher level of energy and enthusiasm than news or weather. But it's impossible (and irritating) to maintain a Dick Vitale-style of anchoring for every show and every story. And it would put the audience to sleep to deliver the show in a boring monotone.

Relaxation and control come mainly from confidence that you've done your homework and now feel comfortable in front of the camera. Viewers can tell when an anchor is confident and in control, just as they can sense when he or she is scared or nervous. So far, the only known cure for nerves is practice. You have to get in front of the camera and keep working on your delivery and style until you feel comfortable with it. This is why it's so important to get as much experience as you can, either with internships or at school. Establishing your comfort level as soon as possible puts you that much farther ahead when you go to get that first meaningful job (Figure 7-1).

Knowledge about the subject also gives the anchor confidence. This is generally not a problem for most people getting into the business, who grew up as sports fans. But the job also demands knowledge of the local sports scene. Viewers can immediately tell if someone mispronounces the name of a school or team, which can create a credibility problem. For example, the athletic teams at Wichita Falls, Texas, High School are the "Co-yotes," not the "Co-yotees" and it's important to know the difference. Television news director Paul Conti says, "Know your material. It's horrible when someone tries to fake it and gets it wrong. Sports viewers are the most unforgiving viewers in TV."

Figure 7-1

Good anchoring means being in control no matter what the situation.

Personality

Without a doubt, the one piece of advice given by most professionals is to be yourself and develop your own style. Too many people starting out try to imitate a successful broadcaster or even sound like him or her. Just as viewers can tell when a sportscaster doesn't know sports, they can also spot a phony. Television news director Joel Streed says, "If you're going to do sports, be yourself and don't copy anyone else's style. There's enough Chris Bermans out there." For some reason, Berman has touched a nerve with local news directors (Figure 7-2). "Don't try to imitate Chris Berman," says Conti. "The student has to have his own style and go with what comes naturally. If you have a sense of humor, that's fine. But don't manufacture one."

On the subject of Berman, NFL Network anchor Rich Eisen worked with him at ESPN and says the act is completely sincere. According to Eisen, Berman has the same personality when he's off-camera as when he's on-camera. "I think that's the key to succeeding or failing," says Eisen. "Be yourself. Anybody can smell a fake and they won't care, they won't watch and they won't trust you."

Because of people like Chris Berman, Stuart Scott, and Kenny Mayne at ESPN, young sports broadcasters now think they have to have some sort of comedy act to get noticed. But those people make it work because it suits their personality. The key is to find what suits your personality and develop it into a unique and distinctive style.

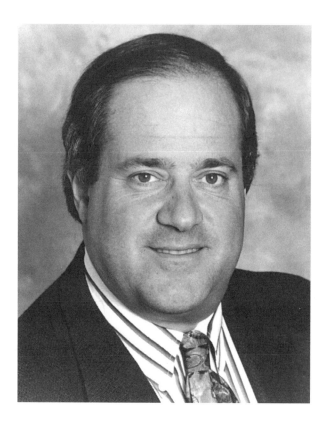

Figure 7-2

ESPN's Chris Berman has thousands of imitators—often to the chagrin of local news directors. *Courtesy: ESPN/John Atashian*

Creativity

"Too many sportscasters look and sound alike or try to mimic national sportscasters," says television news director Ron Lombard. "We like to see people who are natural communicators and can do it with their own style."

There are several ways sports anchors can make themselves unique and set themselves apart from the competition, without going overboard on the personality. You can develop and emphasize a particular aspect of your presentation, such as the photography, storytelling, or interviewing. Most sports interviews consist of sticking a microphone in an athlete's face and asking about a certain play. Very few sportscasters, such as Roy Firestone and Jim Rome, have developed a more sophisticated approach and turned in-depth interviewing into a career.

Many sportscasters develop their own style by doing nothing more than speaking their minds. The trend has really taken off in radio, where opinionated sports talk hosts such as Chris Russo and Mike Francesa have one goal in mind—to provoke the

Figure 7-3

Today's sports talk radio hosts, such as Mike Greenberg (left) and Mike Golic of ESPN, are very opinionated and outspoken. *Courtesy: ESPN/John Atashian*

listeners to react. People who listen to these shows may not agree with the host, but they're still listening and driving up ratings (Figure 7-3).

Anchors on television usually don't act quite as opinionated or brash on the air, but they have the same purpose in mind. "I hear all the time about people who say, 'I don't care about sports, but I tune in to you all the time'," says Ted Leitner, who worked for years at KFMB-TV in San Diego. "That's exactly what I'm trying to do. People will tune in because they just want to hear what this jerk has to say ... or because they think it's interesting or funny or whatever."

Obviously, what works for Ted Leitner probably wouldn't work for Bob Costas, and vice versa. The important point is to find what works for you. Experiment with different styles until you find the one that suits your unique personality and then stick with it.

Entertain

While sports broadcasting is often a difficult and demanding job, you should never forget that it's not life or death. Certainly, sports include some very serious issues involving topics such as money, drugs, and crime. But to most fans and most people who read about it in the newspapers or watch it on television, sports are a form of escapism. Former U.S. Supreme Court Justice Earl Warren once said that he read the front page of the newspaper to learn about man's failures and read the sports section to learn about his successes.

People watch sports to feel good about themselves, share a cultural experience, or see something they've never seen before. In many cases, the actual event itself takes a back seat to the televised experience. Howard Cosell was one of the first to realize this when he worked on *Monday Night Football*. "I bridge the gap between entertainment and journalism," said Cosell. "I'm a communicator with the human perspective." At one point, Cosell even had his own short-lived variety show on ABC.

When Cosell decided to leave *Monday Night Football* in 1984, he did not want a well-known sports broadcaster to take his place, but instead suggested television star Bill Cosby. "He's a brilliant communicator and his performing skills are beyond reproach," said Cosell. "First and foremost, *Monday Night Football* is prime-time entertainment." While ABC decided to pass on Cosby, it broke new ground in June 2000, announcing that stand-up comedian Dennis Miller would join the *Monday Night* broadcast team starting that fall. "We want to make the game relevant to the hard-core fan, accessible to the occasional fan and unpredictable to both," said new *Monday Night* producer Don Ohlmeyer. It was an interesting experiment, but sports fans didn't buy it. Miller was considered too esoteric and lasted only two seasons.

This does not mean that there isn't a place for serious sports journalists on the anchor desk. But you don't have to look any farther than the success of pro wrestling or similar events to realize that sports today have become major prime-time entertainment. Of course, that also doesn't mean you have to forgo the serious sports journalism. But more and more news directors want someone who can present serious information in an entertaining way. Paul Conti says, "I consider sports to be an entertainment product that happens to air in my newscast. Therefore, I want the sports anchor to be entertaining without looking foolish."

Sitting down at the anchor desk to deliver a show is probably the most nerve-wracking experience for young sportscasters. The only sure-fire cure is practice, because very few people are born with the proper control, confidence, and personality to deliver a quality product. Practice as often as you can, keeping in mind the tips listed in Table 7-1.

Play-by-Play

At the other end of the spectrum from anchoring is play-by-play. While both skills require much preparation and research, play-by-play is more spontaneous and less rehearsed. It is sports broadcasting by the seat of your pants, in that anything can happen and sometimes does. And that very quality of unpredictability is what makes it so attractive to many broadcasters. "I love the spontaneity of it," says Charley Steiner, who worked at ESPN and now is the radio voice of the Los Angeles Dodgers. "It unfolds right before your eyes, the complete opposite of the studio experience, which is very scripted and controlled."

Practice under "game" conditions	If possible, practice with all the elements of a professional sportscast in place, including lights, cameras, dress, and makeup. There's something to be said for practicing at home in front of the mirror, but nothing substitutes for the real thing. Ask your university or college to use their studio in nonpeak hours. Get used to sitting in the chair, adjusting your eyes to the lights, and looking on and off camera.	**Table 7-1** Getting Started
Try to avoid getting locked into the teleprompter	The teleprompter is a great device that scrolls your script across the camera while you're reading. But too many young sportscasters use it as a crutch and become hooked on it. The result is a "deer-in-the-headlights" look that appears stiff and unnatural. In many cases, the viewers at home can actually see the sportscaster's eyes moving back and forth during the show. Practice breaking your eyes away from the teleprompter to look down, even if you don't actually read off the copy. These breaks make you seem more relaxed and comfortable.	
Work on relaxed body positioning	One of the symptoms of nervousness is stiff body language, so it's important for the sportscaster to work on relaxing. Many times, a sportscaster is so tight, he or she is physically tired after a 3-minute show. Sit in a relaxed, comfortable position where you're back isn't ramrod straight. Be in a position that allows your head to move easily in any direction. Young sportscasters often seem concerned with their hands and what to do with them. Avoid keeping the hands in a locked, fixed position and instead use them naturally, such as emphasizing a certain point. The hands should comfortably be used to move through pages of your written copy. Much of body language is related to comfort level, and more relaxation comes with more practice and experience.	
Work on tosses and ad-libs	Have an idea ahead of time what you're going to say to the anchors when they introduce you, or you close your show. This "cross talk" doesn't have to be scripted out, but both news anchor and sportscaster should have some idea of what direction to take. Nothing looks worse than long, uncomfortable conversation before a sportscast begins.	
Expect the unexpected	Too many sportscasters believe they have to have a perfect show with no mistakes. As a result, they put so much pressure on themselves, their tension and nervousness increase to the point they make even more mistakes. An experienced sportscaster knows that mistakes are simply a part of the business, especially because so many things are out of his or her control on the set (such as problems in master control, engineering, etc.). The important thing is to roll with the mistakes and keep going. Many sportscasters like to poke fun at themselves during these times, which really helps take the edge off. News directors don't expect you to have a "perfect show" every time, but they are interested in how you handle the mistakes. Learn to find a way to deal with mistakes (yours and everyone else's) that come across positively on the air.	

However, don't let the spontaneity of play-by-play fool you. Announcers don't simply walk into a broadcast booth and do a game without lots of preparation, which in most cases takes much more work than for a traditional studio broadcast. "I would say that for something like baseball, the game preparation is generally between four and eight hours for each game," said Steiner. "Hopefully, you're prepared for any and all eventualities when you're on the air."

Table 7-2

Play-by-Play Preparation
Source/Courtesy:
ESPN/Ron Franklin

Wednesday, October 13			
11:30 a.m.	Virginia conference call		
	11:30 a.m.	Coach	Al Groh
	12:00 p.m.	Quarterback	Marques Hagans
	12:10 p.m.	Linebacker	Ahmad Brooks
	12:20 p.m.	Def. End	Brennan Schmidt
Thursday, October 14			
3:30 p.m.	Florida State practice @ football practice fields		
4:30 p.m.	Stadium technical walk-through		
7:30 p.m.	Production meeting		
	• Distribute graphic packets		
	• Discuss Friday's schedule		
	• Production elements		
	• Promo rotation and copy		
Friday, October 15			
9:00 a.m.	Crew call		
10:00 a.m.	Meeting with Florida State Sports Information		
	• Flip cards – any major injuries or lineup changes		
	• Game timing sheets (pregame and halftime activities)		
	• Stadium map (locations: Family, coaches, VIP's, bands)		
	• Confirm game film viewing time (all 22 clips)		
10:30 a.m.	Florida State coaches meetings		
	10:30 a.m.	Coach	Bobby Bowden
	11:00 a.m.	Offense	Jeff Bowden
	11:30 a.m.	Defense	Mickey Andrews
12:00 Noon	Film session with analyst		
3:30 p.m.	Announcer voice overs (7 p.m. scene set, JIP's, and flashbacks)		
3:45 p.m.	Announcer production meeting		
	• Opening on-camera and production elements		
Saturday, October 16			
10:00 a.m.	Production meeting		
5:15 p.m.	Announcers leave for stadium		
6:30 p.m.	Rehearse promos, lineups, and closing with announcers		
	• Check talk back with all talent		
	• Check TELE-ISO router with analyst		
	• Check communication with sideline reporter		
	• Announcers opening on camera segments		
6:50 p.m.	ESPN News talkback with analyst from the booth		
7:00 p.m.	Air: Roll announcer's scene set into scoreboard show		
7:47 p.m.	Kickoff		
10:45 p.m.	ESPN News Extra and both press conferences		
10:45 p.m.	Feed mini melt, D5 archives to Bristol tape library		
11:00 p.m.	Meal break and strike		

Play-by-play preparation for a live sports broadcast actually begins several days before the game. On Monday and Tuesday, announcers start looking ahead to their next assignment, including reading team reports and press guides. Table 7-2 shows the list of assignments for ESPN announcers who called a 2004 football

Pregame conversations	The broadcaster would probably want to talk to both coaches, both athletic directors, and possibly even some players, if possible. The broadcaster is looking for any scoops, new information, or interesting stories he can relate during the game.	**Table 7-3** Before the Booth
Taped interviews	Interviews with players, coaches, parents, or fans that can be used during the game. This would include information on strategy, how the team is doing, comments about how it's playing, etc. The broadcaster also might want an extended interview to use at halftime. Such interviews should be as interesting as possible and focus on feature-type material.	
Printed information	The broadcaster needs to go over game notes and all information related to the game. This would include rosters, player numbers, and statistical information, all arranged for easy access. During the game, the broadcaster needs to instantly connect numbers to names. Such information also helps in providing background, such as player histories and past performances.	
Technical work	Most bigger stations have engineers working out all the technical details. But in many places, the on-air talent is still responsible for setting up the equipment and making sure it all works properly, with a strong signal going back to the station. This is obviously a much longer and more complicated procedure for television than for radio (see Chapter 8).	
Broadcast responsibilities	The broadcaster must also make sure the call of the game conforms to station standards and policy. Primarily, this means getting the commercials on at the right time and in the right place. The game wouldn't even go on the air if not for the advertisers, and it's extremely important to make sure they're satisfied. Sometimes, the broadcaster will even have to do live commercials or promos during breaks in the game.	

game between Florida State and Virginia, and it is fairly typical of a weekly schedule for a play-by-play announcer. The on-air personnel for the game included a play-by-play person, an analyst, and a sideline reporter.

This preparation usually includes reading newspaper and Internet stories about the event and the athletes, going through game notes supplied by the teams involved, and talking to athletes and coaches before game time. The broadcaster can then use all this information during the game, in the form of statistics, information, or simply interesting stories. John Madden is generally recognized as the most accomplished and successful football broadcaster in the game today and much of his material comes from the preparation he has done before the game starts. "In preparing to do a game," he says, "I always come across stories I can use on the air." Steiner says, "The thing I like most is talking with the players in the dugout three hours before the game. You get a sense of who they are and it helps to tell better stories on the air."

Much preparation goes into doing a play-by-play broadcast, even on the local level. Consider a radio broadcast of a game between two local high school basketball teams, where preparation might include the details given in Table 7-3.

There's also another kind of preparation in which the play-by-play broadcaster uses aids to help him with names, numbers, and statistics. For network events, the

Figure 7-4

Play-by-play requires instant access to all kinds of information.

play-by-play person will have a "spotter," who helps identify players and substitutions. Even if there isn't a spotter, the play-by-play person typically has access to a "spotting board," a visual representation of players, numbers, names, and positions that are arranged for easy access. In a football game, for example, the broadcaster might arrange the spotting board to correspond to the players' location on the field and their position on the team's depth chart. Each broadcaster has his own way of putting together a spotting board and no single way is better than another. The key is to come up with a board that can be accessed easily and quickly and with as little disruption as possible. Most, but not all, boards include things such as a current depth chart, the stat sheets and play-by-play sheets from the previous game, the latest media guides and releases, and a "speed card" for quick, instant information (Figure 7-4).

Whether you're doing a game on radio or television, the preparation is much the same. But after that, the similarities end. Doing games on radio and television are entirely different experiences.

Raised on Radio

Most play-by-play announcers get their start in radio, mainly because the opportunities are so much greater. Almost every local radio station in the country covers some type of sports event, either high school sports, the local college, or minor league baseball.

Because many of these stations don't have large budgets, they rely on young talent seeking to break into the business. Television play-by-play requires years of experience and the field is virtually closed to entry-level applicants.

But there's another distinct advantage to starting in radio. Many current professionals believe radio provides the best training ground for play-by-play because of the unique qualities of the medium. Gary Bender has spent more than 25 years as a play-by-play announcer for network television and radio, and he believes young broadcasters must get their play-by-play start in radio. "Until you have learned the nuances of describing an event on radio, of painting vivid pictures in the listener's mind, you can't do the same for television," writes Bender. "Radio is the cornerstone of a play-by-play career."

Bender and other professionals realize that radio is much different and, in many ways, much more demanding than television. Because the listener can't see what you're seeing, it's important to create an image of the event in the listener's imagination. "Radio is where you are painting the picture," says Steiner. "You are watching the game for millions of people. It's your eyes, your experience, your use of voice and the ability to paint that picture and tell the story."

A phrase like "painting a picture" can mean several different things, but mainly it involves a tremendous amount of description. Radio announcers should describe as much as possible about what's happening. In a typical baseball game on radio, for example, the announcer would go into great detail about things like how the pitcher looks on the mound, how the batter steps into and out of the box, and the size of the crowd. Such information paints a visual picture of the event for the listener. Longtime baseball announcer Jon Miller says, "You're the conduit from the ballpark to (the listener), and the challenge is to put them in the ballpark."

Most of the description will focus on the action and what's actually going on in the game. But radio announcers must convey detailed information about who's doing what and at what moment. This is called "setting the scene," or putting the action into context. Oftentimes, listeners will simply come across a game while tuning in the radio and want to know why this game is important or why they shouldn't change stations. An announcer that does a good job of setting the scene and providing context can keep someone listening, even if that person has no particular interest in the event or the teams that are playing. "TV is right there—you see it, it's easy to believe," says Mark Gastineau of KJR-AM in Seattle. "To me there's more art in radio, you really have to paint a picture for people. It's the most fun of the media because there really are no rules." Says Milo Hamilton, who has broadcast Houston Astros games for nearly two decades, "I don't think it's an accident that (men like) Ernie Harwell and myself have chosen in recent years to do radio only. Maybe it's because we're storytellers."

Despite the importance of storytelling, a radio broadcaster should not forget the role of score updates. Above all else, sports emphasize winning and losing.

An announcer can be as descriptive as possible and paint beautiful pictures of the game, but it doesn't mean anything if the listener doesn't know the score. Hall of Fame announcer Red Barber learned this lesson early on and used an egg timer to remind himself to update the score at least every 3 minutes. If that seems silly or old fashioned, think about the last time you listened to a game on the radio and the frustration you felt if you couldn't figure out the score.

Many young broadcasters get into radio play-by-play thinking it's easier than television because the broadcaster has to deal with less equipment. Often, a radio broadcast can be done with nothing more than a microphone and a telephone line. But in many ways, not having a televised picture to fall back on puts more pressure on the broadcaster. "Radio is the use of words," says longtime television broadcaster Keith Jackson. "It's the creation of images. It's the ability . . . to build a picture for somebody to see."

The Electronic Eye

In 1951, New York Giants radio announcer Russ Hodges won broadcasting immortality with his call of Bobby Thomson's dramatic home run to win the National League pennant. "The Giants win the pennant! The Giants win the pennant!" has become a part of not only baseball history, but American history as well. Less well known is Ernie Harwell's call of the same event. Harwell is best known for his long career as a radio baseball announcer, but on that particular day he did the game on television. "After Thomson hit the home run," he said years later, "I simply said 'it's gone.' And after that, I didn't say anything for a long time."

One event, two announcers and two different mediums. The Thomson home run points out the difference between play-by-play on radio and television, a difference not all announcers understood as well as Harwell. Many professional broadcasters had a difficult time making the transition from radio to television because they thought of television as simply radio with pictures. "In the early days of television, most sports announcers were radio guys and did radio on TV," said veteran sportscaster Jack Whitaker. "The director would always say, 'don't say he swung and missed—we can see that!' "

Eventually, sportscasters learned the nuances of calling a game on television as a completely different kind of art form that required a different play-by-play approach. One of the men who helped define the emerging form was NFL play-by-play announcer Ray Scott. Scott covered the Green Bay Packers during their glory years of the 1960s and developed a "short hand" game description that has become almost the standard today. Instead of saying, "Bart Starr drops back, avoids the rush, throws to Boyd Dowler who catches it on the 20 and avoids two tacklers for the

Radio Announcers	Television Announcers	**Table 7-4**
Play-by-play: "And now with 59 seconds left in the first half, they've got the ball 1st and 10, 33 yard line . . . Isaac Bruce in motion . . . Warner takes the snap and falls down, tackled at the 40 yard line."	Play-by-play: "Isaac Bruce in motion left . . . and Warner falls down. He gets tripped up by one of his own players."	Radio versus Television *Source: Courtesy KSD-FM/St. Louis Rams, Fox/NFL*
Analyst: "When things go like that, it's not going your way. He was backpedaling and just trips and falls. I think he got caught up with one of his linemen."	Analyst: "They have played as bad in this first half as they have all year, including the preseason. Everything that could go wrong, has gone wrong."	
Play-by-play: "I want to bring this up, and we talked about it before the game . . . this is the Rams first game this year on grass."	Play-by-play: "A 7-yard loss."	
Analyst: "He got his leg caught up with either the left guard or center."	Analyst: "You can see Newton's right foot gets caught up with Warner's left foot."	
Play-by-play: "2nd down and 16 at the 39 yard line . . . Warner in the shotgun, takes the snap . . . under pressure, steps up and throws to the left sideline, caught by Roland Williams. He can't even get back to the original line of scrimmage, tackled there by Steve Jackson. Rams in the hurry up, 32 seconds to go . . . they'll have 3rd down here at the 45. Warner shotgun formation, 3-receiver set, back to throw . . . has some time . . . throws to the right side and it's nearly intercepted by Dennard Walker, intended for Torry Holt. And the Rams will have to punt."	Play-by-play: "45 seconds to go. Warner steps up . . . slings it out and the pass goes to tight end Roland Williams; he had a career game last week against the Browns, including a touchdown pass. The Rams now in the hurry-up after the 4-yard pickup with less than half a minute left in the first half. 3rd and 13. There's the pass . . . tipped way by Dennard Walker, intended downfield for Torry Holt. So on 4th down, Jeff Wilkins will come in for a field goal."	
Analyst: "He had Torry Holt. Tennessee rotated a corner up, or had him go way deep and played a man underneath. If he throws that ball a little earlier, it' s a completed pass."	Analyst: "We've seen some excellent play in this first half from the Tennessee defensive backfield . . . they have taken away all the Rams big weapons."	

touchdown," Scott would make the description brutally simple: "Starr . . . Dowler . . . touchdown" and let the pictures fill in the details. Over the years, sportscasters embellished Scott's bare-bones style, but the theory remains the same. "On TV, people are seeing the same things you are," says Steiner. "So you have to find a way—through facts, research, knowledge, and insight—to add to what they're seeing."

Calling a game on radio is completely different than doing the same event on television. A good example of the difference can be found in Table 7-4 in a short series of plays from an NFL game between the St. Louis Rams and the Tennessee Titans. Notice how the radio announcers added much more information, while the television announcers tried to keep their observations to a minimum.

This is another way of saying that the television announcer should rely less on description and statistics and more on "setting the scene" referred to in radio. While detailed description may keep the radio listener connected to the game, in television it becomes annoying overkill. Why describe at length what the viewers can already see? Thus, one of the main jobs of the television announcer is to fill in the details and provide context for what the viewer can't see or doesn't know. Marty Bass works as a morning news anchor at WJZ-TV in Baltimore, but he also does work with the Baltimore Ravens radio broadcasts. "Nothing is bigger than the game," he says, "but the game itself can be dull. A good announcer with style can build the drama and build the story around the statistics." John Madden agrees, up to a point. "There's no such thing as a dull game. The person talking about it might be dull."

Just as a good announcer knows what to say, he or she also knows what not to say. One of the cardinal rules of television announcing is "let the pictures tell the story." That is, let the action speak for itself, especially if the action is compelling or dramatic. It's during these times that the television announcer should keep his words at a minimum, as Harwell did after Thomson's home run or like Al Michaels after the U.S. Olympic hockey win over the Soviet Union in 1980. One of the main problems television announcers must overcome is the temptation to talk too much and kill the pictures. This is especially problematic in baseball, where there are so many natural lulls and pauses in the game. According to Bob Marshall, television has ruined coverage of the baseball playoffs because the network's announcers compete with each other to dominate the broadcast. "They talked incessantly," said Marshall, referring to ABC's coverage, "no matter what was going on in the game. And when they ran out of things to say or there was a pause in the action, they talked some more."

This brings up another essential point: the game should not be a showcase for the broadcasters. Many professionals have fallen into the trap of trying to become bigger than the event. Howard Cosell would tell anyone who would listen that most people tuned in to *Monday Night Football* to watch him, not the game. There may be an element of truth in that, but when a broadcaster puts the focus on himself instead of the event, the broadcast isn't as effective. Even John Madden, arguably the most popular announcer on television today admits, "The game is the thing, not me . . . or the camera angles. The game is what everybody is interested in."

The Role of the Analyst

Announcing teams usually work in pairs (or sometimes in threes), with an analyst or "color" man broadcasting with the play-by-play person. The analyst position usually goes to someone with an in-depth knowledge of the sport or event, which more than likely means a former athlete. While not many professionally trained broadcasters qualify for this role, it's still important to know what the analyst does because the two must work together as a team within their roles in order to produce the best possible on-air performance (Figure 7-5).

Primarily, the analyst provides the "how and why" of the game, whereas the play-by-play person handles the "who and what." Of course, this is an oversimplification,

Figure 7-5

Announce teams usually work in groups of two or three. In this case, the two announcers are on the right and the spotter, who uses binoculars to help the announcers identify players, is on the left.

but it helps explain why the analyst must have such a strong background. He or she is expected to fill in details and explanation that give the audience a deeper understanding. "I tell my analyst to take us beyond what we're seeing," says veteran announcer Marv Albert. "Take us someplace new—someplace we haven't gone before." Adds baseball analyst Tim McCarver, "What can I add to the picture that explains what happened or how it happened?" But while the analyst is concerned primarily with explanation, Albert adds that there's a fine line between being interesting and being redundant. "You want some replays, but not too many. Otherwise, the guy just sits and talks over highlights all night."

That's why so many modern analysts have developed distinct and entertaining personalities. John Madden was one of the first analysts to move the boundaries of the job beyond simple description. Madden diagrams football Xs and Os like any former coach, but it's his presentation that fans remember. "The cornerstone of broadcasting to me is passion," he says. "I don't really think of myself as a broadcaster." The same could probably be said for basketball analyst Dick Vitale.

In some cases, analysts such as Madden and Vitale have become even more popular than their play-by-play partners, which is why a good working relationship in the booth is so important. It's very easy for big egos to get bruised and ruin the on-air product. Frank Gifford admits that during the 1980s, Howard Cosell was virtually impossible to work with on *Monday Night Football* because he insisted on dominating the telecast and tried to drown out his broadcast partners. The partnership works best when all the members understand their roles and their place in the broadcast. "Don't just keep talking," says golf analyst Ken Venturi. "It has to have meaning. On television, it's not what you say but what you don't say."

Final Advice

Some final thoughts about the play-by-play booth, whether it's for radio or television:

Style

Just as in anchoring, it's important to be yourself and not copy anyone else. "Imitation is flattering," says Gary Bender, "but you can't build a career on it. The key is to develop a distinct style of your own, based on your own strengths and weaknesses. Style is a product of being yourself." Longtime announcer Curt Gowdy agrees. "I loved the voices of guys like Ted Husing and Bill Stern," he said, "but I never tried to copy them. That's the worst thing you can do. You have to be yourself."

Practice

Many play-by-play broadcasters started out with a tape recorder, a game program, and a secluded spot in the high school gym. Trying to describe the action seems awkward at first, but that's the point. Smooth out the rough spots at an early age and then you can work on the finer points of style and technique. It also helps to share your work with a trained professional, who can offer advice and suggestions. In many situations, the local radio broadcaster will be more than happy to help out. With enough practice, whether it actually makes the air or not, the fundamentals of good play-by-play become second nature. "What I do has to be instinct and reaction," says Madden. "If you start questioning your instincts, you'll be afraid to make a mistake or say the wrong thing."

People, Not Statistics

Always remember that games are played and watched by people. Young broadcasters often fall into a trap of trying to fill the game with too many numbers and statistics, especially if there's time to fill or the action seems to drag. Marty Bass says that Jim Hunter of CBS radio is one of the best play-by-play men in the business. "But during a baseball rain delay, he fills the extra time with stats. I don't know how many people have driven their cars off a bridge listening to endless talk about somebody's ERA. Contrast that to ESPN's Jon Miller, who is likely to break into his Vin Scully impersonation if things get too slow."

Bass says firmly "stats killed sports." That may be an overstatement, but it's certainly easy for a play-by-play announcer to kill a game by concentrating too much on the numbers and ignoring all the interesting stories. Author Curt Smith adds, "The play-by-play men of today are not as interesting or distinctive as those of two or three decades ago. But thank God, there are exceptions."

Play-by-Play with Ron Franklin

Since joining ESPN in 1987, Ron Franklin (Figure 7-6) has become one of the network's primary college football and men's college basketball play-by-play commentators. Other broadcasting credits include play-by-play for tennis, college

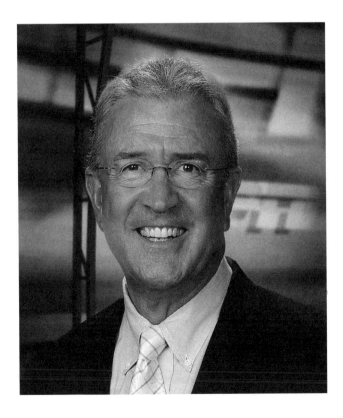

Figure 7-6

ESPN announcer
Ron Franklin. *Courtesy:
Rich Arden/ESPN*

baseball, the U.S. Olympic Festival, and host of ESPN's *Sportsman's Challenge*. Franklin also operates "Ron Franklin Productions," a production company producing various syndicated television and radio sports programs.

Q: I'm not sure people appreciate the work and travel schedule of a play-by-play person. Can you describe a little of what your typical workweek is like?

A: Mondays are usually spent getting depth charts emailed or faxed to my office to start my charts. I use my computer to put together an offensive and defensive chart for each team. Normally, the books from these schools come the week before or I received them at the beginning of the year so I have a source to start making notes on the individual players. Also, I normally use some time on Monday to call a few people with the two teams we are doing to get some different views as to what they are doing and how they are playing, and that helps me prepare for what to look for if it's a team we haven't done in recent years. I use other play-by-play announcers to bounce things off of as well.

On Tuesday, ESPN sends me cut-up video of both teams with offense, defense, and special teams. They also send the last game these teams have played unless I request an earlier game as well. My main reason for using video is to check formations and see how key players are used whether they are on offense or defense. This really helps me. Packets from each school usually arrive on Tuesday and reading takes a good part of the day while getting into the video as well.

On Wednesday every week we set up a conference call with the visiting school and talk with the head coach, offensive coordinator, and defensive coordinator. If the school allows players to talk that late in the week we normally visit with three or four of them. The conference calls usually last anywhere from 90 minutes to 2 hours.

Thursday is travel day. We are required to be at the home team workout Thursday afternoons. Here I get a chance to watch both sides of the ball prepare plus special teams. Also, it's a chance to shake hands with some players and visit if the school allows that and talk with some of the position coaches. I look for stories and side bar stuff and my color man is primarily looking for Xs and Os. Being at practice always adds several stories we can use on the air and it gives me a better idea of how to lead my color guy during the telecast.

Friday mornings are always spent visiting with the home team head coach and his coordinators for both offense and defense. After these meetings, which usually last around 90 minutes, we head into the video room and watch both teams one more time and talk about situational things that could be discussed in the game or things to watch for on special teams. Friday afternoon I go to the trucks and get copy for my voiceovers. We have a tease to record as well and sometimes a scene-set. At least every other week ESPN wants me to do an essay, which requires coat and tie. After recording in the booth I find a dressing room and change into a coat and tie and we record on the on-camera at the same time of day that it will run on Saturday.

We try to find a neat place on campus with a good background to do these to break the monotony of always sitting with the stadium in the background. The day ends with that done for me and we usually finish between 7 or 8 o'clock.

On Saturday, production meetings begin at 9 am. Sideline people first and then production people (graphics, producer, director, and infinite). The announcers are invited in about 45 minutes after the start and we all discuss where we are going with the telecast. We have a game plan just like the coaches do. We go over what will be said in the open and how that can be supported with video or graphics. Our part doesn't really take that long (30) minutes. We have spent so much time visiting during the week and watching video together it's just a matter of making sure everyone is on the same page. Before we get to the stadium we are expected to watch and take some notes on big games that are being played earlier so we can constructively comment on the air about them during our game. We are required to be at the stadium at least 2 hours before the telecast begins. We have last minute things to do. I rehearse the starting lineups so production can go through them as well as myself. We read every promo that will run that night and go over any "in-game" things that might be out of the norm. Then it's the game and 3 1/2 hours later we are done. Normally, ESPN News wants a short cut-in immediately following the game with the two announcers. Probably 5 minutes total on that. Then it's home to bed for an early wake-up call and off to the airport.

Then on Sunday it's an early flight out to get home to family and prepare to do it all over again.

Q: In terms of the on-air performance, what are the attributes a play-by-play person has to have to be successful?

A: People have different opinions about this question. Certainly looks and a decent voice can be a great help, but are far from the most important ingredients to me. Knowledge of the game, knowledge of the teams you are doing, and presentation that is enjoyable for the audience. Viewers want to be comfortable with the person they are listening to and they want to think this person is believable. Overly opinionated announcers generally have a tough time gaining much support from the viewers. My theory has always been that we are not the show, the game is. I will have an opinion and don't shy away from giving it when the situation deserves that kind of remark. Never back off answering a tough question but you're playing with fire if that's all you do. Audiences want to make up their own minds on some things. Be consistent and give the viewers reason to trust you by showing total objectivity. Remember, you have to be able to look yourself in the mirror the next morning.

Q: How would you describe the ideal relationship between the play-by-play person and the analyst?

A: You've got to like each other and trust each other. He is the specialist on the game and you are the specialist on broadcasting and the telecast itself. It would be very hard to work with an analyst who's there only for his own good and cares little about who he steps on to garner attention. I would never hang my color guy out to dry if he makes an error and doesn't realize it and the situation is the same for him. "Team" is the name of the game when it comes to these two people in the booth. You are there to inform and entertain the audience.

Q: We hear a lot about the importance of starting a play-by-play foundation in radio and mastering that medium before doing television. Would you agree with that approach?

A: To have done radio is a great help because of timing during a game. Once a game starts most people have no idea of how fast things really go when you add all the ingredients it takes to make the show work. It's simply a pace that you have no way of preparing for until you've worked some games. I don't think it's essential to have done radio but again it certainly helps. Some people have trouble with the transition because in television the pictures do a lot of the talking. "Layouts" are sometimes more important than words in television, while in radio you are the eyes and ears of the audience. Some find that more creative than doing television. I find myself in that category sometimes. I love doing radio.

Q: Not a lot of schools give students the opportunity to do play-by-play. For someone who has an interest, what is the best way to prepare for a play-by-play career?

A: Find a high school who wants a play-by-play man or buy yourself a tape recorder and go to games and do your own. Come home and listen afterwards and see what you think of yourself. Repetition is the most important thing you can do and it's virtually the only way to learn. Also, close yourself in a room and take game material in with you. See how long you can talk and maybe make up a game and have interludes where ad-libbing is imperative. We are becoming an era of "readers" on television because of teleprompters and nobody knows how to ad-lib any more. Teach yourself how to converse with an audience and not read to them. Talk to them like you're having a conversation with them. Small markets are a very good place to get started. You have to do almost everything in the newsroom in small operations and there's no better way to learn than having done it yourself. It's the same as going to school, but now you are getting paid for it.

References

Bender, Gary and Johnson, Michael L. (1994). *Call of the game: what really goes on in the broadcast booth.* Chicago: Bonus Books.

"Careers in sports journalism: play-by-play announcer." (1999, September 7). *ESPN.* http://www.espn.go.com./special/s/careers/anno.html

"Careers in sports journalism: TV sports anchor." (1999, September 7). *ESPN.* http://www.espn.go.com/special/s/careers/anchor.html

Cosell, Howard and Boventre, Peter. (1985). *I never played the game.* New York: Morrow.

Einstein, Charles. (Ed). (1987). *The fireside book of baseball.* (4th ed.). New York: Simon & Schuster.

Greppi, Michelle. (2000, June 23). 'MNF' runs rant pattern, brings Miller to booth. *Hollywood Reporter.*

Laurence, Robert P. (1999, March 22). Leitner's light touch. *Electronic Media.*

Madden, John and Anderson, Dave. (1996). *All Madden.* New York: HarperCollins.

Marshall, Bob. (1981). *Diary of a Yankee hater.* New York: Franklin Watts.

Martzke, Rudy. (2000, April 28). Albert's NBA schedule filled with traveling calls. *USA Today.*

National Sports Report. (2000, August 25). [Television show]. *Fox Sports.*

Rites of Autumn. (2001). [Home video]. *Lion's Gate Entertainment.* Producers: Don Sperling and Wayne Chesler.

Sportscasters: behind the mike. (2000, February 7). [Television show]. *The History Channel.*

Sports-talk radio host. (1999, September 7). *ESPN.* http://espn.go.com/special/s/careers/sptalk.html, September 7, 1999.

8 *Production*

So far, we've concentrated on the end result of sports media content—the finished story or presentation. But putting together that content requires a tremendous amount of time, energy, and resources. There are two main parts to the sports media production process: getting the individual stories ready for presentation and producing live sports events.

Daily Sports Production

Print

New technology has vastly improved the production process for both print and broadcast. Most of us have seen the old-time movies of the newspaper office, where copy boys take the finished story from the reporter's typewriter and run it down to layout. In those days, the newspaper had to be put together by hand and then sent to the printing press. When reporters were covering games, they either typed their stories in the press box or phoned them in. For a reporter from a morning newspaper covering a night game, the process was so time-consuming that making a deadline was always a constant concern. This was especially problematic considering that reporters also had to get postgame comments from players and coaches.

Longtime sportswriter Roger Kahn began his career in 1948 at the *New York Herald-American* and he describes the print production process that existed at the time:

> Stories came in to a Western Union room, transmitted in Morse code, and transcribed by fast-typing telegraphers. Copyboys carried them to the chief copyreader, or slotman, who gave each a 'slug,' or label. Sitting inside a U-shaped arrangement of tables, the slotman distributed stories to his subordinates, who sat around the rim. Slugged and edited stories went down

a chute to the composing room, where they were set in type. Following hand-drawn layout charts, other printers inserted type into models of pages. The pages were pressed into molds, which were then affixed to huge rotary presses, each capable of producing 35,000 copies every hour. Conveyor belts carried the finished newspapers to ground level, where fleets of trucks, massed like so many Patton tanks, waited to fan out through the city. Joe Herzberg called this process, the production of a newspaper, 'a daily miracle.'

Changes in technology have drastically improved the process, allowing reporters to stay longer at stories and transmit their information more easily. Reporters even at the smallest papers usually have access to a laptop computer they can take to games or stories. They will use the computers not only to write and edit, but also to send the story back to the newsroom. Usually, this involves finding a phone line hookup to get Internet access, but wireless technology now makes it possible to send back stories even when no line is available, such as from airplanes. Many event sites provide media members with computer hookups and Internet lines for story transmission.

It could be argued that such technology has improved the quality of sports journalism at newspapers and magazines. Reporters can stay longer at stories, get more information, and transmit breaking information much more easily. As a result, sportswriters have extended their reach and coverage far beyond the limits of just a few years ago. The same goes for print photographers, who can now transmit their images directly from the scene of the story. Almost as soon as a big play occurs, photographers can have the picture relayed to their newspapers. The newsroom has much more time to get it ready for layout in the paper, which would include such things as cropping, resizing, and positioning. Other newspaper personnel can immediately post the image on the paper's Internet site.

Once the reporter transmits the story from the scene, it goes into the hands of editors and other newsroom personnel. One thing that has not changed is the need for copyeditors, who look over the stories and make typographical and factual corrections. After copyediting, the final version of the story and its headline go to layout for positioning in the sports section. Among the decisions editors must make are how prominently the story will be displayed, how large the headline will be, and how many column inches will be used. Again, technology has completely revolutionized this aspect of newspaper production. Much of today's layout is done with computer software. The individual elements are stored as computer files and moved easily around the page. Once editors make the final determinations for all the stories in the sports section, the section goes to press (Figures 8-1 and 8-2).

The actual process of printing the paper hasn't changed much, and it still takes awhile to get it off the press and out to the public. Morning newspapers have varying deadlines for the paper to get to press, usually somewhere between 11 p.m. and

Figure 8-1

One view of today's
newspaper layout process.

2 a.m. The newspaper staff will create its Internet sports content on much the same schedule as the paper. Stories will be created and posted on the site even as the paper goes to press. But because the printed version is the newspaper's bread and butter, staffers usually do not update the site throughout the night.

This reflects some of the debate in today's newspaper industry over how to treat an Internet site. Much of the concern is economic, and specifically how to get people to buy the newspaper if the same information is available for free online. If people can get all the scores and sports information they need on the Web, why would they bother with the newspaper?

Newspapers have addressed this issue in varying ways. Some have simply started charging a fee for access to their Internet site. Some newspapers, such as the *New York Times*, make today's Internet edition available for free, but charge for access to previous editions. Other newspapers require their Internet users to fill out

lengthy surveys, which almost always include specific demographic information. This helps the paper target readers for merchandising and sales opportunities more directly.

For example, new readers to the Internet sports section of the *Ft. Worth Star-Telegram* have to sign up for access to read the site's contents. The access is free, but the paper uses the information for a variety of purposes. The company's privacy statement notes, "Our main goal is to provide you with a customized and more relevant experience. We review our users' preferences, demographics, traffic patterns, and other information in aggregate so that we can better understand who our audience is, and what it is you want. Tracking user preferences also helps us serve you more relevant advertising."

At some newspapers, access to any and all sports content is free. The thinking at these papers is that the Internet section really serves as a promotional device to encourage people to read the newspaper. Newspaper Internet sports sections usually don't carry as much content as found in the paper. Typically, the site will feature the one or two big sports stories of the day, but much of the "meat" can only be found in the newspaper. By restricting content, even to a small degree, the Internet site can prompt users to find more information and detail in the newspaper.

Finally, there's also the sense that one of the primary benefits of reading the newspaper is the experience of "having something to hold on to." Aside from the problems of messy ink or delivery boys with poor aim, holding and reading a newspaper is a tactile experience that most people enjoy. The format makes it easy for readers to skip around, go back to get more detail, and, perhaps most importantly, take the medium out of the house. With the rise of modern technology, such as the computer and electronic books, many have predicted the demise of the printed media. But newspapers and magazines continue to survive and thrive, especially in terms of sports media.

Broadcast

Producing sports for broadcast falls into two main categories. There is the production of stories and sportscasts on a daily basis, done at television, cable, and radio broadcast outlets. Some of this is national in scope, such as the tremendous amount of sports content created daily by the ESPN networks. Much more of it is local, as almost every television and radio station in the country has some sort of sports programming. The other type of sports broadcasting is the production and transmission of special sports programming. These kinds of shows are usually longer than daily productions and are centered around a special or significant event.

Daily Sports

Just like the newspaper, television and radio outlets must produce a certain amount of sports content each day. While print content is determined by column inches, broadcast content is measured in terms of minutes and seconds, which can vary widely according to each medium. A talk radio station may devote its entire afternoon or evening schedule to sports, but for local television stations, the sports segment of the newscast typically receives around 2 or 3 minutes of time. A national or regional outlet such as Fox Sports devotes its entire schedule to sports content, but still must be mindful of restrictions on time and space.

These decisions are made by a producer, or several producers in the case of large broadcast outlets. The producer is someone who has overall control of the sports content, including such considerations as timing, story selection, ordering, and presentation. Smaller media outlets may only have one producer, who in some cases may also have to double up as reporter or anchor. Big outfits such as ESPN have dozens or even hundreds of producers working on different shows (Figure 8-3).

Of the many decisions producers must make, the first and most important is time or length. This obviously varies depending on the station, the market size, and the situation. Generally, local broadcast executives do not consider sports an important element of the show and almost all research studies confirm their opinion. The sports segment is generally the least-watched part of the local television newscast (behind weather and news) and, according to consulting firm Frank Magid, up to

Figure 8-3

Just a small part of the
production staff at ESPN.
Courtesy: ESPN/Rick Arden

two-thirds of the audience do not find sports a compelling reason to tune in. As a result, sports is left to the end of the newscast and given less time than the other news elements.

Coming at the end of the show affords certain advantages, such as having more time to write and edit material. The deadline for getting such material ready for air is usually around 10 or 15 minutes into the show. But the situation also has several disadvantages. Because the sports segment usually comes at the end of the show, time often gets cut or expanded to make corrections for earlier problems in the newscast. Special situations, such as breaking news or live reporting, can often cut into sports time. For an important event such as election night, some stations will forego sports coverage entirely. Thus, while the newscast producer will try to stick to time as much as possible, the actual time can change often during the day and even during the newscast.

Slug	Format	Tape #	Still Store	Length	Total Time
HS football	V/O	S-147	Football	:40	:40
Scores	CG	----------	----------	:30	1:10
College preview	VO/SOT	S-148	Tigers FB	:45	1:55
Coach Jones	PKG	S-149	----------	1:50	3:45
Baseball trade	RDR	----------	Cubs	:15	4:00

Table 8-1

Typical Sports Segment Rundown

Once decisions about time have been made, sports producers must begin to consider story order and selection. This is where the rundown comes into play, which is perhaps the producer's most important tool in putting together a show.

A rundown is simply a list of the stories you plan to cover for the day (Table 8-1). It generally includes the list and names of your stories, how you plan to present them (highlights only? Sound on tape? A full package?) and other important information for the director. Most newsrooms are now computerized and have software programs to use with your rundowns, although in some of the smaller markets you still might have to do your rundown manually on a typewriter.

There is no one standard for rundowns, but typically they include some standard information. The "slug" is a one- or two-word name for the story that is easy to write and remember. "Format" refers to the type of story, whether a package, V/O, VO/SOT, reader, or whatever (V/O stands for "voice over" when the anchor is narrating over video, and VO/SOT stands for "voice over/sound on tape," which adds a short interview segment to the V/O). "Tape number" indicates whether the story has a tape associated with it and, if so, the tape number assigned. As digitalization increases in newsrooms, tapes are being replaces by computer files.

"Still store" or some similar designation refers to the graphics that many stations use. These are the small pictures on the screen that appear over the shoulder of the sports anchor. "Length" is an indication of how long each individual story runs. The addition of each story's length adds up to a cumulative "total time," which tells the producer how close the show is running to its assigned time. In our example, the show is scheduled for 4 minutes, although weekday sports segments usually get around 2 or 3 minutes.

Before we get to timing, our rundown starts with story ideas. One of your jobs is to reduce the dozens of possible story ideas down to just a few that will actually run in the show. Story ideas come from many different places. Most, if not all, stations now subscribe to the Associated Press broadcast wire, which transmits global, national, and sometimes local sports information 24 hours a day. Many times, a national story can be "localized" to attract more interest with the station's audience. For example, if the AP runs a story that says graduation rates for college athletes are falling, one could go to the local college and university and investigate the situation there.

Stations also subscribe to some form of news feed, affiliated either with their network or with an independent provider, such as CNN. News feeds come almost

Figure 8-4

Recording highlights from a network sports feed at a local television station.

continually during the day, although most of the sports content comes at specific times. Usually, news feed organizations will provide sports feeds at least three times during the day: sometime in the morning, where the feed includes highlights and interviews from the previous night's games; late afternoon, which includes the major sports news of the day and any afternoon games; and finally late evening, which focuses on highlights of games played that night and updates major stories from earlier in the day (Figure 8-4).

The goal of the sports feed is to provide local outlets with video and audio elements that support the big sports stories of the day. The feed includes a variety of story formats, including packages, VOs, SOTs, and VO/SOTs, which give the producer more options in planning sports coverage (Table 8-2). For example, the sports producer may not want to use the entire package on Ernie Els because of time constraints. Instead, he or she may edit it down to a VO or VO/SOT and then use the leftover time on another story.

Time	Slug	Format	Source	Length	Table 8-2
4:30:15	Tyson hearing	VO/SOT		1:30	
4:32:05	Red Sox parade	VO	WBZ	1:00	Typical Network Sports Feed Rundown
4:33:30	FSU preview	VO/SOT	NCAA	3:00	
4:37:00	Illinois preview	VO/SOT	NCAA	2:56	
4:40:15	Ernie Els	PKG	WCPX	1:50	
4:42:30	Pujols file	VO	MLB	:35	
4:43:15	Santiago file	VO	MLB	:30	
4:45:00	Cards preview	VO/SOT	KTVK	1:30	
4:47:10	Jags preview	VO/SOT	WJXT	1:20	
4:48:45	Bears preview	VO/SOT	WFLD	1:45	
4:50:45	Chiefs preview	SOT	KMBC	:45	

Story ideas can also come out of editorial meetings, where producers and reporters gather to discuss what's going on that particular day. Many sports directors also keep up-to-date files of events, people, and contact in their area. This allows them to know in advance if important things are going on. Developing good contacts in your area is also advisable. Many times, people will call you with bits of information that you can turn into workable story ideas.

Once you have settled on story ideas, you can start working on determining how to cover the stories and what order to put them in. Order is usually determined by importance, with the most important story going first. "Importance" in this sense typically means how much relevance and impact the story has for the majority of the audience. There should be some sort of logical connection between stories in that they are similar in terms of style, tone, or subject matter. For example, if your lead is about the Los Angeles Angels, it would make sense that the following story is also about baseball, whether little league, high school, college, or pro. If there are no other baseball stories, a logical follow-up would be something on another sport in the Los Angeles area. Tone or style is also important in that the more serious stories are typically presented first, followed by more feature-style reporting.

How do you determine if a particular story is going to be a package, a live report, or a combination of both? Such decisions are determined by several factors, including your available resources. Make a list of your resources you expect for the show. What stories you want to cover obviously depends on what's available. How many photographers are available to shoot? How much time will it take to edit? What's coming down on the network sports feed? What's on the national wires? What are the most important local events going on? Does anything warrant live coverage? These are some of the questions you should be asking yourself as you start planning out your show.

The importance of the story is also considered in that the more serious and important stories are usually done as packages or live reports. You should also take into account your deadlines. If your sports show goes on the air at 10 p.m., what

Table 8-3	Show	Primary Audience	Elements to Emphasize
Considerations for Local Television Sports Producing	Morning	Men/women headed to work; some kids	Late scores/highlights, unusual or interesting video
	5:00 p.m.	Women, elderly, kids, casual fans	Longer feature stories, packages, personality-oriented stories, visually interesting
	6:00 p.m.	Men, hard-core fans	Harder stories, fewer packages, higher story count, more VO, VO/SOTs
	10/11:00 p.m.	Wide range, usually more interested fans	Scores, highlights, reaction

would be the best way to cover a game that starts at 6 p.m.? What about a game that doesn't start until 9 p.m. or one that goes overtime and runs beyond your deadline? All of these possibilities should be considered when planning out event coverage.

The audience also figures into your planning because broadcast audiences change throughout the day for both radio and television. The people who watch the early morning shows to find a particular score are not necessarily the same group of people watching at 10 p.m. Knowing who's watching or listening will help you figure out how to best present your sports content (Table 8-3).

As your rundown continues to fill out, there are several things you should keep in mind. Remember that the rundown is really just a temporary blueprint for the show and will often change before the sportscast. Some stories will come in late and have to be delayed, whereas others will not come at all and have to be dropped entirely. You may also have to drop stories if the news has run long or if your own show has taken longer than expected. Therefore, it's always a good idea to have some sort of backup plan in mind. You might have to change a story from a package to a VO and consider adding another short reader or story to make up the time. The key to the rundown is flexibility and being prepared to make changes at any time.

Communication is also essential. It's important to work with the newscast producer and let him or her know exactly what's in your show. The newscast producer has the responsibility for the overall newscast, of which your sportscast plays just a part. The sportscaster should provide a copy of the rundown to the newscast producer and keep that person updated on any changes. The newscast producer has the final authority to adjust sports time and approve any last-minute changes. Obviously, this step is unnecessary for all-sports radio and television outlets.

You should be realistic in what you can and can't do. You want to give the best possible coverage to each and every story in your rundown, but there are certain technical and logistical handicaps that make your job much more difficult. It would be great to have a live report from the state championship basketball game, but is it even technically possible to get a live shot from the arena? And what's the cost involved? If you don't go live, what's the next best way to cover the game? A package seems logical, but will your reporter have time to drive back to the station and edit together a piece? Would it be better to rent a satellite truck at the site? Sports producers waste a lot of time spinning their wheels because they try to do too much. Certainly, unexpected breakdowns and problems will occur and more often than you like. But pushing the envelope too far only increases your chances for frustration down the line.

Coordinate your coverage as much as possible. This means coordination at every level—the newsroom, event management, engineering, etc. The news department should be fully aware of what you're trying to do, not only to avoid unnecessary conflict, but maybe to provide some unexpected help. If a news reporter is covering a story in the same town where you need an interview with the baseball coach, you might be able to kill two birds with one stone and save yourself the trip. But don't be surprised if you're asked to return the favor someday.

In today's converged media environment, many times you'll have to work hand in hand with the newspaper or Internet media, or it might be that the story is big enough that is crosses over into news. Athletes can become news subjects for their behavior off the field, such as the legal trials of Ray Lewis and Kobe Bryant. In these cases, you will have to work with the news department to decide how best to cover the story. It could involve you anchoring in the news segment or developing sidebar stories for the news segment.

Many times sports stories become front page news and it's necessary for the news and sports departments to work together on the coverage. Consider a hypothetical example, where a local all-star athlete is arrested on drug charges (Table 8-4). Usually news and sports departments will work together to get the pieces of the story. But what are the presentation possibilities for the station?

It's also important to focus on localism and have as many local stories as possible. Not too long ago, broadcast television stations were the only game in town and the only way for people to see highlights of national sports events such as the Kentucky Derby or Indy 500. Now, there are literally hundreds of cable and satellite channels, some of them completely dedicated to sports. And virtually the same highlights you want to show will run on ESPN, CNN, and the like. Add the Internet and online services, and the viewer can get his national sports stories from almost anywhere.

That's why it's essential that local markets emphasize the local sports scene because it offers your audience something it can't see anywhere else. Certainly, this means the traditional sports, such as football, basketball, and baseball. Many stations have now expanded their weekend sports shows to 15 or 30 minutes with one goal in mind—show as many high school and local college games as possible.

But local coverage also means nontraditional sports presented in nontraditional ways. Feature stories about inspiring athletes overcoming adversity or unlikely champions have become quite popular because they interest the nonsports fan. The hard-core sports segment (remember, only about a third of the total audience) is going to tune in no matter what you do. It's the other two-thirds you need to reach, which can be done with well-crafted feature pieces. Such stories provide much

Table 8-4

Combining Sports and News

Situation	Comments
News anchors throw to sports anchor for story as live shot, on set, or sports office.	This is an extremely popular way to handle the story, although it makes it difficult for the sportscaster to come up with fresh material for the sports segment. Having the sportscaster in the news segment lends the sports department credibility and lets the audience know this is not just another story. The downside is that it can lead to "overkill" on a story.
Sportscaster produces some sort of sidebar or related story that runs in the news block.	This is also very popular and allows each department a fresh angle on the story. Usually, the news department would handle the "harder" edge to the story: the details of the arrest and reaction from community members. The sports department would then handle a related angle, such as the prevalence of drugs in the local athletic community or how the arrest will affect the athlete's status on the team or chances for a college scholarship.
"Team coverage" of the story, involving both news and sports.	Team coverage involves allocating almost all the station's resources to the story, including reporters, photographers, engineers, and the sports department. At least two or three reporters would provide different reports on the story, all covering a different angle. Proponents of team coverage say it allows a station to give a story the in-depth attention it deserves, whereas critics simply call it excessive overkill. Again, the main problem for the sportscaster is that it leaves very little new material to use when the sports segment rolls around.
Story runs exclusively either in news or sports, but not both.	This is done very seldom for a variety of reasons. Skipping the story in the news segment sends the signal that it's not a very important story and also runs the risk of other stations getting the jump on coverage. Running the story exclusively in news might miss the viewers or listeners who don't tune in until the sports segment. It also gives people the impression that the sports department isn't on top of things.

of the real "challenge" of the sports media because they force you to get away from scores and highlights and become more of a storyteller.

Spacing out stories for three or four different sportscasts is one of the main responsibilities of producing. To get an idea of how this is done, let's assume you come into the station on a summer Thursday afternoon. Let's say you work in the Rockford, Illinois, market, with no major league teams, but close proximity to Chicago. A scan of the paper, wires, and other sources reveal the following possibilities for the day:

- Local junior golf tournament begins
- First round of PGA stop (Greensboro, North Carolina)
- Area high school hires new football coach
- Afternoon baseball highlights (Cubs–Brewers)
- Evening baseball scores and highlights

Right off the top, the new coach story sounds interesting. Much depends on the school, its history of success, and its importance in the community. This could be the lead. The local golf tournament doesn't sound exciting, but you may need to fill some time. Is there any way to find an engaging story for a package? Maybe there's a precocious talent playing (a young Tiger Woods?) or some other interesting angle. The PGA story is nothing more than short highlights or a VO, unless something unusual or interesting happens. You know your audience is interested in the Cubs and probably the baseball scores. It also looks like you'll have to fill out the rest of your time with other national stories or some local item of interest.

Given these factors, we could come up with the following rundowns:

5:00 p.m.

1. New coach	SOT
2. Cubs	VO
3. PGA	VO or Reader
4. Local golf	PKG (Live?)

Remember, our audience is primarily women who are more interested in feature-type stories. We can lead with the coach, but keep it short and to the point. Maybe include some highlights on the Cubs or the PGA event. The main focus of the show could be the junior golf. There's a chance to turn an interesting angle into a good story. You might even consider a live shot if the situation warrants.

6:00 p.m.

1. New coach	PKG/live/phoner/in-studio interview
2. Cubs	VO
3. PGA	Reader
4. Local golf	VO or VO/SOT

This is a more "hard core" audience, so it's appropriate to extend the coach story into a package. You might consider a live shot, live talk-back, or even a live, in-studio interview if the story is important enough. People still want to know about the Cubs, and you can go a little longer with the highlights. You have to cut something, which means less time for the golf stories.

10:00 p.m.

1. Night baseball highlights/scores	VO/Scores
2. Cubs	VO
3. New coach	SOT
4. PGA	VO/Reader
5. Local golf	VO/Scores

It's important to lead with something new at 10 o'clock, simply because viewers have already seen your other stories at least twice. Unless the coach story is of paramount importance, you should probably drop it in the rundown. You don't necessarily have to lead with baseball, but you should offer something new and different.

Maybe you could show highlights of a local game of interest. The other stories are reduced accordingly, if only because by 10 o'clock they have almost become "old news."

Special Productions

It has become quite common for sports departments to expand coverage for some shows to 15 or 30 minutes. Sometimes, these shows cover a particular event or topic on a weekly basis, such as a NASCAR weekend wrap-up show or a weekly show devoted to sports coverage of a particular team or city. In some cases, the shows are simply special productions to take advantage of increased demand for a particular event. Super Bowls, college bowl games, and local PGA tournaments certainly fall into this category. Another type of longer production is built around a theme of local interest, such as fishing, outdoor activity, auto racing, or bowling. But no matter what type of show, longer productions all aim to satisfy an increased demand for sports coverage that viewers can't get during a normal weekday newscast.

Stations should try to make sure there's enough interest to justify extended coverage. Even simple productions cost extra money for personnel, equipment, and salaries. If the production has to go out of town or even out of the country, the cost can run into the many thousands of dollars. For that kind of investment, news directors want to know there's going to be enough audience and advertiser interest in the project. The key is getting the advertisers because they'll have to contribute above and beyond their normal financial commitment. Oftentimes, a station will sign up an exclusive or single sponsor for an event, resulting in things like the "Jones Chevrolet Post-Game Show" or "Channel Two's Rose Bowl Show, brought to you by Kroger." Single sponsorships increase visibility for the advertiser, but also increase the possibility of excessive demands or a desire to influence the editorial content. Enlisting the help of several different sponsors is also quite common.

Generally speaking, stations will not undertake a special sports production unless they know they have advertisers in place. However, in some cases stations will take a financial loss in exchange for the promotional value and credibility associated with the production. There's also a danger of listening to the advertisers instead of the audience. Many times, a station will get involved with a production because the sales department has several interested sponsors lined up. But if these "advertiser-driven" shows don't have enough audience appeal, they usually don't last very long. The ratings will suffer and the advertisers will eventually drift away.

Obviously, how these shows are produced depends on the money and resources available to the producer. When a big-market team goes to the Super Bowl or the NCAA basketball tournament, stations usually spare no expense in their coverage. This includes sending dozens of reporters, photographers, and anchors to the scene for extensive live reporting, such as when WTMJ-TV in Milwaukee sent 31 people to cover the Packers in Super Bowl XXXI. A smaller station faced with the similar event would have a much more scaled-down effort, likely including only 1 or 2 people at the scene and some live satellite transmission. But no matter what the market size, sports producers must approach the production in much the same way.

Many stations try to broaden the appeal of these shows by including news and feature reports. From an editorial standpoint, news producers should focus on the people and personalities of the event and leave the hard-core sports coverage to the sports department. For example, when a local team goes to play in the Orange Bowl, the sports department will likely cover team practices, player and coach interviews, and then the game itself. News coverage could include reports of Miami nightlife, interesting tourist attractions, or fan activities.

The sports department has the challenge of trying to make these special shows unique. They should realize that other stations and outlets in the market are probably considering or doing much the same thing. If there's a big professional golf tournament in town, chances are all the other stations will have some sort of special programming. That's why it's important for the show to have its own unmistakable identity and something that separates it from the competition. This can be accomplished in several different ways, including emphasizing the personality of the anchors, the quality of the photography and graphics, or the type of stories presented.

No matter how the station approaches the event, it will require thorough planning and preparation. The sports department should consult with the news director, producers, engineers, and other station personnel to map out a strategy for the entire production. The ultimate success or failure of the production depends largely on planning done ahead of time.

Live Sports Production

When the very first sporting events were televised back in the 1930s and 1940s, the technology was still extremely primitive. That limited the type and location of events, and necessitated simple, no-nonsense coverage. The equipment was big, bulky, and inconsistent, resulting in several breakdowns and other accidents. As a result, boxing and wrestling became staples on early television, mainly because they took place in a confined area and could be covered easily with one camera. Pioneer radio sportscaster Harold Arlin broadcast in the 1920s and said, "Sometimes the transmitter worked and sometimes it didn't. Sometimes the crowd noise would drown us out and sometimes it wouldn't. And quite frankly, we didn't know what the reaction would be—if we'd be talking in a total vacuum or whether somebody would hear us."

Television went through a similar period in the 1950s. The 1958 championship game between the Colts and the Giants is generally recognized as one of the most important and dramatic in NFL history, but fewer people remember an incident that happened near the end of the game, when NBC television cables accidentally got dislodged, knocking the signal off the air. Luckily for NBC, a fan then ran onto the field, creating a distraction that allowed engineers to fix the problem just before the winning touchdown scored. According to an apocryphal story, it was an NBC employee who created the distraction to save the network from 45 million angry viewers.

Flash forward 50 years or so. A typical Super Bowl production now includes about 25 pedestal cameras, six handheld cameras, two remote control cameras, and another camera on the blimp. The production list also includes around 75 monitors, 30 video tape recorders (VTRs), 60 microphones, 20 miles of cable, 35 production trucks, and a crew of more than 300. The Super Bowl is no ordinary show, but clearly, producing live sports events has become much more complicated, time-consuming, and expensive. And it is a frontier that is constantly changing and updating, especially with the impending arrival of digital broadcasting.

Television Production

There are certainly many variables to live television sports production, including the type of event, the venue, and the resources available for coverage. But no matter what the circumstances involved, production actually starts days and even weeks before the event takes place. National television networks have their own equipment and production crews, and they work together as a team, moving from event to event. Keeping the same crew together helps foster teamwork and improves the quality of the live production.

In some cases, usually for smaller regional events, the work is contracted out to a company that specializes in sports production. Several such organizations exist throughout the country and they usually work events on a regional scale, which allows for transportation of the equipment by large trucks. For example, Metro Sports in Kansas City will handle live events in Missouri, Kansas, Arkansas, and Illinois. Companies such as Metro Sports own much of the equipment they use, but often will have to borrow facilities to help meet the demand for their services.

The production crew is responsible for almost every facet of the live telecast, including satellite truck and uplink facilities, equipment, and personnel (although, in many cases, the organization that sponsors the event will arrange for its own talent for the broadcast). The size of the crew depends on the size of the event, but for a regional event such as a college football or basketball game there are usually two dozen or so crew members involved. Full-blown network coverage of a particular game might include up to 50 or more crew members.

Table 8-5 is a list of the on-air, production, and technical people associated with ESPN's coverage of the college football game between Florida State and Virginia on October 16, 2004. To promote teamwork and cohesiveness, most of these crew members travel and work together throughout the season.

Job Description	Person
Primetime Game Director	Scott Johnson
Play-by-Play	Ron Franklin
Analyst	Mike Gottfried
Sideline Reporter	Erin Andrews
ISO Producer	Cathi Cappas
Sideline Producer	Dave Dare
Associate Producer	Steve Ackels
Associate Director	Susan G. Pierce
Show Writer	Jeff Sarokin
Bristol Campus – PA	Dominic DeLeon
Production Supervisor	Nikki Godfrey
Operations Manager	Tom Gianakos
Operations Producer	Joe Wire
Operations Assistant	Barb Hansen
Operations Assistant	Jim Birch
Program Finance	Nick Parsons
Hotel and Meeting Rooms	Judy Frauenhofer
Travel Team "B"	Andrea Beady
Crewing Coordinator	Barbara Cox
Crewing Coordinator	Courtney Dowling
ENG Crewing	Jeff Israel
Assignment Desk	Eric Lynch
Stage Manager/Robotics	Mike Black
Talent Stats	Elven Lindblad
Talent Spotter – Ron	Bill Werndl
Talent Spotter – Mike	John Gottfried
Research and ISO Spotter	Todd McShay
Rules Consultant	Rom Gilbert
MIS Computer Stats	Tom Vigorito
Miniboard Operator	Chan Hartsog
MIS 1st and 10 Spotter	Kyle Brown
ENG Assist/All 22 Cam	Nick Spears
Technical Director	Dean Peare
Audio	Stevie Kaura
A2 – BOOTH	Paul Bush
A2 – FIELD	Rick Maldonado
A2 – RF AUDIO	Ray Steidel
Video	Cliff Davis

Table 8-5

Network Sports Production Crew List
Source/Courtesy: ESPN

Continued

Table 8-5	Job Description	Person
Cont'd.	Video	Al Taylor
	V2	Craig Stevens
	Camera	Mark Griffard
	Camera	Dave Earnhardt
	Camera	Chris Rehkopf
	Camera	Ed Rodriguez
	Camera	Gerry Jennewein
	Camera	Larry Faircloth
	Camera	Jim Vanderford
	Camera	Tim Tew
	Camera	Scott Caldwell
	Camera	Steve Angel
	Camera	Andy Erwin
	Camera	Mike Williams
	JIB Camera	Steve Ritchie
	ENG ASSIST/ALL 22	Nick Spears
	EVS/LEAD TAPE	Rembert Young
	EVS/Editor	Ryan Leimbach
	ON-LINE Editor	Mike Gay
	EVS/SSM	Dave Gallatin
	EVS	Russ McGonagil
	EVS	Keith Bozarth
	EVS	Brad Kendrick
	INFINIT	Susan Hamaker
	EIC/NCP5	Jack Pakkala
	MTC-A UNIT	Brian Donovan
	SPORTVISION	Craig Sepko
	SKYCAM	Tom Landsman

Networks keep their own production personnel and pay them on an annual basis, but when the work is contracted out, most of the crew members are freelancers who work on a per-event basis. Each crew member usually gets around $250 or $300 per day plus expenses, and the cost can go even higher in places that require union labor. The cost of the crew is one of the major expenses of a live sports production and can easily run between $5000 and $10,000 for a single game.

Uplink time and the use of a satellite truck runs around $3500, while the production truck and the use of an engineer usually costs another $5000. The cost of the truck itself runs more than $6 million, about twice the price of a dozen years ago. When you consider miscellaneous expenses and overtime costs, it's not unusual for sports production costs to run about $20,000 per event. The cost runs even higher for network productions, which have more personnel and technology involved (Figures 8-5 and 8-6).

Production trucks usually come at a high price because they contain extremely sophisticated and expensive equipment. Each truck is, in effect, a mobile television studio. It has dozens of monitors, cameras, cables, and microphones necessary for the

Figure 8-5

Interior view of a typical sports production truck a few hours before the game.

production of any live sports event. Production trucks literally come in all shapes and sizes.

Jefferson-Pilot Sports produces hundreds of live sporting events every year. Table 8-6 shows one of the company's "medium range" 48-foot trucks.

Chain of Command

No matter how many people are involved with the production process, everything begins and ends with the event producer. The producer is ultimately responsible for every component of the telecast, although much of his or her work is done before the event ever begins. Producers often work three or four games a week and have a heavy travel schedule. As a result, sometimes they don't get to a venue until the night before the live production, when they will schedule meetings with the crew and talent. This is a run-through to make sure everyone is on the same page and to go over important points that the producer wants to emphasize during the telecast (Figure 8-7).

Most of the producer's work is done the next day in the hours leading up to the event. During that time, the producer will make sure the cameras are positioned properly, do all the preproduction work for the telecast, work on commercials,

Figure 8-6

Exterior view of a typical sports production truck.

Figure 8-7

Producers do most of their work in the hours leading up to the event.

Cameras
  5 HK-366
  3 Canon 55:1 Lens w/2x extender
  2 Canon 55:1 Tele Super Lens w/2x extender
  3 HK-355PA Handheld
  3 Canon 18:1 Lens w/2x extender
  1 Studio configuration
  1 Betacam (by request)
  2 Panasonic CCD LPS Cameras
Production switcher
  3000-T Grass Valley
  36 Inputs
  3 mix effects
Routing switcher
  SMS-64x64 Grass Valley
  48x48 Video
  32x32 Audio
Special effects
  Abekas A-42 Still Store
  Abekas A-51 Dual Channel DVE
Videotape
  2 Sony DVW-A500 Digibeta
  4 DNF Slo-mo controllers
  1 Lance Slo-mo controller
  4 Sony BVW 75 Beta SP
  1 Drastic Disc Recorder
Production
  58 monitors (monitor wall)
  2 Ikegami 19" Color
  4 Color 9"
  42 B/W 9"
  2 B/W Triple
  1 B/W Quad
  Additional monitors
  3 Color 13"
  4 Color 11"
  5 Color 9"
  2 B/W 9"
Other equipment
  7 Frame syncs
  2 Lowell-D light kits
Audio
  Yamaha PM 4000 console w/52 inputs and 24 outputs
  2 6-input sub-mixers
  8 compressors
  Two channel Yamaha digital
Effects
  1 Digicart II

Table 8-6

Typical Sports Event
Production Truck
*Source/Courtesy:
Jefferson-Pilot Sports*

Continued

Table 8-6

Cont'd.

1 360 Digital Audio editor
1 CD player
1 DAT recorder
Microphones
4 Sennheiser 816 (shotgun)
7 Sennheiser 416 (shotgun)
6 ECM 44B lavs
1 Lectronics HH mic
3 Lectronics body packs
Full complement of hand mics
18 Bantam patch panels
40 Audio D.A.'s
4 QKT lines to patch field
Gentner digital telephone
Interface
Communications
RTS 9 channel intercom
RTS IFB
Intercom w/4 stations
1 Wireless IFB w/2 receivers
Receivers
2 Telos links
4 Clear Com Adaptacom
6 Walkie-talkies—5 watts
2 base units—45 watts
11 10-line AT&T telephones
Graphics
Chyron Infinit! 13.5MHZ/68060 CPU
Bernoulli 230 Meg Drive
1 Gig JAZ Drive
General
Power requirements: 220 volt/200 amp

and make the final decision with regards to any questions concerning the preparation for the telecast. Preproduction work takes up the bulk of the producer's time and includes all the prerecorded elements that will go into the show, including previous highlights, game day interviews, and special feature segments. For a large-scale event, it's not unusual for the preproduction to take 3 or 4 hours or longer. The producer must also make sure that the commercials are ready to go and positioned in the proper place. Depending on the type of event, the length of preparation before a telecast can run anywhere from 3 to 6 hours. For televising games of the Chicago White Sox, Fox Sports Chicago starts its pregame production process about 7 hours before the game starts (Table 8-7).

Once the game starts, the producer serves mainly as an overseer for the telecast. Again, one of the main responsibilities is making sure that the commercials run in their proper places, and there is sometimes a tape coordinator on hand for this

12:00	Park and power
1:00	Crew call, Infinit! Load
2:00	VT transfers, editing
3:30	FAX
3:45	Camera and tape meeting
4:00	Pregame field interviews
4:45	Dinner break
5:45	Full truck and booth/rehearse
6:30	Air (pregame show)
7:00	Game
10:00	Approximate end of game/VT meltdown, strike

Table 8-7

Typical Baseball Preproduction Meeting Schedule *Source/ Courtesy: Fox Sports Chicago*

Position	Duties
Producer	Responsible for show content
	Communicates plan to production crew and Announcers
	Dictates story lines
	Selects replays
Director	Executes producer's plan
	Instructs camera operators and selects camera
	Inserts graphics
	Communicates with audio and tape personnel
Technical director	Puts director's plan into operation
	Executes and coordinates technical elements
Associate director	Coordinates commercial breaks and times
	Monitors sponsored elements
	Times all show elements
Tape producer	Assists with replays
	Assists with highlight packages
	Assists in tape production

Table 8-8

Behind the Scenes *Source/Courtesy: ESPN2*

purpose. The producer will also help the director run the telecast and communicate with the talent. The latter mainly involves keeping the announcers informed as to the general direction and flow of the telecast.

On August 28, 2004, ESPN gave viewers a unique look at what goes on during the production of a live sports event. While ESPN carried the football game between USC and Virginia Tech, ESPN2 carried video and audio feeds from the production truck, the announcer's booth, and the sideline. The show highlighted the split-second timing and technical sophistication that goes into today's live sports production. Of the dozens of people involved in the game production, some of the most important positions and their responsibilities are noted in Table 8-8.

While the producer does most of his work before the game starts, the director does all his work after the game begins. The director charts the pattern of the game by calling the sequence of cameras to be used, an often difficult job that involves a half-dozen or so cameras placed in various positions around the event. The director must be aware of not only what is going on, but also what is coming up, for he or she has to decide which cameras to use and for how long. In addition to cameras, the

Figure 8-8

The director is responsible for executing the producer's plan during the game.

director must also integrate other elements of the telecast, such as videotape, replays, audio, and the like (Figure 8-8).

While the director calls the shots, the technical director actually pushes the buttons during the telecast. Also called a technical manager, this person also checks out all the monitors and equipment inside the production truck to make sure they're working properly. As many times as the crew has to set up and break down the equipment, the settings will often change or something will simply malfunction. The technical director must also make sure that all the equipment is set to his or her specifications, which can become changed by other producers and directors working previous events in the same truck.

Each event generally has at least two people working audio. The first person (often called A1) is responsible for the internal audio in the production truck. This person must make sure that all the audio settings inside the truck are correct and allow for proper internal communications and processing of the live signal. The second audio person (A2) usually handles the external audio at the event site. This would include the proper positioning of all the audio cables and microphones related to the event. Audio can be a difficult job because every venue is wired differently and requires a unique set up. Cables that fit together in a certain way at Yankee Stadium in New York could be completely different than the setup at Shea Stadium across town (Figure 8-9).

Figure 8-9

Cable hookups and configurations can vary from venue to venue.
Courtesy: Mary Lou Sheffer

Also inside the production truck are the graphics operator and the tape replay operators, two positions that are fairly self-descriptive. The graphics operator is responsible for all the printed information that will appear on-screen during the telecast. This means loading the graphic information in the hours before the game, including names, statistics, and the like. During the game, the graphics operator will work with the director and technical director in getting the proper graphics on the screen at the right time. Tape replay operators are responsible for capturing, loading, and displaying video replays during the game. Again, these positions work with the director and technical director. Because of the frequency of replays in live sports events, it usually takes more at least two replay people to handle the load (Figure 8-10).

Some of the most visible members of the crew are the camera positions. With the exception of major events such as the Super Bowl or World Series, most live sports productions use six or fewer cameras per game. The camera locations are fairly static, although much depends on the configuration of the venue and some cameras may have to be repositioned or moved slightly (Figure 8-11).

Camera operators listen to the director to help them figure out what shots to get. A director might want a player close-up on a particular camera and a wide shot of the arena on another, but most experienced camera people already know what shots they need ahead of time. Either way, it's important to remember that the camera

Figure 8-10

A graphics operator loads her information several hours before game time.

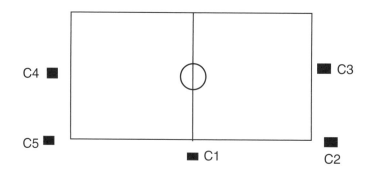

Figure 8-11

Typical five-camera setup for a basketball game.

operator is not "freelancing" to shoot whatever he or she wants. Usually, the operator has very detailed and specific instructions on how to shoot from a particular location. These instructions are discussed in the hours before the game and vary depending on where the camera is located (Table 8-9). You can also tell that the camera operators have to have some sort of basic knowledge about the game or the sport they're shooting. If the director calls for a wide shot of a possible suicide squeeze play, the camera operator has to know exactly what to look for to set up the shot properly (Figures 8-12 and 8-13).

Figure 8-12 and 8-13

No matter where they're stationed in the arena, camera operators must know their exact assignments.

Table 8-9

Typical Baseball Camera Assignments
Source/Courtesy: Fox Sports Chicago

Camera 1/Lower Third baseline: LH batters waist shot for stats; after tally goes out zoom back for head-to-toe shot; if LH batter bunts, give batter more looking room on the left side of screen and go with ball; RH pitchers, both dugouts, if you have a batter and there are two men on base you have the backup runner after the ball is in play. If you do not have a batter you will have the lead runner. If bases are loaded and you have the lead runner, you score the lead runner and then pick up the runner on first trying to advance. If you don't have a batter or lead runner, shoot the pitcher. If batter was on other team, look for infield hero shot. Always shoot runners head-to-toe.

Camera 2/High Home Plate: Follow the ball; play-by-play; cover appeals at 1st and 3rd base, umpires, infield and outfield defense; put home plate in lower right corner and then pan left to right. If you have a runner at 2nd base, please be sure to include runner in your battery shot. Always include the outfielders in the picture when the ball is hit to the outfield; you have to see where the ball is going and who's going to catch it.

Camera 3/High First baseline: Shag infield and outfield; defensive pull across; go for infield or outfield hero shot after play. If the drama is at 1st base when the out is made, keep a look out for the 1st baseman/runner/umpire reaction. Two shot runners at 1st and 2nd; pickoffs at 1st base; if runner steals, go with runner; pitcher–runner shot at third base; show the whole thing when there is a chance of squeeze bunt or sacrifice at home. If there are runners at the corner, you may be asked to cover the potential pickoff play at 1st base.

Camera 4/Centerfield: Pitcher, batter, umpire shot; go with ball on passed balls, wild pitches, pop ups behind the plate, and steals of 2nd base. Go with the ball if ball is on ground between 2nd and shortstop. If ball is in air, wait until tally light goes out then go for shag/defense. Routine or great play stick with for hero shot. If pitcher strikes out batter to end inning, follow off pitcher, otherwise follow batter back to dugout. On home runs, listen to the announcers, you have three options—follow the batter and push in tight after swing for reaction; pause, then go for ball looking for diving catch, etc.; or zoom right to pitcher for reaction shot of ball being launched.

Camera 5/Low First baseline: RH batters waist shot for stats; after tally goes out zoom back for head-to-toe shot. If RH batter bunts, give the batter more looking room on the right side of screen and go with ball. LH pitchers, both dugouts. If you have a batter and there are two men on base, you have the back-up runner after ball is in play. If you don't have a batter you have the lead runner. If bases are loaded and you have the lead runner, you score runner and then pick up runner trying to advance. After pitcher goes into windup, shag the entire field. Cover plays at 1st base, if routine follow player back to dugout. After play look for infield hero shot. When following runners, always shoot head-to-toe.

Camera 6/Low Home Plate: Tight shot of pitcher; pitcher/batter shot; LH batters, you need to move to your left; RH batters, you need to move to your right. Follow ball when your tally goes out. Look out for behind the plate action; runners with good speed cover the runner at 1st base; if he steals, go with the runner. If the ball is hit up the middle and a runner crosses in your path, then pick up the runner trying to score. What really looks good here is the 3rd base coach trying to hold runner or giving the advance sign to home plate.

Every crew must have an engineer, but hopes it never has to use one. An engineer must be available to repair any equipment breakdowns or malfunctions, and there are very few times when a crew will not need his services. "We deal with very expensive and finicky equipment," says Curtis Lorenz of Metro Sports. "Things are bound to break down and go wrong." An engineer must not only be available at a moment's notice, but must also have a current and in-depth knowledge of a wide variety of broadcasting equipment. Technology changes constantly and the engineer must keep on top of the latest developments. Except at the network level, most engineers work on a freelance basis.

Each crew usually has two people to handle the statistics involved with the game. It generally requires more than one person because of the flood of numbers that can overwhelm a director—averages, ages, height, weight, personal histories, and the like. All of it must be sorted through and presented in a coherent fashion for the broadcast. The production truck also has at least one liaison that works down on the field. For a basketball game, it's the time-out coordinator who notifies referees and game officials about designated breaks in the game for commercial spots. The time-out coordinator or liaison also keeps officials aware of any situations that necessitate a change in the action. One of the more famous examples came in Super Bowl I, when broadcast networks stayed too long in commercial and missed a kickoff. After notification, the referees simply ordered the teams to kickoff again. Such instances are extremely rare, but the production crew must have a way of communicating with the officials in charge of the game.

The final members of the crew are the utility people, usually about a half dozen or more for each game. Their responsibility is to do all the necessary but unglamorous work associated with the telecast. This includes such things as handling cable, keeping track of certain pieces of equipment, or running errands for other members of the crew. Utility crew members are usually local volunteer workers who take the job more for the experience than the pay. Many times they are students from the local university or college.

Radio Production

Live Events

As with the medium itself, live sports production on radio has a much longer history than events on television. There's some debate as to exactly when the first sports broadcast went on the air, but a reliable estimate is July 2, 1921, when RCA founder David Sarnoff arranged a heavyweight boxing match as a way to promote radio. Later that same year, the World Series went on radio for the first time and, again, Sarnoff played a leading role. Recognizing that the new medium needed programming, Sarnoff made sports one of the cornerstones of the industry. "We had to have baseball in order to sell enough sets to go on to other programming," he later wrote.

Radio sports was extremely successful both on a local and on a national level up until the 1950s, when television began to take away advertising dollars and radio sports had to make changes in the face of economic reality. The niche that sports eventually found on radio was the local sports audience. Because of technological improvements and the nature of the medium, radio found it was the perfect venue to broadcast local high school and college games. The development of telephone lines for radio use and later the emergence of more sophisticated delivery systems made broadcasting games easy, quick, and relatively inexpensive—especially compared to what it would cost for a local television broadcast. The only major cost is the talent, which still doesn't add up to much because most of the announcers already work at the station in some capacity. Thus, broadcasting live sporting events has become the bedrock of local radio sports.

Most live radio coverage still depends on transmission by telephone. In the earliest days, a radio station would order a telephone line a couple of weeks in advance of an event and the phone company would string a line into the event venue. Once the line was strung, the announcer would attach a telephone and use the handset to give the play-by-play. This proved to be quite a challenge in some cases, where lines did not exist or the venue proved difficult for technicians to reach, and it eventually led to the development of permanent, dedicated phone lines. Because of the simplicity and inexpense of this system, the production did not require a large crew. Many sports broadcasters covered events by themselves or occasionally used the services of engineers. The development of remote trucks for long-distance coverage added a few more people to the mix, but sports broadcasting on radio remained very much a one- or two-man operation.

Despite all the technological advancements of today, many stations follow this same production process. It is especially helpful for smaller stations because of the costs, which usually only involve paying the talent and the price of the phone service. For a typical out-of-town game requiring long-distance service, a 2- or 3-hour radio sports broadcast normally runs between $100 and $150 in phone charges. A local broadcast using only local lines would obviously cost much less. Thus, any radio station in America, regardless of size or finances, can broadcast live sports events using only one person and a phone line. Today's stations will often utilize a phone with a jack on the side to send its signal back. The production is simple, effective, and inexpensive, but it does not offer the best sound reproduction. Using phone lines in such a manner usually results in tinny or scratchy audio. Yet, such a means of transmission remains a staple for thousands of small stations across the country.

For bigger stations that can afford better equipment, there are a variety of options. For years, the Marti was the basis for much radio sports production. The Marti does not depend on telephone relay, but sends the signal back to the station via a microwave signal. This provides the advantages of broadcasting from venues where telephone lines are unavailable and because it does not require lines, the costs are almost zero. But the Marti also requires a line-of-sight relay connection to the broadcasting station and the path must be free of obstacles that could impede the signal, such as buildings or trees. It also is considered somewhat big and bulky and has a dependable range of only about 20–25 miles. Another development along these lines is known as the Cellcast. Because the Cellcast uses cellular phone technology, it can go anywhere in the country where cell phone service is available. The obvious drawbacks are the uncertainty of cellular service and the expense associated with it.

The Comrex Corporation has worked on audio transmission systems for the past 40 years and has developed several digital and wireless models now in use by radio stations around the world. Current digital technology works much like other forms of transmission in that it sends the signal out over telephone lines. But new systems compress the signal digitally, which is sent back to the station for decompression and transmission. As a result, the audio signal has the highest professional quality and sounds much better than traditional transmission methods. Such systems also allow for closed-channel communication between people at the studio and the broadcaster at the event, and have memory to send back recorded interview segments. Workers back at the station can inform the broadcaster of score updates from other games or other important information related to the broadcast. New digital and wireless remote systems generally do not run less than $5000—a relatively minor expense given their flexibility, and certainly only a fraction of what television stations pay for live remote coverage.

Regardless of what system the radio broadcaster uses, almost all stations have some sort of mixer as part of their production. A mixer is a device that lets the broadcasters on the scene "mix" in other sound elements in addition to their own voices. First and foremost, this includes other microphones at the event. In addition to the ones used in the booth by the broadcasters, a station will place a variety of microphones at an event to capture crowd noise, sideline activity, and the like. The mixer allows the broadcasters to control the type and amount of extraneous noise going on the air. It also allows them to record audio at the event for delayed playback or to playback previously recorded material as part of the broadcast. Many stations handle this with cassettes, but more and more are switching to digital discs or "mini-discs" because of the better sound quality. With such technology, broadcasters can instantly replay any key moment or any other sound element from the game.

Despite such sophisticated technology, radio sports production still does not require nearly the amount of support personnel as television. Many stations continue to utilize two- or three-man crews, primarily the people who handle the play-by-play and color duties. These same people take care of the technical details as well, although they may consult a radio engineer for an especially difficult situation. The third person is usually someone back at the station who handles the incoming transmission for rebroadcast. That same person punches the audio board, runs the commercials, and makes sure the broadcast conforms to the prearranged format found in the broadcast log. Bigger stations with more elaborate productions may require dozens of support personnel. A typical NFL radio pregame show, for example, can involve switching back and forth from several live venues involving half a dozen performers. Such a production obviously requires much more planning and technical support and, of course, comes at a higher cost.

Sports Talk Radio

The other major staple of radio sports is talk—and lots of it. Talk radio began in California in the 1960s, but really didn't hit its stride until the late 1970s. By the mid-1980s, radio talk exploded with the emergence of Larry King, Rush Limbaugh, Tom Snyder, and Sally Jessy Raphael. By the end of the 1990s, talk radio had become a solid force in radio broadcasting, with millions of listeners tuning in to talk about politics, current affairs, pop psychology, and sports.

The appeal of talk radio is simple—listeners can voice their own opinions and become active rather than passive users of the medium. Sometimes people call in to vent their frustrations or to comment on a certain topic. But many times, people just want their voices heard. In a highly fragmented society, many people want to know that their opinion counts, no matter what the topic. And if there are any doubts about the importance of interactivity and active participation in a medium, witness the phenomenal growth of the Internet.

Sports talk and call-in shows really boomed in the mid-to-late 1980s. In 1987, Emmis Broadcasting started WFAN, an all-sports talk format. WFAN operated in the red for a couple of years, but by the 1990s had become one of the most profitable radio stations in the country. In 1991, Infinity Broadcasting bought WFAN for $70 million—at that time a record for a stand-alone AM station.

The success of WFAN led to a rising tide of competition. By the mid-1990s, 28 stations of the nation's 100 largest markets ran a sports talk format, and that number has now grown to 421 stations. Other sports-oriented programmers, such as ESPN and Sporting News Radio, soon began delivering national talk and call-in shows. The growth of sports talk radio has not come without controversy. In an effort to cut through the clutter of so many sports talk shows, hosts have become increasingly controversial, critical, and loud-mouthed. Supporters would say that's exactly what they're supposed to do. "There is an element to these shows of 'you top this,'" says Mike Lupica of the *New York Daily News* and contributor to ESPN's *Sports Reporters* roundtable. "People expect you to say something strong," says Mike Greenberg, cohost of ESPN Radio's *Mike and Mike in the Morning* with Mike Golic. "You have to know where the line is and go right up to it but not cross it."

But the beauty and simplicity of the format remains its local orientation. Any small station in any market can build a loyal audience simply by opening the phone lines and asking fans what's on their minds. "I think the biggest thing to remember about local sports talk radio is that local is what works," says veteran sports talk show host Mike Gastineau of KJR-AM in Seattle. "I can go on this afternoon and talk ad nauseum about what is going on nationally, but I've got to somehow relate it to the people here in Seattle. That's a key, finding the local angle that will provoke calls."

In late 2004, *Sports Illustrated* listed the best (or at least the most interesting) of the talk show hosts that dominate local sports radio. The common characteristics

Host(s)	Station (on AM dial)	Comments
Ralph Barbieri and Tom Tolbert	680, KNBR, San Francisco	"The Razor" and "Mr. T" aren't afraid to tackle tough issues
Mike North	670, WSCR, Chicago	Passionate Chicago sports talk veteran since 1990
Glenn Ordway	850, WEEI, Boston	Hosts the "Big Show" and lets listeners vent their frustrations
Mark Madden	1250, WEAE, Pittsburgh	Former pro wrestling announcer who can get nasty
Angelo Cataldi	610, WIP, Philadelphia	Identifies with blue collar listeners at the expense of local sports figures
Kevin Kietzman	810, WHB, Kansas City	Specializes in breaking "scoops" in KC market
Mike Francesa and Chris Russo	660, WFAN, New York	Duo has worked together in tough NY market since 1989
Mike Rhyner and Greg Williams	1310, KTCK, Dallas	Baseball fans in football crazy Texas
Paul Finebaum	960, WERC, Birmingham	Advertises his show as the place "where coaches are fired"
Hank Goldberg	560, WQAM, Miami	Lots of scoops because owners and coaches like to use him as a sounding board

Table 8-10

The Mouths That Roar
*Source: Mighty mouths.
(2004, November 8).
Sports Illustrated, pp. 68
and 69.*

seem to be passion, criticism, and, perhaps most important, a willingness to listen. On a clear night, you might be able to pick them up on your AM dial (Table 8-10).

The Future

There is no reason to think that the demand for live sports production will do anything but increase in the coming years. Deregulation and legislation have opened the door for more and more opportunities in the industry. The proliferation of new media, such as the Internet, satellite, and cable, has provided the means to satisfy growing consumer demand. There are currently more than 300 sports event televised on networks and cable each year.

But costs also keep going up, primarily due to all the new television technology. For example, the "First and Ten" effect you see on football games—the digitized yellow line that indicates first down—costs more than $25,000 per game to use. "Digital gives a better picture, no doubt about it," says Lorenz. "The cameras are smaller and easier to work with, the audio is better sounding, and the entire size of the operation shrinks down. But we need to get ready for this digital revolution and rethink the way we do things."

In an age when most media outlets are trying to improve the bottom line by doing more with less, live sports production is no different. While the number of televised sports events goes up each year, the amount of equipment produced for each project has decreased, especially at the regional level. "In the past, if a network was using two trucks to feed different regions of the country, it would use two completely separate crews and cameras," said Phil Garvin, owner of two mobile production companies. "Now there's an effort by the networks to save money by only duplicating the things that distinguish one show from another." Another cost-saving device is having advertisers sponsor expensive technology. In 2004, both America Online and Overstock sponsored the First and Ten lines on network football broadcasts.

There's also the question of what to do with high-definition television (HDTV). HDTV has a much clearer and visually exciting picture than regular television, especially in terms of sports programming, but the conversion to digital television has been delayed in the United States for several years. Programmers are reluctant to invest in HD content with so few people owning HD sets, and consumers aren't buying the expensive sets because there isn't much HD programming.

HD programming and equipment are also much more expensive than traditional analog equipment, and content providers still aren't sure how to recoup all the money they're pouring into new HD cameras, transmitters, and production trucks. "We're doing [HD production] not as an experiment, but because we had a client that wanted to pay for it," said Ken Aagaard, CBS Sports VP of technology. "CBS is in the business to make money, not lose it. We're also in the business of figuring out how to get multiple revenue streams. [HD sports production] gives CBS some leverage that the other networks don't have right now."

Despite these issues, the movement toward high-definition production continues. ESPN has made a major commitment, broadcasting not only games and other content, but also dedicating two channels to HD service. Together, ESPN HD and ESPN2 HD offer viewers more than 6000 hours of originally produced HD content and more than 2000 original programs. Sean Bratches, president of Disney and ESPN Networks affiliate sales and marketing, said "ESPN HD is driving our affiliates' high-definition business, and the addition of ESPN2 HD makes the consumer proposition that much more compelling. Our affiliates, our advertisers, and most importantly, our viewers are requesting more HD content, and as we've seen the demand skyrocket, we're committing to fulfilling that need."

In 2001, Garvin and Mark Cuban, owner of the NBA Dallas Mavericks, launched HDNet, the first national television network to broadcast all its content in high definition. Live HDNet sports productions include National Hockey League games, Major League Soccer games, *The HDNet Horse Racing Challenge*, NASCAR and Champ Car auto racing, *HDNet Boxing*, and NCAA football and basketball games. "There are people like Mark Cuban that are really pushing the envelope and not waiting until there's a clearly defined revenue stream from this," said Dick Vardanega, vice president of broadcasting and production for the NBA's Portland Trailblazers. "That is what it is going to take to get significant set penetration." Said Garvin, "Mark Cuban and I agreed that if I could bring the cost of HD production down dramatically and he was willing to risk a long-term investment, then we could make sports in HD a success. That's what we plan to do."

References

Catsis, John. (1993). *Sports broadcasting*. Chicago: Nelson-Hall.

Ditingo, Vincent. *The remaking of radio*. Boston: Focal Press, 1995.

ESPN2 HD set to launch in Jaunary. (2004, September 7). *ESPN*. http://sports.espn.go.com/sports/tvlistings/espnhd/espnHDStory?id=1876748

ESPN college football behind the scenes. (2004, August 28). [Television show]. *ESPN2*.

Grant, Jim. (2000, February 25). The dual-cast in Atlanta held many challenges, but ABC technicians and crew were up to the task. www.tvbroadcast.com/issues/2000/0225/ 02.25.4.htm

Grotticelli, Michael. (2001, December 3). Demand for mobile production units rises, but rates stay flat. *Broadcasting & Cable*. http://www.tvinsite.come/broadcastingcable/index.asp? Layout= print_page&doc_id=58958&articleID=CA184321

Hilmes, Michelle. *Radio voices*. Minneapolis: University of Minnesota Press, 1997.

HNet facts. (2004). *HDNet*. http://www.hd.net/factsheet.html

Kahn, Roger. (1997). *Memories of summer*. New York: Hyperion Books.

Martzke, Rudy. (2003, May 9). Talk shows' tendencies make crossing line inevitable. *USA Today*. http://www.usatoday.com/sports/columnist/martzke/2003-05-09-martzke_x.htm

Mighty mouths. (2004, November 8). *Sports Illustrated*, pp. 68 and 69.

Patton, Phil. (1984). *Razzle-dazzle*. New York: Dial Press.

Privacy policy and terms of use. (2004). *Ft. Worth-Star Telegram*. http://www.dfw.com/mld/dfw/contact_us/terms_of_use/

"Sports-talk radio host." [Online]. Available: http://espn.go.com/special/s/careers/sptalk.html, September 7, 1999.

Economics

If you've read through the text up to this point, you should have somewhat of an understanding of the relationship between sports media and economics. We're now going to explore that relationship more in-depth on a variety of levels. Advertising figures prominently in this relationship, which has undergone important changes in the past several years.

The Bottom Line

Let's start with a controversial view of both sports and the sports media—in today's society both exist primarily to make money. Of course, the media have always tried to make a profit, but not necessarily to the exclusion of all other functions. This causes problems for some people, especially those who believe in the journalistic traditions of public service or those who feel athletes and coaches should serve as positive role models for today's youth. To the extent that those conditions ever existed, they do not exist today.

Much has been made about the relationship between sports and socialization of American youth. It has been believed and taught that kids learn important lessons about fair play, sportsmanship, sacrifice, and hard work from playing in sports. That may still be true, but in terms of watching, reading, and consuming sports, the increasing emphasis on commercialization and profit has caused any positive social-ization effects to be nearly abandoned. Where once star athletes went on radio and television to tell kids to eat right and get plenty of sleep, today's generation hears Charles Barkley say, "I am not a role model" in a series of ads for Nike. To be fair to Barkley, he went on to say that parents should have the most influence in a child's life. But according to a survey by the Kaiser Family Foundation, many American kids are mirroring the behavior of famous athletes—good and bad—both on and off the field.

The media take much of the blame for these changes because they are the primary transmission agents for changing values. CBS, the NFL, and MTV all took a lot of criticism after the 2004 Super Bowl for the halftime show that featured singer Janet Jackson. At one point in the show, Jackson exposed part of her breast. The next day, sportswriter Mike Lupica noted rhetorically, "What did (NFL Commissioner Paul) Tagliabue, and CBS for that matter, think was going to happen when they invited Jackson—some kind of hip-hop version of 'Up With People?'"

Lupica's point was that CBS, MTV, and the NFL all knew what they were getting—a Super Bowl geared more toward profit, entertainment, and commercialism than actual competition. The game is dominated by commercials, high-energy entertainment acts, and promotional announcements. "Jackson was only around Super Bowl Week at the end," wrote Lupica, "but apparently it was long enough to figure out that the whole event —except for the football game, which always comes as a relief —is a monument to wretched excess. Maybe the league would have been more comfortable if she'd sung her song riding around in the Campbell's Soup Chunky Chuck Wagon."

The situations involving Charles Barkley, Janet Jackson, and a host of others have developed for a simple reason—for better or worse, we live in a world where revenue has taken over sports and the sports media, and where it is getting much harder for both to turn a profit.

The Ratings Game

Several factors have combined to make it much more difficult for sports teams and leagues to make money. Much has been said and written about the escalation of player salaries, which have now jumped into the multimillion dollar range for many professional sports. In 2000, baseball player Alex Rodriguez signed the richest individual contract in sports history, worth $252 million over 10 years. Athletes such as Tiger Woods and Shaquille O'Neal probably make close to that figure when you add in endorsement money.

Other rising costs include facilities, equipment, and stadiums. Several teams have built new stadiums in recent years in order to attract more fans, with the costs reaching up to and beyond $500 million. The $52 million renovation of the University of Texas basketball arena and complex included individual lockers wired for television sets and computers so that players can watch game tape at their seats, do their homework, and even get on the Internet. "As a business decision, wiring lockers for computer access and high-definition TVs makes perfect marketing sense," says sportswriter Kirk Bohls. "Hard to blame UT for doing it. But are college sports a business? You bet your Nike shoe contract they are." That's hard to argue considering the university's $75 million athletic budget.

Many of the sports media are experiencing the same financial problems. Just as sports teams have to put money into facilities, the media have to invest in new equipment and technology. For example, high-definition television can deliver unparalleled pictures of sporting events, but the transition costs for stations to convert to digital formats have been estimated at around $16 billion. The Internet is now an established medium for sports content, but a consistent revenue model for it has yet to emerge. The same thing goes for satellite radio, which will try to make money offering live NFL games. The entire media industry, including sports media, faces a time of great uncertainty because of issues related to new technologies and economic models.

The traditional revenue model for the sports media has been advertising. It has been a perfect marriage almost from the very beginning—sporting events deliver the middle class, male audiences that advertisers love, while the advertisers provide a stable source of profit and revenue. In the early days of sports broadcasting, one company or advertiser would often become the official sponsor of a team or event, such as Ballantine Beer did with the New York Yankees. Longtime Yankee announcer Mel Allen would seamlessly work ads and promotional announcements into his game broadcasting, saying something like, "A great defensive play there for the putout . . . and fans, make a great play for yourself by going to the refrigerator for a delicious Ballantine beer."

For years, sports and the sports media appeased advertisers in an effort to keep the revenue rolling in. Starting times of games were moved later in the evening so as to attract large, prime-time audiences. The World Series did not have its first night game until 1971, but by 1985 all games were played exclusively at night. In the 2002 World Series, the games played in California all went well beyond midnight in the east, but they also made money for the Fox network. Despite the fact that it was the lowest rated series in history up to that point, Fox Sports President Ed Goren observed, "It's less about the ratings and more about the volume of ad inventory and the length of games. Sales are so strong, it gave us an oversold situation in the early games. With more pitching changes than expected, we were able to get in extra ads. If we hadn't gotten in all the ads, we would have left money on the table."

In addition to changing game times, sometimes the games themselves have been changed. Owners and leagues made concessions and rule changes to help their games fit into the fast-paced electronic format. College basketball added television time-outs at predetermined intervals to make sure the networks could get in all their commercials. Even today, several coaches complain that the unnatural time-outs create a different and often difficult game. In the 1980s, the NCAA added a shot clock and a three-point line, in reality because slow downs and stall tactics had threatened to hurt television ratings.

Sometimes the influence of television goes beyond simple tinkering with rules and involves an entire sport. Some events—notably professional wrestling, roller derby, indoor soccer, and arena football—exist solely because of their television potential. The derisive term is "made for TV sports," which implies that such events have all the quality and production value of a tired movie of the week. In reality, these events can and do make a lot of money, especially pro wrestling.

Essentially, made-for-TV sports are created because of their appeal to advertisers. Roller derby certainly has a higher visual and entertainment quality than say billiards. Usually, such events are fast-paced, aggressive, and have formats that translate well onto a television screen. The Major Indoor Soccer League (MISL) shrank the game down and put it on a basketball-sized field, complete with sideboards that produced all kinds of strange bounces. The idea was that compressing the game would speed it up and create more scoring, thus making it more acceptable to television audiences. But the MISL could not overcome America's relative lack of interest in pro soccer and the league eventually folded. Arena football has enjoyed more limited success with basically the same concept.

Advertising remained an essential part of the sports media throughout the 1960s and 1970s. As audience interest and ratings continued to increase, so too did the cost of a commercial bought within a game telecast. The 30 seconds of commercial time in the Super Bowl that cost $239,000 in 1967 went for $2.3 million in 2004. Of course, the game reaches nearly 40% of all U.S. television households.

The problem for the sports media is that except for the NFL and the Super Bowl, broadcast ratings have declined, and when ratings decline the media typically make less money in ad revenue. According to sportswriter Richard Sandomir, television sports ratings are "down. Whether it was the World Series, the NBA finals, all four Grand Slam golf tournaments or the United States (Tennis) Open, network ratings tumbled." In 2004, ABC announced that *Monday Night Football*, once the premier prime-time sports show on any network, had its ratings sink to the lowest level in the show's history.

There are several explanations for this decline, but the most likely seem to be the growth in media options and the fragmentation of sports audiences. Sports events could pull in huge audiences when networks were the only viewing options, but that exclusivity no longer exists thanks to cable, the Internet, satellite, and VCR machines, which allow fans to tape and replay shows at their convenience or even watch replays of old games. Mass audiences have splintered into distinct "niche" groups of sports fans, and dozens of magazines, cable, and satellite channels now program specifically for them (Figure 9-1).

The last few years have seen the creation of networks dedicated to the NFL, outdoor sports, and college sports. Many of these have become extremely successful, such as the Golf Channel (into 67 million homes as of 2005), Speed Channel (63 million), and Outdoor Life Network (62 million). These networks are offering specialized content, including original programming and more live events.

Figure 9-1

Figure 9-1

Many sports magazines now target smaller, niche audiences.

Channel	Content
ESPN Classic	Footage of old games and interviews with retired athletes; very appealing to aging "baby boomer" audiences
The Golf Channel	Coverage of golf tournaments, news shows, and instructional programming; its *Big Break* series gives winners exemptions on professional tours
NFL Network	Studio news programs and content from NFL Films library; discussions under way to carry live NFL games
NBA TV	Live NBA games and other original programming
Speed Channel	Motor sports, with an emphasis on NASCAR
Fuel	Advertised as "television that showcases the best in action sports culture"
The Tennis Channel	Tournament action, news, and instruction
Outdoor Life Network	Focuses on hunting, fishing, and outdoor adventure; its major attraction is the Tour de France bicycle race, but added the Boston Marathon and Iditarod dog sled race in 2005

Table 9-1

Niche Sports Channels

"Event organizers realize we can dedicate a lot more time to their events compared to bigger networks," says Amy Phillips, OLN's director of public relations.

Table 9-1 lists part of the growing list of "niche" sports channels now available on cable and satellite. Because these channels appeal to distinct, targeted audiences, the list does not include general-appeal sports channels, such as ESPN and Fox Sports Net.

Rising costs and sagging audiences have also impacted professional and college athletics. Typical of the problem is the NBA, which saw attendance rise in 2004, but revenues drop. "We're still in a negative position, but obviously that's not true of every team," said NBA Commissioner David Stern. "Overall, the league remains in a negative position, in a negative cash position." In 2002, major league baseball reported that the operating losses for its 30 teams would reach in excess of $450 million. "The problem is that the owners are relatively less wealthy than they were 10 years ago," said Sal Galatioto, managing director of Lehman Brothers' sports practice. "So there's more stadium debt than ever before and these owners are worth less and less as their stocks plummet. That's why you've got a formula for disaster."

And that's bad news for all parties concerned because there is a very direct connection between the financial health of sports and the financial health of the sports media. Broadcast fees are a major source of income for most professional and college teams. For example, in 2001 the New York Mets reported an operating revenue of $182 million, of which nearly $71 million came from national and local broadcast rights. The more money a team makes in broadcast rights, the more money it can spend on players and the more competitive it can be on the field, theoretically increasing merchandising and ticket revenue.

There are billions of dollars today in broadcast sports fees, but networks are having trouble making money because of declining ratings and a lack of return on the investment. The major networks are paying from $500 to $700 million a year for the NFL. In 2004, Fox and CBS extended their NFL deals for 6 years at a staggering cost of $8 billion. Fox also pays $417 million annually for baseball, and ESPN and TNT combine to pay an average of $767 million a year for the NBA. According to sports media analyst Rudy Martzke, "Only Fox has publicly declared losses—$397 million for the NFL and $225 million for baseball—though some other deals are regarded by industry experts as either wallowing in or headed for red ink." Financial losses led ABC to dump its costly contract with the college football Bowl Championship Series (BCS) after 2006 and to drop its signature sports show—*Monday Night Football* (MNF). ABC has lost $150 million per year on MNF, and the contract has been picked up by ESPN for 2006. Disney president Bob Iger admitted that even though MNF had "been a cornerstone of sorts for ABC over the years, we've said for a long time that economics were a consideration as well."

New Approaches

To borrow a horrible sports cliché, it's a whole new ballgame today for sports economics. As the cost of sports and sports media goes up, both sides look for new ways to increase revenue. Given the drop in viewer ratings, advertisers are not necessarily willing to pick up the slack in terms of paying more for access or buying more commercial time. As a result, the media, sports franchises, and advertisers are all searching for new approaches and alternative revenue streams.

In some cases, the easiest and most cost-efficient thing to do is simply pull the plug. We have already discussed how sports segments in local newscasts across the country have been shortened, streamlined, or eliminated. The Fox *National Sports Report*, which was the only serious challenger to ESPN's *SportsCenter*, was cancelled in 2002 after 6 years on the air. Time-Warner cancelled the Goodwill Games in 2001, reportedly because of falling ratings and losses of $150 million. "After reviewing the business of the Goodwill Games, we determined that our viewers will be better served by reallocating the resources into other sports opportunities," said Jamie Kellner of Turner Broadcasting.

Advertisers also try to end run the media and go directly to the sports franchises and players. This technique of product placement is not uncommon, as witnessed by the professional golfers, tennis players, and race car drivers who display corporate logos. Events themselves, such as the Nokia Sugar Bowl and Fed Ex Orange Bowl, have also been sponsored for some time. Advertisers also get exposure through stadium naming rights, which provide high visibility for a modest cost that averages about $2 million per year.

However, there is a sense that these trends are growing and becoming more of the rule rather than the exception. In 2003, the Chicago Bears, the oldest and most traditional franchise in the NFL, officially became "the Bears presented by Bank One." Bank One paid an undisclosed amount to be the team's "presenting partner," which means for the dozen years of the contract the company will get signs all over the Bears' stadium, advertisements on Bears' radio broadcasts and nongame television programs, the team's banking business, a presence at training camp, and a sponsorship role in the team's community outreach efforts. The team will often make use of the phrase "Bears football presented by Bank One" on the air and in newspapers. "This strikes me as a dangerous precedent, maybe one step too far," said Paul Swangard, managing director of the Warsaw Sports Marketing Center at the University of Oregon. "We've reached the point where to generate more revenue, everyone's diving into what seems to me to be a gray area."

Product placement is also becoming much more common, helped greatly by advances in technology. Digital manipulation can increase advertising exposure by superimposing images into a game telecast. The practice has become extremely common in televising baseball games, and such virtual billboards helped promote companies that are official sponsors of major league baseball. "It's an enhancement that gives an advertiser increased value, especially in what has been a very difficult advertising marketplace," said Lou D'Ermilio of Fox Sports. "We have a tremendous demand from other sponsors" he said, but Fox has had to turn them down.

Advertisers have also found other ways to integrate their products into sports media content. Product placement has found its way into the broadcast booth through sponsorship of shows or segments of shows. This is quite common on the local broadcast level, where sports segments have natural tie-ins with sporting goods companies, foods and beverages, or sports health clinics. Such commercialism has existed for years, but now it's starting to overshadow content instead of complementing it. Commenting on recent changes in *Monday Night Football*, sportswriter Phil Mushnick observed, "Football seems to have become a down-graded priority. The higher goals now seem to be selling John Madden, selling what John Madden sells, selling Disney (ABC/ESPN) programming, and selling the kind of incivility that has laid sports low."

The media understand that they have to find new ways of increasing value for advertisers, no matter how blatant the effort. In 2002, Fox went on location in Detroit with its NFL pregame show, while the network's number-one announce team handled the game between the Lions and the Packers. The game had little to do with Fox's decision, considering that the Lions were winless at the time and had gone 2–14 the previous year. Instead, Fox went to Detroit as a favor to the Ford Motor Company, using animated virtual advertising during the game, as Ford trucks popped up on the field. According to Fox Sports chairman David Hill, "We try to go an extra yard for our advertisers, and Ford has been with us for a long time. We do something like this for advertisers once or twice a season."

According to Mushnick, "The next sport on TV's desperate agenda appears to be golf. It, too, seems to have been designated for destruction. Cross-promotion—corporate synergy—and the stop-at-nothing quest to attract younger viewers have begun to shove competitive golf from view. During the Bob Hope Classic, ABC's high-priority, on-site effort was to sell ABC's "Bachelorette." A featured bachelorette, as if by magic, even showed up on the course, where she was interviewed by Terry Gannon—while a PGA event was being contested a few feet away."

Creative product placement and sponsorship are ways the media can increase revenue, but they also look for ways to cut costs. One priority has been reducing commitments to long-term and expensive broadcast rights fees. We have already noted the billions of dollars involved in television and radio deals between networks and sports leagues. According to a Morgan Stanley report released in 2003, CBS, ABC, and Fox will lose $5.5 billion combined on baseball, football, and basketball contracts between 2000 and 2006.

NBC came under criticism when it lost its rights to televise the NFL in 1998, but the network has purposely embarked on a "smaller is better" sports philosophy. The network now features properties such as the Arena Football league, which doesn't pull much in the way of ratings, but also doesn't cost much. "We're already assured a profit," said Kevin Sullivan of NBC Sports after the first AFL telecast. Even high-spending CBS seems to have learned a lesson, as the network just renegotiated a

10% decline in rights fees for the next 4 years of the U.S. Open tennis tournament. "Chances are, the other networks will scale back their future bids on the bigger leagues," says sportswriter Filip Bondy. "(That would affect) ticket prices, salaries, expansion and all the runaway economics of sport. Maybe not a lot, but the escalation definitely stops."

As a last ditch effort to save money, the sports media can always rely on an old strategy—pushing increasing costs off to the consumer. We've seen this with the Internet, where sports sites and newspapers have begun requiring a fee or personal registration to access content (Chapter 5). More and more sports content on cable and satellite is becoming pay-per-view or requires a commitment to purchase additional channels or tiers of programming. The NFL has had great success with its "Sunday Ticket" service, which offers access to every Sunday game for around $250 a year. "Sports fans across the country will pay through higher cable fees," says sports reporter Richard Wilner. "Cable companies say they have no choice but to pass along (rights fees) increases. ESPN is said to be asking cable companies for a 20% increase in carriage fees. Other networks are right behind them."

ESPN has had a contentious time dealing with carriage fees, which is the charge ESPN levies on cable and satellite companies for carrying ESPN programming. Some cable companies such as Cox and Charter Communications threatened to bump ESPN off the basic cable tier, thus reducing its audience, because of what they called unwarranted price increases. The situation was resolved in early 2004 when Cox and Charter agreed to lower price increases in exchange for adding more ESPN channels.

Economic Synergy and Breakdown

By now, you should have some sense of how all of this ties together and the synergy among sports, the media, and advertising (Figure 9-2). Sports athletes and events provide content the media so desperately need, especially in today's competitive media environment. In turn, the media promote sports and increase their visibility and revenue. Promotion leads to more audience interest, which increases ticket sales, concessions, and merchandising. In some cases, as with network broadcast contracts, the media pay directly for access to the sports content.

Advertisers are interested in the sporting events because of the audiences they attract, which are primarily young males with disposable income—very attractive audiences for advertisers of certain products such as beer, automobiles, and video games. Advertisers contribute revenue to the sports franchises and events through commercial tie-ins, sponsorships, and direct payments. The high visibility of sports events ensures that advertisers will want their names attached in some form or fashion.

Finally, media provide advertisers with access to much bigger audiences. Only a few thousand people will watch a particular game in person, but millions more

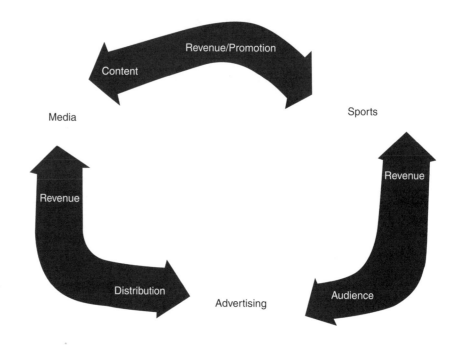

Figure 9-2

The relationship between sports, media, and advertising.

will be able to access it through television, radio, newspapers, or the Internet. Historically, these audiences have been very large, but recently they are becoming smaller and more targeted because of more media options and consumer choice. Advertisers pay handsomely for this access, and traditionally this money has been the media's primary revenue stream.

The problem is that in today's environment, there are breakdowns at different parts of the system (Figure 9-3). The media are facing increasing costs, largely because of new technology, and there is a real danger that advertising might not be able to shoulder enough of the revenue burden. Revenue is also a problem for sports leagues and franchises, many of which are in serious economic trouble. The major league baseball strikes of 1981, 1985, and 1994 were directly a result of inequitable revenue distribution from broadcast revenues. Some teams were making millions off local television and radio rights, while teams in smaller markets were going broke.

Advertisers have also suffered because of lower ratings and fragmenting audiences. Except for big events like the Super Bowl, advertisers have difficulty reaching the large, mass audiences they need. Although the Super Bowl still attracts a healthy audience, it has seen its ratings decline steadily over the past two decades. As a result, many advertisers are turning to niche outlets that cater to smaller, more targeted audiences, such as specialty magazines, Internet sites, and cable channels.

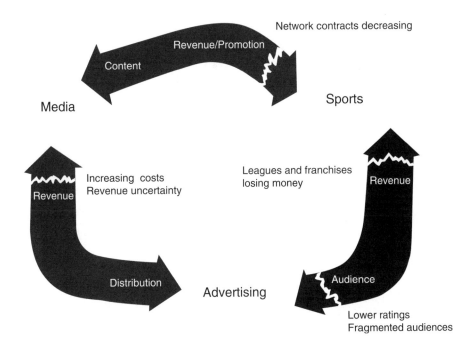

Figure 9-3

Breakdown in the relationship between sports, media, and advertising.

The bottom line is smaller audiences for advertisers, which means they have to spread around their buying to multiple outlets. That leads to less money for individual media, which depend on this revenue stream to deliver sports content. If the media make less money, they have to scale back their broadcast rights fees contracts, and the sports teams and franchises make less money.

It should be obvious that there's a problem in the system, but it's just as obvious that advertisers, sports franchises, and the media are not in business to lose money. When businesses are faced with rising costs or decreasing revenues, one of their strategies is to try and push the problem off onto someone else. We have already seen, such as when ESPN wanted to raise its cable carriage rates, how the partners in the system can try to solve economic situations by attacking one another.

However, it's much more likely that the system will try to push costs off to a fourth party—the consumer—and in fact this is already happening (Figure 9-4). The media solve the problem of rising costs by raising access fees. Subscriptions for magazines and newspapers have gone up, as have cable and satellite fees. More and more Internet sites are requiring a fee to access content or are demanding personal information they can use to help with their advertising.

Advertisers transmit costs through the "corporatization" of sports, which is more of an indirect cost. This indirect cost has traditionally been in the form of commercials and advertisements, but fragmenting audiences and the development of

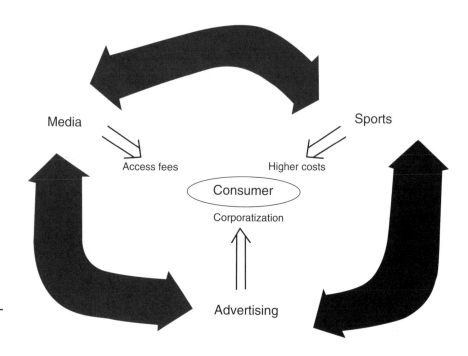

Figure 9-4

Industry pressures push costs off to the consumer.

technology that allows consumers to avoid commercials, such as the remote control and TiVo, have forced advertisers to focus more on product placement, sponsorships, and corporate tie-ins. Virtual billboards are one example, such as when viewers of the Indy 500 see digitally created advertisements placed strategically around the track. More events and even athletes will become corporately sponsored, and there will be more of a corporate presence in the broadcast booth and in the sports section of the newspaper.

You may have already noticed how much it costs to go to a sporting event today. Teams and leagues are raising prices on tickets, concessions, parking, and merchandise. "The middle-income and lower-income fans are being priced out of the game," says Andrew Zimbalist, a professor of economics at Smith College. "It threatens the mass character of sport, and over time there is a gradual loss of interest, which hurts TV ratings and licensing deals."

Team Marketing Report of Chicago has tracked fan costs over the past dozen years, calculating things such as the cost of tickets, parking, and concessions. The figures listed in Table 9-2 are the family cost index (FCI) for each league. The FCI includes four average-price tickets, four small soft drinks, two small beers, four hot dogs, two game programs, parking, and two adult-size caps. Overall, the costs of attending a game today have escalated far beyond normal inflationary increases.

	2004	1991	Percentage Increase	Table 9-2
National Football League	$301.75	$151.33	50	
National Basketball Association	$261.26	$141.91	46	
National Hockey League[a]	$253.65	$195.79	23	
Major League Baseball	$155.52	$79.41	52	

Rising Fan Costs *Source: Team Marketing Report (www.teammarketing.com)*

[a] No 1991 figures are available for the NHL, and figure listed is for the 1994 season.

Of course, there's a sense that consumers can be pushed around only so far. Attendance at many professional sporting events has declined, and even NBA Commissioner David Stern admits, "You would like your teams to have tickets at prices families can afford, but the average sports fan is now a television fan." Frank Stadulis, a former IBM executive and president of Florida-based United Sports Fans of America, a fan-advocacy group with 500,000 members, agrees. "Fans are much more in tune with being gouged," he said. "They are much less inclined to go see a bad product and see the home team get its brains beat out."

Growing consumer dissatisfaction and the shift toward an "electronic fan" suggest that the system continues to evolve. Consumers, the media, advertisers, and sports franchises and leagues are all trying to figure out what the economic future will look like. While there is much discussion on that topic, there is almost no debate on one important fact: The old days are gone and not coming back. "It's like comparing apples to artichokes," said Dennis Howard, a nationally known professor of sports marketing at the University of Oregon. "In my judgment, the golden era is over, but I'm not sure the owners are paying attention. Even if the economy sustains itself, the nature of professional sports has fundamentally changed."

References

Bank One to be Bears' presenting sponsor. (2003, June 24). *ESPN.* http://espn.go.com/sportsbusiness/news/2003/0624/1572282.html

Bock, Hal. (2003, February 5). College sports television to launch Feb. 23. *Associated Press.*

Bohls, Kirk. (2003, August 24). Big games, big money, big troubles. *Austin American-Statesman.* http://www.statesman.com/horns/content/sports/bohls/0803/082403.html

Bondy, Filip. (2003, February 4). Whole new arena. *New York Post.* http://www.nydailynews.com/sports/story/57032p-53418c.html

Cuts at Fox Sports. (2002, January 17). *Associated Press.*

ESPN reaches deals to stay on basic cable tier. (2004, February 20). *Ft. Worth Star-Telegram.* http://www.dfw.com/mld/dfw/sports/7998644.htm

Hiestand, Michael. (2004, January 30). Super Bowl hype: part of the game. *USA Today.* http://www.med.sc.edu:1081/superbowl2004.htm

Horn, Barry. (2004, November 9). Fox, CBS to pay $8 billion for NFL through 2011. *The Dallas Morning News*. http://www.dallasnews.com/sharedcontent/dws/spt/stories/110904dnsponfltvdeal.c9b.html

Kaiser Family Foundation Survey of Kids (and their Parents) About Famous Athletes as Role Models. (2000, October 12). *Kaiser Family Foundation*. http://www. iyi.org/library_reference/reports_details.asp?TopicID=68&offset=50&ReportID=153

Kapadia, Reshma. (2001, December 21). AOL Time Warner pulls plug on Goodwill Games. *Yahoo News*. http://dailynews.yahoo.com/h/nm/20011221/en/industry-goodwillgames_1.html

Lupica, Mike. (2004, Feb 3). Jackson's stunt exposes league. *New York Daily News*. http://www.nydailynews.com/sports/story/160869p-141111c.html

Marchand, Andrew. (2003, January 17). 'Monday night' falls. *New York Post*.

Martzke, Rudy. (2005, January 26). Golf Channel, other niche networks, get good reception. *USA Today*. http://www.usatoday.com/sports/columnist/martzke/2005-01-26-martzke_x.htm

Martzke, Rudy. (2004, December 9). ESPN's Earnhardt biography is off track, misses points. *USA Today*. http://www.usatoday.com/sports/columnist/martzke/2004-12-09-martzke_x.htm

Martzke, Rudy. (2004, September 13). Deion Sanders makes TV presence known. *USA Today*. http://usatoday.com/sports/columnist/martzke/2004-09-13-martzke_x.htm

Martzke, Rudy. (2003, February 25). Deals affirm NBC's direction. *USA Today*. http://www.usatoday.com/sports/columnist/martzke/2003-02-25-martzke_x.htm

Martzke, Rudy. (2002, October 25). With pitching changes, Fox counts more change. *USA Today*. http://www.usatoday.com/sports/columnist/martzke/2002-10-25-martzke_x.htm

Martzke, Rudy. (2002, September 19). Fox goes all out in Motor City favor. *USA Today*. http://www.usatoday.com/sports/columnist/martzke/2002-09-19-martzke_x.htm

Mushnick, Phil. (2004, February 9). Good walk spoiled. *New York Post*. http://www.nypost.com/sports/16180.htm

Mushnick, Phil. (2002, September 27). 'MNF' shows off its crass. *New York Post*. http://www.nypost.com/sports/48242.htm

Sandomir, Richard. (2003, September 10). The decline and fall of sports ratings. *New York Times*. http://www.nytimes.com/2003/09/10/sports/10ratings.html

Saunders, Patrick. (2001, April 8). Sky-high ticket prices are keeping many fans from arenas, ballparks, stadiums. *Denver Post*. http://www.surveyusa.com/ArchivedArticles/dposttickets.htm

Special report: economics of baseball. (2001, December 7). *New York Mets*. www.mets.com.

Stern: league in negative cash position. (2004, April 15). *Associated Press*. http://sports.espn.go.com/nba/news/story?id=1783311

Wilner, Richard. (2001, July 11). Soaring cable fees will fleece fans. *New York Post*. http://www.newyorkpost.com/sports/29063.htm

Wollenberg, Skip. (2001, November 1). Advertisers use backdrop of World Series billboards visible only to TV viewers. *Yahoo Business News*. http://biz.yahoo.com/apf/011101/world_series_ads_1.html.

Public and Media Relations

In terms of the sports media, there are two sides to the issue of public relations. On one hand, there are a number of professional public and media relations outlets whose primary job is to provide media members with information and access. The other side is from the perspective of the sports media, which must work with these outlets and sort through the seemingly endless amounts of material they provide. The key to success on both sides is developing a good working relationship and an understanding of what each side is trying to accomplish.

The Sports Media Perspective

When a sports media person sits down at the computer to decide on content for the day, there is an endless possibility of choices. Much of the information will come from the local news wires, the daily video news feeds, and even from other media. But an important source of information is the professional media specialist. Media relations organizations employ thousands of people and spend millions of dollars every year with one goal in mind—to get their events, products, or services mentioned on the air in the best possible way. It's the job of the sports media person to sort through all this information and decide how much of it, if anything, will become part of the day's content.

Sometimes, the efforts of media relations companies are nothing more than blatant attempts to pitch products. The sports reporter will often receive unsolicited press releases or video news releases (VNRs) in the mail. These might have information about a new golf ball that will travel 500 yards or an unbreakable wooden baseball bat. The VNR will have video and interview segments that sportscasters can put directly on the air. Sometimes, these releases include items of genuine interest to the public, but one should always keep in mind where the VNR comes from and who's distributing it.

It's relatively easy to spot a media release and decide whether it presents any useful information. More typically, the sports media person will deal with three types of media relations specialists: local, college, and professional.

Local Media Information

Generally speaking, there are very few media organizations dedicated to promoting purely local events. Most fall in the category of "event-specific" organizations: groups devoted to promoting one particular event, such as an annual triathlon or golf scramble. In such situations, the publicity is usually handled by a part of the sponsoring organization. For instance, if the local United Way has an annual charity "fun run," someone from the United Way will serve as a contact point for the organization and be responsible for working with the media.

It's important to remember in such situations that these organizations don't view the event the same way you do. To them, it's the most important thing going on and merits lots of coverage. To you, it's just another event competing for time and space. This can create some obvious tension, especially if the organization doesn't think you're giving the event the coverage it "deserves." Your job is to balance the needs of the organization with the best interests of your audience, and sometimes that means saying "no thanks." Much of the coverage issue has to do with timing. A local event planned during Super Bowl week or during the state basketball tournament will not get as much coverage as it would during the long, boring summer months. Most organizations recognize this and try to schedule accordingly.

Another source of tension occurs when the event itself becomes less important than something that happens during the event. Every year, Wichita Falls, Texas, hosts a bicycle race called the "Hotter 'n Hell Hundred." One year, the course was poorly marked and several of the race leaders became lost, resulting in enormous confusion at the finish line. Thus, the major story had shifted from the race itself to the confusion surrounding the winner and the local media rightly played up that angle, much to the frustration of the event organizers. The issue is one of control and at such times, organizers lose control of event coverage.

Most high schools do not have full-time personnel dedicated to event promotion and so the responsibility falls with the sports reporter. Coaches and administrators can be extremely helpful in delivering information on schedules, scores, and athletes, but they usually don't come to you. It's wise to develop contacts at the school that can provide this information. Sometimes, this contact is the head coach or athletic director, but it can also be other school officials or even parents of the players.

Again, it's important to remember that local schools have the same vested interest that other organizations do and want to see them presented in the best possible light. No school wants to publicize a drug problem or an abusive coach, which can create very difficult situations for the sports reporter. Some schools take preemptive action, such as St. Marys in Ohio. During his long tenure, legendary football coach Skip Baughman would not allow his players to talk to the media during the season.

Even though some schools and coaches may be overly protective, at the local level you're dealing with kids, not professional athletes. There is a temptation to be critical or break the "big" story, but often it can have serious consequences for young athletes, most of whom are playing for the fun of it.

On Campus

Almost every media market includes a major university, college, or junior college. Unlike high schools or other local organizations, all of these institutions have full-time, professional staff to disseminate media information. A few of these people work for university public relations, but most work in the sports information department or in the athletic department.

The sports information department varies in size, depending on the size of the school. Larger schools will have dozens of employees, each with a specific area of responsibility. Some will be in charge of certain sports, whereas others work on publications or behind the scenes. Smaller schools may only have a few people who have to do everything. But no matter what the size, sports information departments all perform the same basic functions. They provide information, give media access to players and coaches, and serve as liaison between the school and the local media.

Information and access are what sports media people need most. The development of technology makes it much easier and faster for sports information departments to disseminate information. The traditional printed press release has all but disappeared and has been replaced by e-mail releases and Internet sites. One tradition that remains is the media guide, which is usually a book-sized production that includes pictures, statistics, and photos that media people can keep for easy reference (Figure 10-1).

As much as information, sports media people need access to players and coaches. This includes access for interviews before and after games, and the ability to report from games at home and on the road. Colleges and universities have a system in place for who gets to cover the games and where they will sit. Legitimate media outlets usually don't have any trouble getting credentials to cover a game, unless there are unusual circumstances. If it is a game with a lot of media interest, there might not be enough room to accommodate everyone. The sports information director (SID) has the final say on who gets in and who doesn't. All during a game, sports information

Figure 10-1

Providing information is one of the primary duties of the sports information specialist.

people will provide media members with updated information, statistics, and even food and drink.

Newspaper and magazine reporters, along with television and radio play-by-play people, watch from the press box or a designated press area. Press box space limitations dictate that television photographers and other reporters cover the game from ground level. There are restrictions as to where photographers can stand and where they can shoot, and most arenas and fields are marked to keep field personnel within the rules. For example, most college and professional football fields have a 5-yard buffer zone marked by a dotted line around the entire field, and the media are not allowed in this area.

While sports media outlets usually do not have much difficulty in getting credentials to cover games, the same cannot always be said for getting access to players and coaches. Media members obviously need interview access to these people several times a week—right after the game to talk about what happened and at times during the week to discuss the upcoming opponent or for feature stories (Figure 10-2).

The problem for media people is that access to key players and coaches is often tightly controlled. Postgame access is usually not difficult, but even then not all players may be available and there are certain time restrictions. Most schools set up a news conference with important players and coaches during the week, but the media

Figure 10-2

The sports media need access to players and coaches, which is often controlled tightly by sports information people.
Courtesy: Mary Lou Sheffer

complain that these interviews are often too stiff and don't provide any interesting information. If a media member wants to interview a player or coach outside the news conference, the request typically has to go through sports information, and there is no guarantee the interview will be permitted. The player could be injured, have a scheduling conflict, or might not even be allowed to speak to the media.

This last point suggests that coaches and athletic department personnel have a tremendous amount of power in granting access and often tie the hands of the sports information people. No matter how accommodating the SID wants to be, if the coach doesn't want a player to talk, he or she won't talk. Many coaches have very strict rules about interviewing players, especially younger players or freshman. And it goes without saying that it's much more difficult to get access during a crisis or after a tough loss. After his team was beaten badly in a 2004 game, Texas Tech football coach Mike Leach would not allow his players to be interviewed afterward. "We're not mentally tough enough to talk with the media," said Leach, who cut off his own press conference after only one question, and then cancelled player interviews for the rest of the week. According to Tech defensive coordinator Lyle Setencich, "I don't like any of the guys giving interviews. Anything they say may be construed to be a smart-aleck type thing. If you're a football coach, that's like cancer."

That kind of attitude often puts the SID squarely in the middle between the coach and the media, and it can makes things quite uncomfortable. While the media are screaming for access to a particular player, the head coach is just as determined to keep a lid on things. The SID certainly wants to help the media as much as possible, but you should never forget that sports information people are employed by the school, and that's where their loyalty lies. For example, you can imagine the almost impossible demands placed on the sports information department at Ohio State University during that school's recent football scandal in which former player Maurice Clarett alleged that he and other players received illegal benefits. As much as the school's sports information people wanted to help the media covering the story, their primary goal was to control access and information in accordance with university goals and policies.

Recognizing this, reporters should be aware when they're getting "stonewalled" in terms of investigating serious stories or allegations regarding the school. In the Ohio State case, the sports media simply can't wait until the school SID hands out information. Reporters realize that SIDs have a vested interest in promoting the university and its agenda, and they often look elsewhere for the information they need.

Ideally, the SID should serve as a middleman or liaison between the school and the media, and have good working relationships with both sides. That means it's very important for those in the sports media to create good working relationships with media relations based on trust and respect. The relationship is not necessarily a friendship, but both sides can create a situation where they make clear their expectations. Trust also involves respecting the guidelines and restrictions imposed by sports information departments, most of which come directly from the coaches. The sports media should observe and respect these conditions, despite the obvious temptations not to do so. Circumventing the rules may work in the short run, but it will destroy the trust of the sports information department and have serious consequences down the line. Sports information departments will be much less willing to share information and work with reporters who have "burned" them.

Sports Information with Mike Lageschulte

Mike Lageschulte (Figure 10-3) is in his 10th year on the sports information staff at the University of Utah. In 1999 he was promoted to associate SID, taking over as the primary media contact for the Runnin' Ute men's basketball team. Lageschulte is also the media contact for the Utah women's soccer team and assists with football. In addition to his media relations duties, Lageschulte has worked as a sportscaster in the Salt Lake City market. He handled play-by-play for Ute women's basketball for three seasons. Lageschulte has also filled in as the play-by-play announcer on KALL-700 and as an analyst on KJZZ-TV for Ute men's basketball broadcasts.

Figure 10-3

Mike Lageschulte,
Associate Sports
Information Director,
University of Utah.

Q: *How would you describe the duties of an SID or someone in media relations? Is there one part of the job that's more important than the others?*

A: As much as technology has changed the way we go about doing our job over the years, the foundation of what media relations directors strive to accomplish remains the same—to promote the good news while handling the bad news with dexterity. I think sometimes all of us in the profession are guilty of spending too much time on trying to produce the perfect media guide or the best set of game notes. But doing those things is just part of the process, not the end result. The ultimate is to promote your student-athletes, coaches, and athletics department as a whole. You could write the best press release that has ever been printed, but if you don't get it in the hands of the right people in a timely manner, it won't be very effective. If you don't have a good relationship with your local sports media, your story won't be told no matter how good it is.

Having good relationships with members of the media is particularly important when something negative surfaces. Generally, if reporters have a negative story that will sell papers and draw an audience, they are going to go with it. But you want to have a good enough relationship with them that they will let you know what's coming—and give you more than just a token phone call. You want to have the chance to tell your side of the story, to give some good information to counterbalance what they have and defuse the situation as much as you can.

Taking care of the media so that they can do their job as effortlessly as possible on a daily basis, and developing a working relationship with them is the best way to get that done. As coaches go about their daily routine, the question they continuously pose to themselves is, "Will this help me win games?" As a college SID, you have to ask yourself, "Will this help us get positive publicity?" It's as simple as that.

Q: Do you feel like your prime responsibility is to the school? The media? The coaches? How do you balance all that?

A: No question, college media relations directors work in a unique environment. You interact with the university administration, the athletics department administration, the coaches, the student-athletes, the media, and some cases the fans. Balancing the best interests of those entities can be one of the most challenging tasks of an SID, because it's a rare occurrence when the same thing benefits all of them.

When it comes to working with the media, ultimately you have to remember where your paycheck comes from. It comes from the university, so doing what's best for the institution, the athletics department, the coaches and the student-athletes—and in that order of importance—should be your primary responsibilities.

The media tends to see you as a friend of the coaches. And, even though you work under the same roof, some coaches will see you as a friend of the media. If you're doing your job well, you exist somewhere in the middle—as tough as that may be sometimes. The administrators, coaches, and student-athletes are too busy doing what it is they do to build great relationships of their own with the media. And to be quite honest, some of them don't want to. Being able to work effectively with everyone involved is what makes you valuable. And, getting a coach or student-athlete together with a reporter to do an interview, providing information to both sides, and seeing a finished product that everyone is happy with is the most satisfying thing you will do.

Q: What is the most difficult aspect of dealing with the sports media?

A: For the fans, watching and following sports is a form of entertainment. It's an escape from their daily lives. But, for those who work in sports, it's a business. If you get into athletics media relations, especially at a major college or with a professional team, thinking it's going to be all fun games, you'll be in for a rude awakening. Don't get me wrong, being in the locker room or on a flight home after a big win is the ultimate thrill. I think that's why a lot of us get in the profession and stay in it. But coordinating interviews after a tough loss, or working with a team that is having a tough season, can be extremely difficult.

Just like their colleagues who cover the White House or City Hall, the job of a sports reporter is to beat the coverage of their competition. They cover their beat thoroughly, work to get stories, and are always on the lookout for exclusives. There's no better way for reporters to make a name for themselves than to break the story on a coach getting fired or hired. Understanding that the sports media is just like the rest of the media is one of the first things you must learn.

Another difficult part about dealing with the sports media is that you tend to have a different relationship with them than you would in other areas. People in all areas of media relations get to know the reporters they work with. That's part of building working relationships with them. But I think in sports, it can be easy to get too comfortable around them. Just like you, they enjoy sports. You sit next to them at games and watch practices with them. You have to be conscious not talk to them like they are another fan. You have to remember that they have a job to do, and finding sources of information is a part of their job. As someone who they are in contact with on a regular basis, you become a source of information for them. That can be a good thing when you want to get your message out, but you have to be careful to not say too much or unintentionally give something away during a casual conversation or while venting your frustrations over a loss.

Q: How would you describe your relationship with those in the local sports media?

A: I make an effort to get to know everyone the best I can. I'm a strong believer in that you're more effective when you work with people on a personal level. Sometimes I feel like my relationship with the local sports media is too good. My office, home, and cell phone numbers are all over the place, and unless I make it a point to get away from them, members of the sports media can reach me pretty much anytime, anywhere. That can be somewhat of an inconvenience at times, but I still wouldn't have it any other way.

I can't tell you how many times I've been able to get coverage for the teams I work with, or have been able to defuse—even slightly—a negative situation because I've been accessible. When a TV reporter gets a hot tip on a story 1 hour before his 10 o'clock show, by the time I'd get his message at the office the next morning, the story has already aired and the rest of the media is on to it. I want to be able to do whatever I can as soon as I can. And, when a newspaper reporter sits down at his computer to write a negative story, I want them to remember how helpful I've been to them. It certainly can't help.

Q: What effect has technology, specifically e-mail and the Internet, had on the job?

A: Recent technological advances allow us to do our job more effectively and efficiently than ever. The Internet has even allowed us, in some cases, to cut out the media as the "middle man" in our promotional efforts.

E-mail allows us to distribute information faster than ever. No more waiting for fax machines or sending encrypted data files through a dial-up modem. And with group e-mail lists, we are efficiently able to target our media outlets according to local and national coverage, and sport-by-sport coverage. One of the best technical advances that work hand-in-hand with e-mail is the ability to send large documents as an attachment in PDF format. For instance, I can e-mail a 20-page basketball release in PDF format to someone clear across the country, and the recipient can print out a copy within minutes that's as clean as the one I would hand them in person.

The Internet has revolutionized the media relations profession. We still rely heavily on the mass media to promote our athletics programs. But with our own Web site, we in essence have our own newspaper, radio station, and television station—and complete editorial control. We can post an endless amount of news releases, feature stories, media guides, photo galleries, and link up live stats from our games and events. Friends and family of our student-athletes can go to our Web site for in-depth coverage, and this is especially valuable for nonrevenue sports that struggle to get attention from the mass media. We also do live audio broadcasts for seven sports. In a media market the size of Salt Lake City, getting our baseball games on the radio, for instance, has been a tough sell. Now we can broadcast those games live and at a relatively low cost. In the future we might look into putting together sponsorship packages for our Internet broadcasts, which will allow us to offset our costs entirely or perhaps even generate revenue. We are also air streaming video of all home and select away women's gymnastics and women's volleyball contests.

The evolution of all sports radio stations has also changed the business entirely. Between national shows and local shows in all areas of the country, it seems like there is a never-ending demand for guests. Especially for student-athletes, who have academic commitments and also want to enjoy that stage of their life, there aren't enough hours in the day as it is. It can be tough to convince them that it's important to go on a live radio show for 5 minutes. I also think that talk radio has fueled a lot of negativity in sports. Fans now have a public forum to vent after a loss. If you're considering buying a ticket for an upcoming game, hearing opinions from other people about how bad a team is has to make you think strongly about parting with your hard-earned money. Even continuous positive talk can build up unrealistic expectations. Talk show hosts and callers also will toss out rumors or second-hand information about a coach or an athlete. There might not even be a shred of truth behind what they are saying, but it can be as equally damaging as fact.

Q: We saw the SIDs at Colorado put in a terrible position with the recent media firestorm over the football program. From an SID perspective, how do you deal with something like that?

A: Handling a crisis situation needs to be a collaborative effort. The first step is to get the coaches and student-athletes involved to disclose what the problem is to the administration. Ideally, this will take place before the media gets hold of the story. As the media contact, you will often be the first person contacted about potential legal/criminal issues. Even though you may not have the legal clearance, or in some instances be far enough along in the investigative/fact finding process where you are ready to release details or make any lengthy statements, just being prepared for what is coming, and being able to confidently tell the media that you are aware of the situation and that it is being dealt with internally is a major plus. When the media senses they have you scrambling, they have a tendency to become even more aggressive.

Once the administration is aware of the potential issue, you must strategize how best to deal with it publicly. Everyone who will be involved, including the president of the university, university legal advisors, the head spokesman for the university P.R. office, the A.D, and the SID, needs to be a part of this process. In addition to the individuals directly involved in the incident, all of the aforementioned people will be drawn into a crisis situation. And, they all have something to contribute based upon their area of expertise. Everyone needs to be up front with one another about what they're thinking and what they're feeling, and not be afraid to make suggestions. Then a strategy needs to be formulized as to what will be announced to the public and when, and who will do the talking.

Unlike the normal day-to-day situations that arise in athletics, it is likely that the university public relations department will want to take over handling the media in a major crisis situation. Along those lines, I think one of the best things you can do is to limit the number of people that will be talking to the media. The more streamlined your communication is, the better your chances are of getting your message across and getting the same information to everyone. And, perhaps more importantly, it limits the chances of incorrect information and/or details that you don't want to be made public getting out.

The Big Leagues

Ask any athlete and he or she will tell you the difficulty in moving from college to the pros. The players are bigger, the game is faster, and it's a completely different culture. Much the same can be said when comparing media specialists who work for colleges with those who work for professional organizations or teams. It's a whole new ball game.

The biggest difference is one of control. At the college level, the university (meaning the coaches and the sports information staff) has a strong degree of control over the athletes. When a coach tells the player to talk to the media (or not to talk), the player usually complies. When someone from sports information sets up an interview with a player, that player usually shows up and does the interview. Only in rare circumstances does the player (or the coach, i.e., Bobby Knight) rebel against the system.

Not so in professional athletics. Players make a lot of money and enjoy a tremendous amount of personal freedom. Whether or not they cooperate with the media and to what degree is entirely up to them. Several athletes, most notably former baseball stars Steve Carlton and Albert Belle, have simply refused to have any dealings with the media, except on their terms. Other players will cooperate to a degree, but show open hostility to reporters. The relationship between the media and athletes, which once bordered on friendship, can now best be described as cautious, or even adversarial.

This puts team media specialists in a difficult situation. Every professional team has someone in charge of dealing with the media, but in no way can that person control or dictate to the athletes. By way of example, the 2000 Boston Red Sox clubhouse had become something of a war zone, involving players, the manager, and the media. One of the main instigators was moody outfielder Carl Everett. In late September, according to writer Peter Gammons, "Carl Everett had launched into an obscenity-filled, threatening tirade at *Boston Globe* writer Gordon Edes. There were club officials present, but they did nothing until Edes replied, 'Nice game, Carl' and walked away so (Everett's) teammates could have some peace. Edes was then confronted by those club officials and accused of a 'cheap shot.' When you're in the big leagues, you're on your own."

Sports PR with Gregg Ellis

Gregg Ellis (Figure 10-4) has worked as a sportswriter for the *Indianapolis Star* and the *Northeast (MS) Daily Journal,* where he currently is the paper's beat writer for Mississippi State athletics. But before moving into sports journalism, he spent time as a media relations specialist with the Indianapolis Colts. Having worked both sides of the fence gives him a unique perspective on the relationship between the media and sports information departments.

Q: *How would you describe your duties with the Colts?*
A: I was the liaison between the players and the media. When interview requests were made, it was my job to see the reporter got the interview, whether during the week in practice or on game day. We were also responsible for putting together game notes, media guides, and yearbooks.
Q: *From your perspective, what was the most difficult part of the job?*
A: Dealing with high-priced players who didn't respect what I did or the media.
Q: *How would you describe your relationship with the players? The coaches? The media?*
A: For the most part, I got along great with everyone involved. Of course, there is always going to be that one person. But it's important you establish trust from Day 1. If you can achieve that, your job will be much easier.
Q: *Did it seem like the players' big salaries and independence made it more difficult to get them to cooperate?*
A: Not in every case. Most of the time, the guys understand the importance of self-promotion. And it was never a problem when money was involved. It's amazing; they

Figure 10-4

Gregg Ellis, *Northeast (MS) Daily Journal.*
Courtesy: Adam Chapman

make all this money, yet won't do a public appearance unless they are paid. Some would even be satisfied with as little as $100.

Q: *Having now worked on both sides (media and PR) does that give you a better appreciation of what each side is trying to do?*

A: No question does it give me an appreciation. Now being the one needing the interviews, I try to plan ahead to make it easier for the media relations person. I also try not to take more time than needed with players and coaches, knowing just how valuable their time is.

Control is also a two-way street. At the college level, if a reporter violates media policy, it could result in serious repercussions, which range from loss of credentials to simply getting "cut off" from information and stories. At the professional level, however, media managers have no such control. In some dire situations, teams have barred certain reporters from practices and other events, but it's certainly not a major threat. At this level, many reporters simply ignore the team media specialist and get stories on their own, especially if it's a controversial or sensitive topic. Reporters realize that the team media specialist doesn't have the power to give them the coverage or the access to the athletes they need.

That is not to say that such media specialists are totally powerless in these situations. They can establish and try to enforce guidelines for interviewing coaches and players, but their abilities in this area are often hampered by situations outside their control. In certain situations, such as "media day" at the Super Bowl or NBA Finals, the league will step in and order players and coaches to cooperate with reporters. Failure to do so usually results in a fine, but given today's huge salaries, it's not unusual to see players simply refuse to show up.

Despite such lack of control, professional media specialists still have many of the same responsibilities as their collegiate counterparts. Mainly, this includes preparation and dissemination of information. Sports reporters need to know statistics, facts, times, and other pertinent information, all of which comes from the team's media director. Another function is credentialing: making sure supply for game credentials meets demand. Media organizations that cover teams on a regular basis will take up the bulk of the credentials, sometimes up to a dozen for each game. The rest go to reporters in town for special assignments or stories. There are very specific rules for getting game credentials and each organization has its own way of handling the situation.

Sometimes, the job involves public relations in its purest form—simply trying to get reporters out to cover the team. In the 1940s, when interest in pro football still lagged behind the college game, Tex Schramm of the Los Angeles Rams wrote stories for local newspapers that didn't bother to send reporters to training camp. Obviously, the NFL doesn't need any more publicity today, but dozens of other fledgling sports do. Professional soccer, women's basketball, arena football, and similar ventures have all suffered attendance and financial problems. In these situations, the work of the media or publicity director can have a huge effect on the success of the team or even an entire league.

The key to a good working relationship with media specialists of professional organizations is to realize that fundamentally they have very little power. Media directors can supply important information, but remember that they have a vested interest in their own position and their own organization. The big stories and the important stories are going to come from old-fashioned reporting—day-to-day coverage of the coaches, owners, and athletes involved with the team. New York reporter Dick Young had the reputation as one of the best baseball writers of the 1950s, 1960s, and 1970s. Young passed away several years ago, but his advice on good reporting still applies today—not only for writers but sports broadcasters. "If you put in time, if you're there, you'll get things that other guys don't get. (The team) won't call you up and tell you. There are no shortcuts. You get stories by working. There's no substitute."

The Public Relations Perspective

Sports information specialists and public relations outlets have several different priorities. Their primary function is to keep the media informed of upcoming events and to provide necessary information. At a university, the sports information department is responsible for keeping track of all the facts and figures related to the school, the players, and the coaching staff. This involves sending out enormous amounts of information—box scores, statistics, feature stories, media guides, and the like. And now most schools have added a Web site to include much of the same information on the Internet. Bobby Parker is a typical sports information director at Bradley University. He says, "My primary duties involve producing media guides for volleyball, soccer, men's and women's basketball, baseball and softball, as well as keeping our official Web site up-to-date, maintaining statistics and records for all sports in general and sport-specific release writing."

Perhaps a more important function is acting as a liaison among the university, the media, and the school's athletic teams. Bill Lamberty, SID at Montana State University, says, "The most difficult component of the profession, I believe, is to balance the needs of the media with what is best for the coaches and athletes. In a sense, the SID must maintain a loyalty to the media without sacrificing the best interests of the school."

Oftentimes, the balancing act becomes extremely difficult, especially in the case of a negative story. It's important to remember that sports information people work for the school and will always put that interest first, but they also recognize the media's responsibility. "There has been a big change in the way the local media report events," says Washington State SID Rod Commons. "They are much more critical than in the past, which isn't always bad." Maxey Parrish, former SID at Baylor University, says, "I've been in the business long enough to remember when sportswriters were friends with whom you could share just about anything. Today, there are only a handful still like that. Almost everybody is out to move up the ladder by breaking the big story; the worse the circumstances, the bigger the story."

Interestingly, many SIDs say their own coaches are harder to work with than the media. Ohio University SID Heather Czeczok says, "For the most part, the media are only difficult when they're 'snooping' or you have a 'bad' situation to deal with. Athletes can be temperamental, but I really think coaches are harder to deal with in most cases, because his or her sport is the most important thing and no other sports matter."

Media and industry professionals say the key to working in this atmosphere is to develop trust, especially difficult in this age of increased media attention and emphasis on celebrities. "Trust is huge," says University of Arizona SID Tom Duddleston. "The SID must be able to convince the staff at the university that the media are not a necessary evil, but a fun part of the whole experience." Parker says, "Trust remains the foundation. The media trust that the SID is providing accurate information in a timely fashion and the SID must trust the media to report on that information fairly."

Work as a college or university SID has changed from a 9-month job to a position that demands 60- to 100-hour workweeks almost year-round. The people who work in sports information have a unique and demanding position that provides them special insight into the relationship between athletes and the media. Several college and university SIDs offered their opinions on a variety of topics, which media practitioners will hopefully find useful and thought- provoking (Table 10-1).

Table 10-1

The Public Relations Perspective

How would you describe the duties of an SID?	"Years ago it was much more of a public relations position than it is now. Today, all athletics departments have promotions and marketing directors, jobs the SID did in years past. Now, the SID is more responsible for NCAA reports, conference reports, and the like. It's much more demanding."—Fred Huff, former SID, Southern Illinois University
	"Our primary area of responsibility is with the media and good public relations can't be beat. We also work a lot with coaches and a willingness to work with them is critical."—Rod Commons, Washington State University
	"Sports information is at its essence a service industry. The first and foremost function is to disseminate information, but at the same time to maintain relationships with media members and provide them with the information they need in a manner which fits their needs."—Bill Lamberty, Montana State University
What is the most difficult part of your job?	"Typically, SIDs put in stretches of about 100–120 days twice a year in which they work 7 days a week without a break. That's 60–70 hours a week. And time and circumstances make it impossible to please everybody."—Maxey Parrish, former Baylor University SID
	"Time management. No one other than other SIDs realizes the amount of time required for the job today. I'm in the office or on the road with the team every day, including Saturdays and Sundays, from August to April."—Fred Huff
What is the ideal relationship between an SID and the media?	"The ideal relationship is built on trust. The media have to trust the SID to be fully factual, whether the news is good or bad. The SID has to trust the media to treat his school fairly."—Maxey Parrish
	"There needs to be a personal element to the relationship. This has lessened over the years with the move to faxes, fax-on-demand, e-mail, and the Internet."—Heather Czeczok, Ohio University
How has the media changed in the way it has covered sports over the years?	"The growth of sports talk radio and the Internet have created a more negative approach to coverage. The Internet has provided another avenue for the media to get information, but it's not always reliable."—Bobby Parker, Bradley University
	"Media demands have changed dramatically. With the advent of the fax machine, e-mail, and the Internet, the world wants news faster and faster. The technology has caused more and more media outlets to arise and require information."—Joe Hernandez, Associate Athletics Director, Ball State University
	"A whole lot of technological improvements keep the business changing all the time. But a good reporter still covers an event the way a good reporter did 30 years ago—with an objective mind and hopefully some writing talent."—Tom Duddleston, University of Arizona

References

Gammons, Peter. (2000, September 23). The mess grows in Boston. *ESPN*. www.espn.go.com/gammons/s/0923notes.html

Golenbock, Peter. (1984). *Bums*. New York: Pocket Books.

Notebook: Tech stops talking. (2004, October 24). *Austin American-Statesman*. http://www.statesman.com/horns/content/sports/10/24texnotes.html

Phillips, Troy. (2004, October 26). Texas Tech football notes. *Ft. Worth Star-Telegram*. http://www.dfw.com/mld/dfw/sports/colleges/10017571.htm

Seventy-five seasons. (1994). Atlanta: Turner Publishing.

Ethics

The *New York Times*, usually considered the gold standard in terms of journalistic practice and integrity, has found its reputation severely tarnished in recent years. Most of the controversy focused on reporter Jayson Blair and his admissions that he fabricated and plagiarized several stories in 2003. The situation forced the resignations of several powerful *Times* executives, including executive editor Howell Raines.

The year before, Raines had found himself in a less serious, but no less controversial, situation. It was during the heated debate over the Augusta National Golf Club and its policy of not admitting female members. Martha Burk of the National Council of Women's Organizations called for a boycott and then protest against the Masters tournament. Masters chairman Hootie Johnson was equally as firm in holding to club policy.

As for the *Times*, it ran several editorials criticizing Augusta National and suggesting that defending champ Tiger Woods sit out the Masters in protest. No problems there, but then the *Times* killed columns by two of its star sports reporters that contradicted the paper's editorial stance. One of the columns was by Dave Anderson, a Pulitzer Prize winner. Raines said the editors decided to kill Anderson's column because it appeared to indulge in a squabble with the newspaper's editorial board that made the paper look self-absorbed. The other column, he added, was scrapped due to problems of structure and tone. "There is not now, nor will there ever be, any attempt to curb the opinions of our writers" or to "get them to agree with the editorial page or any other section of the paper where an opinion is expressed," Raines said.

But others in the media believed otherwise, and when word leaked out what the *Times* had done, it touched off a free speech firestorm. The *Times* found itself attacked from all sides, and eventually published "revised" versions of the columns. For his part, Anderson said that the whole controversy could have been avoided if the *Times* had just published the columns in the first place. The episode vividly pointed out the fact that sports journalism, even though it is often considered "less important" than traditional news, is no less immune to ethical controversies.

It is not hard to find books, articles, and theories about journalism ethics. There is a tremendous interest in the industry and many major universities now teach classes in the subject. But the narrower focus of sports journalism ethics is a little more shadowy and harder to define. Certainly, many of the ethical dilemmas that face news departments also pose problems in sports. For example, hidden cameras and checkbook journalism have long been hot topics of debate in television newsrooms. The issue came to a head in sports in 1996, involving KXAS-TV in Fort Worth, Texas. The station paid $6000 to a friend of Dallas Cowboys receiver Michael Irvin for footage of Irvin allegedly handling illegal drugs. In a panel discussion that took place after the story aired, former Dallas Mayor Ron Kirk called it "the most disgusting thing I have seen on TV."

Conflict of Interest

By far the most pervasive ethical issue in sports media is conflict of interest. Conflict of interest can take many forms, but essentially it's when sports coverage is compromised because the media outlet has some sort of interest or stake involved. In the *New York Times* case, the conflict was internal, but external conflict of interest is much more common. Some of the most obvious conflicts occur when media outlets own sports teams or leagues. For example, the Tribune Company owns not only the Chicago Cubs, but also *The Chicago Tribune*, and radio and television stations WGN, both of which carry Cubs games.

Media Ownership

It has become quite popular for media outlets to own sports teams as a financial investment because it allows the company to control both the content and the distribution of sports programming. In recent years Fox has owned the Los Angeles Dodgers, Disney has owned the Anaheim Mighty Ducks, and Cablevision still owns both the New York Rangers and the New York Knicks (Table 11-1). In some cases, such as with Fox, the media company has sold off the team, but more for financial reasons than any concerns over conflict of interest.

The danger is that media conglomerates can and do exert certain pressures on media outlets, especially if they own them. In June 2000, radio station WIP in Philadelphia suspended host Mike Missanelli for 2 days after critical comments he made against Flyers management, specifically general manager Bobby Clarke. WIP is owned by Infinity Broadcasting and owns the rights to the Flyers and 76ers basketball games. "We have a deal with WIP," said Flyers executive Ron Ryan. "We don't have a problem with them criticizing how we run the team. It's the personal attacks we don't want." In the new media environment, some broadcast outlets have a vested

Team[a]	Owner
Atlanta Braves	Time-Warner
New York Knicks, Rangers	Cablevision
Philadelphia 76ers, Flyers	Comcast
Chicago Cubs	Tribune Co.
Toronto Blue Jays	Rogers Communication
Anaheim Mighty Ducks	Walt Disney Co.

Table 11-1

Media Ownership of Major Sports Franchises in 2004
Courtesy/Source: Forbes/espn.com

[a] Several teams, including the New York Yankees and New Jersey Nets, have created their own media outlets to televise and distribute games.

interest in making sure the home team plays well, which is something of a disturbing trend for those sports reporters who try to practice objectivity and criticism.

Marv Albert found that out the hard way. After 36 years as the play-by-play voice of the New York Knicks, Albert left in 2004 because he wasn't afraid to criticize the Knicks when they were playing poorly. According to Albert, Cablevision boss Jim Dolan ordered him to back off the criticism and use the broadcasts to tow the company line. "I knew there was no way I could work under those conditions," said Albert, "and I'm sure Jim Dolan has different views about the way broadcasts should be. If you follow his view, I don't know how you can live with yourself in terms of objectivity and credibility."

Boosterism

At its most fundamental level, conflict of interest can be nothing more than booster-ism. The theory goes that local fans and viewers want the local teams to win. When local teams win, it creates excitement in the community and generates much more interest for local papers and broadcast outlets. Players on winning teams are much more relaxed and media-friendly. It certainly makes the job more fun and prestigious for the local media to cover a winning team. What newspaper or station wouldn't want to follow the team to a Super Bowl or World Series? When the team is win-ning, it seems everyone else wins as well, including the sports reporter. Sportswriter Roger Kahn covered the Brooklyn Dodgers in the 1940s and 1950s and remem-bers how he handled covering the 1952 World Series, when the Dodgers played the Yankees. "I was rooting," he said. "Rooting silently in the press box. Rooting visibly in my story. Rooting wildly in my heart. I never knew a worthy baseball writer who wasn't—at the core— a rooting fan."

Veteran sportswriter and journalism professor Howard Schlossberg gives some real-life examples of the pressures on the sports media to make the local teams look good (Table 11-2).

Table 11-2

To Cheer or Not to
Cheer?

Let's say you've been the local beat writer, covering the local high school, where for years the football team has been a perennial winner and the coach a local legend. Then you find out he's a drunk who's been stopped many times by the local police for driving while intoxicated, but has been let go by his good friend the local police chief because of their close relationship and the coach's good standing in the community because of his impressive winning record. You even have proof of the story. Do you run it?

A reporter in a small Midwestern town did not, knowing the backlash he'd feel from a community that already knew all that anyway and turned a blind eye to it because of the coach's great record. But do players and fans expect you, the beat reporter, for preps or pros, to be a force for the positive? Sometimes. It's why San Jose Sharks' General Manager Doug Wilson called *espn.com*'s reporting that he was about to trade one of his players ". . . the dumbest comment I've read in a long time."[a]

It's why the Cubs' Sammy Sosa told the local beat writers, "We need some more support from you guys," when the team was in a mid-season slump.[b]

It's why Curt Schilling, in the middle of his first season as with the Boston Red Sox in 2004, complained regularly that he was reading things about himself that either never happened or weren't true.

And it's why Toronto Maple Leafs' star Tie Domi told the media that he doesn't do talk radio, because, as he put it, "When you listen to morons, you start turning into one."[c]

But you have to be careful out there. The *Chicago Tribune* regularly gets criticism, deserved or not, that it shows favoritism toward the Chicago Cubs because it owns the Cubs. *Tribune* reporters will deny that to their deathbeds, but reporters for other outlets in town will tell you, some out loud and some only in whispers, that the *Tribune* clearly favors the Cubs and always features them over the crosstown rival White Sox.

There's something to being a cheerleader though. Local media have an interest in having the local teams succeed, on the field, that is. The better they do, the more papers they sell. Major metropolitan newspapers regularly sell thousands more papers on Mondays during the football season when the local-market team wins on Sunday.

Still, favoritism or not, cheerleader or not, outside the lines or not, the basics of journalism must be adhered to, whether you're crossing media or not.

[a] *Daily Herald* (Paddock Publications), Feb. 3, 2004.
[b] *Daily Herald* (Paddock Publications), July 11, 2003.
[c] *Daily Herald* (Paddock Publications), Oct. 21, 2003.

Boosting the home team or playing it straight carries several ethical considerations. Namely, how can a reporter or broadcaster report truthfully or critically against a popular home team? In the early 1970s, a sportswriter in Oklahoma named Frank Boggs uncovered an NCAA investigation into the football program at the University of Oklahoma. Boggs published a series of articles detailing the investigation, which centered on an alleged ticket-scalping scandal. But he severely underestimated the popularity and power of the Oklahoma football program, which had regularly contended for the national championship. The criticism began when Oklahoma coach Barry Switzer called the reporting a "conspiracy" and angry fans turned against Boggs. He and co-writer Jack Taylor received 30 death threats in 1 hour. Even friends and co-workers avoided him. The situation got so hot, Boggs eventually transferred to another paper in Colorado.

Contrast what happened with Boggs with the way the *Los Angeles Times* covered the financing of the city's new sports arena, in which the paper later admitted ethical wrongdoing. The *Times* had agreed to become a "founding partner" of the $400 million Staples Center, but failed to tell readers about the arrangement. The deal included working with the arena on a joint project and splitting ad revenue from a special newspaper issue. In return, the *Times* got signs, vending rights, a luxury skybox at the arena, and a record $2 million in advertising revenue. *Time* magazine said it "seemed like a dangerous compromise of the paper's objectivity." *Forbes* magazine called the deal "bad for business and bad for journalism, but boosterism as usual."

With the huge amounts of money involved these days, it's easy to see why some media choose to take sides. If media criticism becomes too hot, a popular star player might decide to leave town for another team. If the team itself decides to leave, it can create an economic vacuum that could cost the community millions of dollars. When a new team moves into town it usually enjoys a "honeymoon" period, where the owners, players, and coaches receive continuous praise for their "courage" in making the move. But when a team leaves town, like the Cleveland Browns did in the mid-1990s, then the media criticism comes out full force. Browns owner Art Modell was generally vilified by the Cleveland media for moving the team to Baltimore, although some reporters made an effort to include all sides of the story.

It's also ethnically questionable to take the opposite approach, which is to be critical just for the sake of ratings or readers. This is especially dangerous given today's media climate, where dozens of voices now feel they have to be as outlandish and negative as possible to be heard above the competition. Veteran sports talk show host Mike Gastineau of KJR-AM in Seattle admits, "There can (also) be a negativism that is really discouraging at times (and) there are too many guys in the business trying to build careers on that. I've heard guys in the business refer to themselves as 'coach killers.' I think that's wildly out of line. It's not our job to get guys fired. I think it's egomaniacal to think you know as a talk-show host everything that's going on. I don't care how much research and behind-the-scenes privileges you have."

Relationships

Another common conflict of interest is the personal relationship between the media and players, owners, and coaches. Sports writers and broadcasters have almost unlimited professional access to athletes. They often travel together on the same plane or bus, they obviously spend time together at the game, and then many times they will see each other afterward. This can create a situation where the business relationship can become more like a friendship, with its obvious ethical considerations.

Back when the media weren't so numerous or sophisticated, players and reporters could develop strong attachments. Reporters would often protect players, sometimes from themselves and the things that might end up in print. The times when reporters did say something critical, they could often cool off the offended player with a round of drinks at the local bar. "Then as now ballplayers read the paper," says Kahn. "(But) during the gilded era when I started covering baseball, working conditions were too intimate for sustained hostility."

This situation has changed drastically in recent years, thanks greatly to the proliferation of media. There are dozens of microphones vying for the attention of a player, who naturally becomes more defensive and distrustful. But even without the close relationship, reporters still have good reason to stay in a player's good graces. There's always the danger of a player "cutting off" a reporter and simply not talking to him anymore, which can be quite difficult if it's the star player of a popular team. Reporters also face the possibility of verbal or even physical abuse from players.

All of this adds up to a situation in which the sports reporter or broadcaster might feel compelled to report more favorably on a player or to omit damaging information. In January 2000, New York Rangers hockey player Kevin Stevens was arrested on charges of drug abuse and prostitution. That combination might seem like a sure-fire screaming headline, but the reporting was somewhat low key. An article in *Sports Illustrated* expressed surprise, describing Stevens as someone "(who) . . . carried sunshine in his back pocket. He never big-timed anyone and he laughed loudest and longest in the dressing room." Author and journalist David Krajicek called the coverage "surprisingly tame" because of Stevens' reputation as one of the league's most popular players. Krajicek went on to say that of the four beat writers covering the story, only one mentioned the fact that Stevens had already spent time in the league's substance abuse program. "The ribald tabloids that usually go nuts on sexy celebrity stories displayed uncharacteristic reserve," he noted. "The pussyfooting stories could be seen as suck-up journalism by the beat writers."

Such situations probably happen more regarding coaches and owners than the players. From the reporters' standpoint, players are expendable commodities; they come and go frequently. But coaches and owners have much more longevity (relatively speaking) and considerably more power. Thus, many broadcasters find it profitable to develop stronger ties in this area. One of the most famous reporter–coach relationships involved former Indiana University basketball coach Bobby Knight and Bob Hamel, a long-time reporter for the *Bloomington Herald-Telegraph*. In his excellent book, *A Season on the Brink*, author John Feinstein described the relationship between the two as unusually strong, almost like brothers. They would take long walks together the night before road games and Knight would often volunteer information to Hamel before he told other media members. In this situation, one could understand how Hamel would be reluctant to report any damaging information about Knight or the basketball program. According to Feinstein, Hamel never considered it a serious ethical issue, but he did admit to having a rooting interest in the games.

Either Knight or Hamel could have abused the situation to his own benefit, although apparently neither one did. But other coaches and players have no reservations about using a relationship with a reporter to further their own cause. Coaches routinely "plant" stories with reporters when they want to send a message to a player without confronting him directly. The reporter becomes an unwitting agent, caught in the middle of team dynamics. Owners can also use the media for a very simple reason: to blunt the sharp edge of a reporter's sword. Sportswriter Dick Young had one of the keenest, most critical writing styles in all of baseball. But according to Roger Kahn, once new owners took over the Dodgers in the 1950s, they began cultivating a personal relationship with Young and feeding him exclusive information. As a result, said Kahn, "(Young) was in the Dodger pocket all the time. Young gave the Dodger line and the guys he liked were the guys management liked. The (*Daily News*) became a Dodger house organ."

Perks

A much more subtle form of influence is all the free perks that go to sports reporters. At almost every event, reporters enjoy access to all kinds of goodies, the most common being the free meal. Free food has become the standard at professional and college events and has now even become common at the high school level. While most organizations offer the food as a common courtesy, it does come with its own ethical implications. Are reporters more willing to speak favorably about the event on a full stomach? When the event does not offer food, does that make the reporter more suspicious or critical? Oftentimes when teams skimp on the meals, they gain a reputation in media circles as being "cheap" or "low class." Some organizations, most notably major league baseball teams, have cut off the ethical debate by charging for food in the media room (which has caused more than its share of grumbling by reporters). On the other side, the *St. Petersburg Times* decided the free buffet at Tampa Bay Buccaneer football games was a conflict of interest and paid the team for meals eaten by its sports staff. ·

At the other end of the scale are the more permanent gifts, which come in all shapes, sizes, and colors. Teams and organizations routinely shower media members with hats, jackets, bags, briefcases, pens, pencils, coasters, and thousands of other "mementos" to mark a particular occasion. Most of the items are relatively inexpensive and usually end up in the bottom of the reporter's closet, but the ethical questions remain. And yes, sports reporters look at these gifts the same way they view the food—almost like an entitlement program.

Many organizations have made serious effort to cut down on freebies. Several professional teams used to give free tickets to sports personnel who wanted to go to a game in their spare time. Now, most teams have ended the practice and extend courtesy privileges only to working media.

Homers

One of the most confusing examples of conflict of interest concerns play-by-play announcers, many of whom work as employees of the team they cover. Organizations are usually very open about this and provide a disclaimer for each game that indicates the broadcaster works for the team and not the broadcast station.

But disclaimers aside, the practice is loaded with ethical problems. How can any broadcaster criticize or downgrade a team that signs his paychecks? The temptation is to become a "homer," an unabashed and usually uncritical fan of the home team (see Chapter 2). Bob Prince of the Pirates and Harry Caray of the Cubs are just two examples of broadcasters who had no trouble taking sides. The situation becomes even more confusing when you consider how sports and broadcasting entities have merged in recent years. The Tribune Company owns not only the Cubs, but WGN-TV, which televises many of the games. So does a Cubs announcer work for the Tribune, for WGN, or for the team? And how can one remain independent in that situation? Several media outlets offer partial or full sponsorship of events, such as the ties between the *New York Times* and the U.S. Open tennis championship.

Local teams have always believed it's important for their own broadcasters to present the team in the very best light. Red Barber finished up his distinguished career with the Yankees in the mid-1960s, when the team fell apart on the field after decades of dominance. Barber was uncompromising in his description of the team and the lack of fans in the stands, and for that Yankee management forced him out. If Marv Albert had not left the Knicks on his own, it's quite possible Cablevision management would have forced him out.

Such occurrences are a disturbing trend in the industry, which has seen much more tolerance of critical announcing in recent years. Today, if an announcer wants to become a "homer," he usually does so out of choice, not because he feels pressure from the home team to do so. Men like Caray and Prince had personalities that suited rooting for the home team and used it to their advantage. But the ethical dangers still exist, especially at the college and high school level. In those situations, the pressure comes more from listeners, viewers, and station management. An announcer who doesn't back the home team may get himself in trouble for the most basic of broadcasting reasons—not enough people will watch or listen.

Advertising

The influence of advertising has long been a concern among professionals in the broadcasting business, and certainly sports are not immune. Advertising and sports have gone hand in hand almost from the very beginning, but we seem no closer today to answering the same old ethical questions.

To an advertiser, sports provide a vehicle to reach potential customers. It can be something as covert as putting ads on the outfield wall at a baseball game or as something more obvious like outfitting tennis and golf players as walking billboards.

However advertisers go about it, their main goal is to present their product in the most favorable light to viewers and listeners. And they spend millions of dollars every year to do it.

This can present all kinds of challenges for the broadcaster, who may feel pressure to protect or promote important advertisers. It has become routine for play-by-play broadcasters to give a list of sponsors during the telecast. Who hasn't heard an announcer say, "Today's game is brought to you in part by Budweiser, the King of Beers?" Usually, broadcasters have no problem with this arrangement. But what happens if a broadcaster has moral reservations about promoting certain products, like beer? What if the broadcaster drinks beer, but hates Budweiser?

Huge conglomerates such as Anheuser-Busch and R.J. Reynolds often spend money for sponsorship of an entire event, a common practice on the professional golf and tennis circuits. How often does a broadcaster feel compelled to repeat the name of the "Fed Ex St. Jude's Golf Classic" or the "Nokia Sugar Bowl?" In recent years, tobacco advertisers have lost many of their advertising outlets because of government regulation. Does this mean broadcasters must promote or endorse these products? More importantly, what happens if the broadcaster says something the sponsor doesn't like?

A partial answer came at the Masters golf tournament in Augusta, Georgia. The Masters has positioned itself as an "upscale" sporting event, attractive to sponsors such as Cadillac. CBS has an annual contract to televise the event and uses a dozen or so broadcasters positioned in different places around the course. One of these broadcasters was Gary McCord, who has a rather relaxed and flippant attitude about golf. One year, McCord made several comments about the course conditions, including a reference to the Augusta greens as looking like they were "waxed with bikini wax." After the tournament, Masters organizers made the decision to ban McCord from further telecasts. It's not known whether Cadillac or other sponsors brought pressure in this instance, but it wasn't the first time an announcer had been kicked out. In 1966, veteran CBS announcer Jack Whitaker was canned for referring to Masters patrons as a "mob."

At the other end of the spectrum are the broadcasters who openly embrace endorsements. Usually, the spots are for innocuous products such as John Madden's pitches for a hardware company or Terry Bradshaw's ads for a long distance phone service. Madden or Bradshaw would never think about openly endorsing the products during a game telecast (there are very strict broadcasting rules against such practices as plugola and payola), but they would certainly never criticize the products, either.

For these and other reasons, the very idea of broadcasters doing commercials has raised serious ethical issues. When broadcasters align themselves with a certain product or service, it automatically affects their credibility and integrity. Broadcasters and reporters have reputations based on neutrality and impartiality. Those reputations can take a serious hit when they step into the world of commercials, such as the recent series of beer commercials featuring Rich Eisen, the host of the NFL Network, and former Denver Broncos quarterback John Elway.

But at least Elway was retired. A much more serious situation arises when broadcasters appear in promos or commercials with active players. ESPN runs a series of very creative promotions for its *SportsCenter* shows, many of them involving current players. To Al Tompkins, former TV news director now with the Poynter Institute, this is an uncomfortable situation. "How would it be if you appear in a promo with an athlete one day," asks Tompkins, "then the next day you have to do a difficult story about that athlete's cocaine use? It would be quite difficult." Responds Bob Eaton of ESPN, "We had some questions about the promos. We ultimately structured it so we make a donation to the charity of the athlete's choice. We don't pay them and don't give them any special treatment."

Almost every station and news organization has strict rules against "plugola" and "payola," forms of ethical violations that go back to the very beginning of broadcasting. In exchange for behind-the-back compensation, the announcer would "plug" or promote the advertiser's product on the air. Despite today's legal safeguards, plugola and payola still present serious problems. It's not unheard of, for example, for someone in sports media to cut a side deal with a local advertiser. In one such instance, a sportscaster featured a series of tips from the local tennis pro in exchange for membership in an exclusive tennis club. Another sports person used his position to reward certain friends with Masters golf tickets. In each case, the offender was discovered and punished, but the practice and the temptation remain.

The endorsement doesn't have to be so sinister to raise ethical eyebrows. In 1999, former ESPN anchor Robin Roberts, who now hosts *Good Morning America*, emceed a fundraising event for presidential candidate Bill Bradley. Roberts later said that she was surprised at receiving criticism for the appearance. Tompkins says anything that waters down or damages credibility hurts in the long run. According to ESPN executive editor John Walsh, "Certainly the fallout has given us cause to look at the issue. I think Robin was a bit naïve."

Other Issues

Manipulation and Honesty

It would seem to go without saying that the sports media should report truthfully and honestly. If 25,313 people show up to watch a game, then the attendance should be reported as 25,313: Simple and straightforward.

But maybe not. There are a growing number of gray ethical areas in sports journalism, many of them created by sophisticated technology. Watch any baseball game on television and you'll see an ad for one of the game's sponsors plastered on the wall behind the batter's box. There doesn't seem to be anything wrong with that, except that the image has been digitally created and superimposed. It doesn't exist in the real world, and the viewer's perception of reality has been altered.

A digital ad for Viagra shown at a baseball game might not seem like a big deal, but what about the photo manipulation regarding O.J. Simpson? In 1994, *Time* magazine darkened the mug shot photo of Simpson that appeared on its cover. The altered photo gave Simpson a sinister, almost guilty appearance. Even in the face of almost unanimous condemnation, *Time*'s managing editor defended the photo, writing, "The harshness of the mug shot—the merciless bright light, the stubble on Simpson's face, the cold specificity of the picture—had been subtly smoothed and shaped into an icon of tragedy."

Less dramatic images have also become controversial. In 2003, *Sports Illustrated* digitally altered a photograph that ran in its magazine, touching off a debate between its art and photograph departments. The deception wasn't necessarily egregious—the photo involved soccer star Mia Hamm, and the magazine simply removed another player from the background. SI spokesperson Rick McCabe called the incident a "mistake" and said the magazine often alters photographs, but clearly labels them as illustrations. "You can't explain it away by calling it an illustration," says John Long, ethics chair at the National Press Photographers Association. "What you're trying to do is use words to explain a visual lie. No self-respecting journalist would do that with a story. If you respect pictures the way you respect words you don't [publish] visual lies" (Figure 11-1A and B).

It's possible to publish "visual lies" in many forms today that go beyond digital manipulation. A good photographer can make a crowd of 100 look like 100,000 and vice versa. Any good reporter can turn a dull game into the most exciting contest of all time. Are these ethical violations? The issue is that reporters, photographers, producers, and anchors all are human beings with their own unique sets of personal biases, values, and beliefs. What may be a gray area to one reporter might be as simple as black and white to another. Roy Peter Clark, Senior Scholar at the Poynter Institue, has a simple answer: "[There are] two cornerstone principles: Do not add. Do not deceive."

Privacy

Many of the issues under discussion are not unique to sports, and newsrooms often struggle with the same problems. For example, privacy has long been an ethical consideration for journalists in news, but only recently has it become much of an issue in sports. The growth of technology and consumer demand has led to a culture of the "celebrity athlete," with status to rival that of rock stars and politicians.

A

Figure 11-1

Many sports journalists think it's a serious ethical breach to alter photographs, even if it's something as seemingly unimportant as removing a scoreboard (B). *Courtesy: The Daily Mississippian*

B

In many cases, celebrity athletes such as Dennis Rodman and Deion Sanders demand the spotlight. But the spotlight also finds many athletes who would just as soon remain private. In 1992, *USA Today* believed it had a major story—the newspaper had reason to believe that former tennis great Arthur Ashe had the AIDS virus. When a sports reporter from *USA Today* called Ashe for confirmation, Ashe stalled. He asked executive sports editor Gene Policinski to delay the story for 36 hours. Policinski would not give a guarantee, so Ashe held a press conference the next day to announce that he did indeed have the AIDS virus, most likely contracted during a blood transfusion.

The situation provided a textbook case of media and privacy. "I am sorry that I have been forced to make this revelation at this time," said Ashe, who died from AIDS in 1993. "After all, I am not running for some office of public trust, nor do I have stockholders to account to. Keeping my AIDS status private enabled me to control my life." But on the other side of the argument was *USA Today*. "When the press has kept secrets ... that conspiracy of silence has not served the public," said USA Today editor Peter Prichard. "Journalists serve the public by reporting news, not hiding it. By sharing his story, Arthur Ashe and his family are free of a great weight. In the days ahead, they will help us better understand AIDS and how to defeat it."

There are powerful ethical arguments for both positions. But as sports journalism continues to focus more on legal and social issues, it's apparent that such cases will only increase. For example, in 2004 several sports media outlets suggested that baseball stars Barry Bonds, Jason Giambi, and Gary Sheffield had received and used illegal performance-enhancing steroids. Bonds was also implicated by the manufacturer of the steroids, although he continued to maintain his innocence. Just how far will the sports media push into Bonds' life in pursuing the story? If Arthur Ashe is any guideline, the answer is very far.

A Double Standard

The issue of privacy cuts across both news and sports, but in other areas do different sets of ethical rules exist—one for sports and one for news? Many long-time journalists think so. Tompkins says, "I come from 25 years in television (and) I personally treated sports more leniently than news. I let my sports guy do stuff I wouldn't let the news anchors do." Sports writer and broadcaster Frank Deford says, "Sports journalism is held to a different standard. Visualize Tom Daschle and Trent Lott teaming up to do a promotion on ABC for Peter Jennings. That's the equivalent of what ESPN is doing (with its promos for *SportsCenter*)."

The other argument is that sports simply aren't on the same level with news because of its relative unimportance. Don Skwer of the *Boston Globe* says, "Sports isn't politics and that's where I draw the line. There's a public trust involved, but it's a totally different thing." Many sports broadcasters agree. "Stuart Scott and I have the same philosophy," says NFL Network anchor Rich Eisen. "This is just sports. It's serious at some point, but it's still just a game."

The Bottom Line

There are no simple answers to these ethical problems, which the industry continues to debate. Almost every newsroom in the country has ethical guidelines in place, but such guidelines don't address all the important issues, aren't consistently applied, and usually don't carry a mechanism to punish offenders. As a result, serious ethical decisions still remain in the hands of the individual. "Every person in this business has to answer to himself," says ESPN's Bob Ley. Most ethical decisions will continue to be made by each sports person on a case-by-case basis, given the lack of a standard body of codified conduct. But there are several resources available to help in the decision-making process.

Professional organizations such as the Radio Television News Directors Association and the Society for Professional Journalists devote regular columns and forums to ethical issues. The same can be said for journalism industry and watchdog publications such as *Broadcasting and Cable, Electronic Media, The Columbia Journalism Review,* and *The American Journalism Review.* Other organizations have also emerged to include discussions of ethical sports reporting and broadcasting.

Even so, these resources can provide only guidance and can't begin to answer the difficult kinds of ethical issues that sports people face everyday. For the foreseeable future, those remain newsroom and individual decisions. The problem is that today's sports and news journalists aren't getting much in the way of ethical training. In a recent study conducted by the Radio and Television News Directors Foundation, 65% of news directors say their organization has some formalized code of ethics. But only 59% of news directors feel such training is "very necessary," and only 56% of the news executives require their reporters to take some sort of ethics training. Perhaps more telling, the plurality of news directors say their new employees do not go through formal ethical training.

That pretty much leaves it up to the individual sports reporter, who must either learn ethical codes of conduct in school or, more commonly, in the workplace. "The ethics situation is finally being addressed by the entire industry," said newspaper sports editor Tom Tebbs. "The public's image may not improve because of their view of our integrity, which they assimilate to that of lawyers. This, however, cannot be fought." The fight, it seems, has really just begun.

References

Bassman, Virginia. (1996, June 6). Irvin debate reborn with SPJ chapter. *Dallas Morning News.*

Booth, Cathy. (1999, November 15). Worst of times. *Time.*

Braves tell broadcasters to fly commercial. (2000, June 27). *Associated Press.* http://www.espn.go.com/mlb/news/2000/0626/605703.html

Clark, Roy P. (2002, January 24). The line between fact and fiction. *The Poynter Institue.* http://www.poynter.org/content/content_view.asp?id=3491

DeFoore, Jay. (2003, October 2). Photo manipulation highlights internal feud at 'SI.' *Photo District News Online.* http://www.pdn-pix.com/photodistrictnews/headlines/article_display.jsp?vnu_content_id=1993503

Ethics in the age of digital photography. (2000). *National Press Photographer's Association.* http://www.nppa.org/services/bizpract/eadp/eadp2.html

Farber, Michael. (2000, February 14). Life of the party. *Sports Illustrated.*

Feinstein, John. (1989). *A season on the brink: a year with Bobby Knight and the Indiana Hoosiers.* New York: Simon and Schuster.

Golenbock, Peter. (1984). *Bums.* New York: Pocket Books.

Heard, Robert. (1980). *Oklahoma vs. Texas: when football becomes war.* Austin, TX: Honey Hill Publishing.

Houck, Jeff. (2000, June 23). Philadelphia story; Philadelphia radio host suspended for criticizing Flyers GM. *Fox Sports.* www.foxsports.com/business/bites/ z000623flyers_critic1.sml, June 23, 2000.

Journalism Ethics and Integrity Project. (1998). *Radio Television News Directors Foundation.* http://www.rtnda.org/issues/survey.htm

Kahn, Roger. (1997). *Memories of summer.* New York: Hyperion Books.

Krajicek, David. (2000, January 27). Sportswriters need to take kid gloves off. http://www.apbnews.com

Oukrop, Carol. Arthur Ashe and the right to privacy. Unpublished media ethics case study. Kansas State University. http://arapaho.nsuok.edu/~scottd/ashe.htm

Postrel, Virginia. (2000, February 7). The ethics of boosterism. *Forbes.*

Previously rejected columns were to run Sunday. (2002, December 7). *Associated Press.*

Raissman, Bob. (2004, October 28). Marv found out truth hurts as MSG. *New York Daily News.* http://www.nydailynews.com/sports/story/247422p-211917c.html

Salwen, Michael and Garrison, Bruce. (1994, January 15). Survey examines extent of professionalism in sports journalism. *Editor & Publisher.*

Scanlan, Christopher. (2000). *Reporting and writing, basics for the 21st century.* Orlando: Harcourt.

Shea, Jim. (2000, January-February). The king: how ESPN changes everything. *Columbia Journalism Review.*

"Sports-talk radio host." (1999, September 7). *ESPN.* http://espn.go.com/special/s/careers/sptalk.html

12

Gender and Race

We have discussed at length how sports media continue to evolve on a variety of levels. Some of this evolution is economic, as media outlets look for new revenue models and streams in a changing industry environment. As large media companies search for ways to stay competitive, they are increasingly turning to niche or targeted sports audiences. Another part of the evolution is technological, as new media platforms, such as digital radio and satellite, continue to emerge. In a cultural sense, as society continues to change and evolve, so do the sports media.

But perhaps the most significant changes are taking place on a human scale. Once exclusively the province of white males, sports media have slowly started to accept women and people of color. The increase of women and racial minorities in sports media has been accepted as a positive move, but it has also raised several important issues.

Women's Work

Crashing the Men's Club

Up until the 1970s, women had virtually no presence in the sports media. Sports were considered a "male" domain—played, coached, watched, and reported on by men. The few female sports reporters, women like Maureen Orcutt of the *New York Times* and Jeane Hoffman of the *New York Journal-American*, were considered rarities who covered obscure women's sports or wrote fluff stories. Sports journalism was considered an exclusive male club, in which writers covered games by day and then hung out in bars with the ballplayers at night. One of the most popular nightspots was Toots Shor's in New York. Author David Halberstam described the place as "a men's club, one that reflected the age. It was white, male and boozy—hard-liquor boozy. Women were most decidedly not welcome."

This stayed as the status quo until cultural values began to change in the 1960s and 1970s. Women athletes became more noticeable and women slowly began to drift into the sports reporting field. Finally, in 1975 Phyllis George broke through the barrier and became the first female sports figure on a national network when she began hosting *The NFL Today* on CBS. Just a few years later, Gayle Gardner occupied a high-profile anchor position on ESPN. And in 1990, Robin Roberts became the first black woman to anchor at the network sports level when she also went to ESPN. "It's something I'm proud of," says Roberts, who eventually moved up to become a news anchor on ABC's *Good Morning America*. "(And) I'll be happy to see more women of color at the network level."

While cultural values certainly played an important part in this process, one cannot ignore the role of legislation. In 1972, the government enacted as federal statue a series of education amendments designed to level the athletic playing field between men and women. Title IX of those amendments prohibited sexual discrimination in educational institutions that received federal funds. More specifically, the law required that colleges and universities must demonstrate equality in one of three ways: the number of women's sports programs must be equal to the number of men's programs, the number of women athletes must be equal to the number of men athletes, or the percentage of male and female athletes at a school must be proportional to the percentage of the student body as a whole.

Such requirements have generated a firestorm of controversy among educators, athletes, administrators, and reporters. Many argue that the requirements place an undue burden on men's sports such as wrestling, gymnastics, and swimming. Hundreds of these programs have been eliminated at schools across the country in an effort to reach Title IX compliance. For example, in 2004 Southern Methodist University eliminated its track and cross country programs. Athletic director Jim Copeland said the school's options were to save an estimated $5.4 million over the 4 years by eliminating track and cross country or to spend $1.2 million each year to keep track and add a women's sport. "This is a lost season," said middle-distance runner Lukas Musil, a senior at the time. "It's sad; we don't understand what the reason is. They told us it was gender equity and about money."

As part of the backlash, several organizations have unsuccessfully tried to get Title IX overturned. The National Wrestling Coaches Association filed suit in 2000 to have the law thrown out, and the College Football Association has lobbied for the same thing. Such efforts have failed, but will likely continue. "It's a quota system, pure and simple," says former CFA executive director Chuck Neinas, who adds that colleges are trying to get women to participate in athletics in "unrealistic" numbers. Critics also point to the unequal revenue generated by men's and women's sports. In college sports, for example, football is the dominant moneymaker at almost every university and at Division One schools it accounts for nearly a third of all athletic revenues.

Supporters of women's athletic programs would counter that Title IX has done exactly what it set out to do—end the domination of athletics by men by opening more doors to women. In 1971, the year before Title IX became law, fewer than 300,000 girls participated in high school sports, about 1 in 27. Today, the number approaches 3 million, or approximately 1 in 2.5. The number of women participating in intercollegiate sports in that same span has gone from about 30,000 to more than 150,000. In the last 20 years alone, the number of women's college teams has nearly doubled. Many people say the resulting explosion in women's sports has directly led to the success of American women athletes in international competition, most notably in the Olympics, where U.S. women have dominated in soccer and hockey. "I could not have been an Olympian without Title IX," said sprinter Evelyn Ashford, who won four medals in track and field. "Title IX allowed me to run on the boys track team."

Despite such dramatic advances, women still have a long way to go to catch up. According to 2000–2001 figures, men's college programs still maintain significant advantages over women's in average scholarships (61%), operating expenses (65%), recruiting expenses (68%), and head coaching salaries (60%). Only 44% of the head coaches of women's teams are female, an all-time low that represents less than half the pre-Title IX figure.

The debate has also been a mixed blessing for female sports reporters. It has increased the importance, viability, and popularity of women's athletics, with a corresponding positive effect on women in the media. As female athletes became more empowered, so too did female reporters. Again, the courts played a major role. In 1977, major league baseball refused to let *Sports Illustrated* reporter Melissa Ludtke in the clubhouses at Yankee Stadium. Ludtke and the magazine successfully sued and won the right to gain access, but the fight took its toll. "This crusade has worn me down," she later said. "I'm a little disappointed by my own situation" (Figure 12-1).

This points out one of the unexpected results of Title IX: a strong and continuing resentment on the part of men who see women encroaching on "their turf." Legislation might have cleared the way for more female sports reporters, but it did not solve the most difficult part of their jobs. Michelle Kaufman wrote for the *Detroit Free Press* in the early 1990s and said she endured constant verbal and emotional abuse in the Detroit Lions locker room. "The locker room isn't a nice place to do business for women or men," she later said. "(But) I have earned the right to do my job with being harassed. When male reporters are treated poorly, it's usually because they wrote something the athlete didn't like or asked a question that the coach didn't like. I wish we had that luxury."

The most infamous incident of harassment took place in the fall of 1990 and involved Lisa Olson, a reporter for the *Boston Herald*. Olson claims that one of the players for the New England Patriots exposed himself and made lewd comments to her in the locker room. Olson complained to the team and to the NFL, assuming

Figure 12-1

There are more women working in sports media, but they still face many difficult challenges and obstacles. *Courtesy: Mary Lou Sheffer*

that the matter would be handled and quickly die out. Instead, the story became a national referendum on women in sports, with Olson cast as the villain. She received death threats and physical abuse that made it impossible to work, forcing her to take a job writing sports in Australia. Olson returned to the U.S. and now writes for the *New York Daily News*, but the scars remain. "How do I describe what happened," she said, "not just the original incident, but the public's reaction and the media circus that followed? It wasn't worth the energy."

It's tempting to describe these incidents as ancient history, but a strong undercurrent of resentment remains today. In 2004, Dallas Cowboys receiver Keyshawn Johnson criticized Pam Oliver of Fox for a report in which she said Johnson got into a shouting match with his coach. "I almost wanted to get on a plane, find where she is at, and sit her down and spank her with a ruler really, really hard," Johnson said. He added that he had been "all for" female reporters on the sidelines, but not if "they can't get their story straight." Fox said it stood by the report, and when asked what she would do if Johnson tried to spank her, Oliver said she would "punch him in the face."

It's not just the athletes doing the criticizing. Many male sports reporters also resent women's intrusion into "their" world and, to a larger extent, the overall effect of the growth of women's sports. A bizarre incident along these lines took place in 1995 involving CBS golf commentator Ben Wright. A female reporter overhead Wright commenting about what he perceived as rampant homosexuality on the women's professional golf tour. Wright did not make the comments on the air and later said they were taken out of context. Nevertheless, the comments were published and Wright became the center of a growing controversy, which led to his suspension and ultimately his dismissal from CBS Sports. LPGA commissioner Jim Ritts later commented, "It's not issues about alternative lifestyles and all the other silly comments that have been made. (It's about) a time in our society when women are given the same opportunities as men; when women are treated equally as a man."

That point was hammered home in 2002, when *60 Minutes* contributor Andy Rooney made some ill-advised comments on a cable talk sports show. "The only thing that really bugs me about television's coverage (of football) is those damn women they have down on the sidelines who don't know what the hell they're talking about," said Rooney. "I mean, I'm not a sexist person, but a woman has no business being down there trying to make some comment about a football game." The comments evoked comparisons to Al Campanis and his 1987 televised statements that blacks "didn't have the necessities" to make it as baseball executives.

Public reaction was swift and almost universally negative. "The first thing that came into my mind is, does anybody take Andy Rooney seriously anyway?" ESPN anchor Linda Cohn said. "He doesn't take himself seriously half the time anyway. The second thing is, why is he stereotyping all women? God knows if he watches *SportsCenter* and has ever seen me. You have to judge each person separately. The third thing is, when was the last time he followed any of these sideline reporters around doing their job?" The real importance of the Rooney incident is not the merits of his comments, but rather how they reflect the tremendous resentment and resistance still prevalent in today's society.

The problem is ongoing because males still dominate the ownership, production, distribution, and consumption of today's sports media content. In a recent survey conducted by the Annenberg Public Policy center at the University of Pennsylvania, women account for just 14% of top executive spots and 13% of board members at 10 major entertainment companies—among them Walt Disney Co., Viacom, Time-Warner, and USA Networks. Representation was slightly higher at publishing companies, where women accounted for 22% of the top executive spots and 17% of board seats, but on the programming side, out of 120 broadcast and cable channels, women account for just 16% of top executives.

"[Men] are buyers and sellers and have a tremendous power base," notes Sci Fi Channel President Bonnie Hammer. "Women are employed within or under that structure." "The classic 'pipeline' explanation—there aren't enough qualified women to promote—is getting tired," says Discovery Communications President and COO Judith McHale. Certainly, there are qualified women who have worked in the industry more than 20 years. "But until you have more women in leadership positions," says McHale, "it will be difficult to make changes and make progress."

That's one of the many things that make the job of a female sports journalist so difficult. Just to get into the business is tough enough, as witnessed by some of the employment figures. While recent research indicates that women make up about 40% of the television news workforce, the number of female sportscasters and sports writers is still only about 10%. The small group that makes it faces more challenges trying to turn a job into a career. "I found the sports-writing life wholly incompatible with motherhood," said Jennifer Frey, who left the *New York Times* to have a baby in 1998. "I can't tell you how many 40-something women sportswriters came up to me in press boxes when I was pregnant and said 'Good for you, I really wish I had (done the same thing).' "

Joan Ryan was one of the nation's first female sports columnists and worked at both the *Orlando Sentinel* and the *San Francisco Examiner*. But she got out of the field in order to spend more time with her family. "There are men who grew up and all they wanted to do was play or be involved in sports in some capacity," she said. Many of them are now sports editors. Women, she believes, feel differently about the role of sports in their lives and careers. "Men don't leave," says sportswriter Nancy Cooney. "They do it all their lives and are thrilled to do it. But women get to a certain level and say, 'What's next?' "

For those that do have the dream, there are a number of groups and organizations trying to level the playing field. Ryan was one of the founding members of the Association for Women in Sports Media (*www.awsmonline.org*). Created in 1987, the AWSM now claims more than 600 members and offers scholarships, job placement, and networking for women interested in the sports media field.

The women who have succeeded on their own terms are a rare combination of skill, determination, hard work, and persistence. One day, women such as Heidi Soliday (Figure 12-2) will not be thought of as oddities, but rather like any other journalists trying to make a living in the demanding world of sports media.

Sports Information with Heidi Soliday

You may not recognize the name Heidi Soliday, but in many ways she's blazed as many trails for women sportscasters as Hannah Storm or Robin Roberts. In 1991, Soliday became the sports director at KCCI-TV in Des Moines, Iowa—one of the first women to hold such a position at any station in the country. Soliday started

Figure 12-2

Sports director Heidi
Soliday of KCCI-TV in
Des Moines, Iowa.

part-time at the station in 1976 and has now gone on to cover the Masters golf
tournament, Rose Bowls, the World Series, the Final Four, and many other national
sporting events. She shares some of the things she's learned from nearly 30 years in
the business.

*Q: Were you really the first woman sports director at a local television station anywhere in
the country?*
A: I'd like to find that out, because I don't know for sure. I know I'm probably the
first one ever in the greater Midwest and certainly one of the first in the country. In
my travels around the country I haven't seen anyone else in a similar position. It seems
most of the women in sports are at the network level, not in local markets. Until
recently, a lot of local news directors still believed that guys would not want to watch
a female sports director on television.

Q: How did you get into sportscasting?
A: I can't say this is something I always wanted to do. In fact, in college I was pretty
sure I wanted to be a film director. But I started watching the Sunday sports one night

and thought it really stunk. I figured it couldn't be that hard, so I applied at all three television stations in Des Moines and KCCI hired me the same day.

Q: *What has it been like as a woman in what has traditionally been considered a man's position?*
A: For me, it hasn't been that big a deal. I'm from Des Moines and that made it a lot easier, because so many people knew me or my family. I'm also not stupid. I realize that in certain ways a woman actually has an advantage over a man in covering sports. A lot of the guys in sports are former athletes and extremely jealous of the athletes they cover. As a result, many of the athletes feel like the men reporters are always on the attack, always out to get them. With women, there's no envy or jealousy. I also think it's easier for a woman to get a story in some situations compared to the men.

Q: *You describe yourself as an aggressive reporter. Do you feel like women in the sports media have to be more aggressive to handle the position and the pressure?*
A: If you're a shrinking violet, you're not going to get the story, which is especially true in sports. I made a concerted effort to be that way when I started out. Being a woman and a blonde, there's a great danger that you won't be taken seriously, even today.

Q: *How would you describe your style on the air?*
A: By nature, I'm sort of a wild person with a bawdy sense of humor. But I'm certainly not a clown and I dislike all the entertainment stuff that's going on in places like ESPN. The trend today in sports, and even in other areas, is toward the wacky and nutty. It's all about look and presentation, rather than substance. I much prefer the straightforward delivery.

Q: *Do you consider yourself a role model for aspiring female sportscasters?*
A: It's not that I don't want to be a role model, but I'm really uncomfortable with that part of the business. I always get embarrassed when someone comes up and asks for an autograph. I say, 'Are you really sure you want one?' I do know that I might have inspired a few people along the way, but I'm not sure my job is really one people should aspire to.

Q: *You've certainly had the opportunity or desire to go to a bigger market, or even the networks. Why did you stay in Des Moines?*
A: I actually did have some opportunities in several other places. I interviewed with CNN for the position that eventually went to Hannah Storm. I also had interviews in places like Chicago, but in a lot of situations it always seemed like a man beat me out. As for the future, what I'd really like to do is work on a news magazine show, where you can really do something in-depth. I'd love to be able to research, write, and develop a story for a show like *HBO Real Sports*. You know, in some respects I actually consider myself a failure, because I never got beyond where I started. But now I feel like I was ahead of my time.

"Sexploitation?"

Traditionally, media coverage of women's sports does not get high ratings or readership. For example, despite decent attendance figures, the Women's National Basketball Association has struggled to attract viewers for its network and cable television packages. When the Women's United Soccer Association folded in 2003 it had national ratings of 0.1 and 0.2 on the PAX Network, numbers that indicated only about 100,000 viewers. Television ratings of 0.6 forced the Professional Women's Bowling Association to cancel its 2003 fall season (one ratings point represents a little more than one million television households).

Numbers like those dictate how the sports media cover and present women's athletics to audiences. In their study of women and television sports, researchers Messner, Duncan and Cooky reported that women's sports are still "missing in action" in television newscasts in comparison to men. Their findings indicate that not only are women underrepresented in terms of the amount of television sports coverage they receive, but also what coverage they do receive is relegated to either nonserious sports or sexual objectification. The results also show little or no change from similar studies conducted in 1990 and 1994.

Interestingly, there has been greater focus recently on reaching female audiences. Sports viewers and readers are overwhelmingly male, and media executives see untapped female audiences as a way to increase revenues. Many sports outlets have worked to reach these female audiences through more feature- and entertainment-oriented content. For example, ABC's coverage of the Super Bowl in 2003 focused heavily on entertainment, including performances by The Dixie Chicks, Celine Dion, Santana, Bonnie Raitt, Shania Twain, Sting, and Bon Jovi. "I think the women component certainly likes the entertainment acts," said ABC producer Curt Gowdy, Jr. "We (also) have stories that appeal to women and are of interest to women."

To the extent that the media cover female athletes, they are typically presented for their ability to attract the heavily male audiences. Going back to the 1970s, golfer Jan Stephenson was one of the most visible and promoted players on the women's professional golf tour, but much of it was due to her beauty and not necessarily her talent. Thirty years later, the same thing happened with tennis player Anna Kournikova, who received much more media attention than any other player, even though she had never won a singles title.

When sex doesn't sell, sometimes novelty does. In 2003, Annika Sorenstam received loads of publicity for playing in a men's professional golf tournament. For years, television had gotten plenty of ratings mileage from special "battle of the sexes" golf events, but this was something out of the ordinary. Sorenstam's appearance in the tournament helped drive up USA's ratings, leading many to conclude that more such gimmicks would follow. "To be an above average student of sports today is to be a student of television," noted sportswriter Phil Mushnick. "And to be a student of TV is to know that good-to-better ratings can and will make anything happen more than once—often as many times as it takes until the shine wears dull. To state, in the same breath, that Sorenstam's inclusion will increase ratings but be 'a one-shot deal' would be the same as suggesting that the success of 'Survivor' wouldn't instantly inspire the creation of other such shows, and that 'Monday Night Football' wouldn't begat 'Sunday Night Football.' Whatever ratings can do, they will do—until, and even beyond, the point of diminishing returns."

According to Messner, Duncan and Cooky, "We speculate that an increase in professional, responsible, equitable coverage of women's sports on these shows would actually hold the large, diverse audience that has tuned into the news shows." That's certainly an issue under debate in the sports media community. However, given current media ownership and viewership patterns, it's unlikely that it will be put into practice anytime soon.

The situation is not much different for women working as sports journalists or reporters. To be sure, women such as Lisa Olson, Sally Jenkins, and Christine Brennan have carved out successful careers based mainly on their ability and hard work. And while more women continue to follow in their footsteps, there still remains a portion of the industry that is hired more for looks than for abilities. ESPN's Jeff Hollobaugh noted, "In a world where women's sports grows in importance daily . . . we have to expect that the media will focus its attention on beauty instead of achievement from time to time. The public wants it."

Consider the 2000 contest *Playboy* called "Choose America's Sexiest Sportscaster," in which the magazine asked readers to vote on its Web site for the 'hottest' among 10 female sports personalities. The magazine would then invite the winner to pose for a nude pictorial. According to *Sports Illustrated*, none of the 10 contestants denounced the vote or asked to have herself removed from the Web site. Winner Jill Arrington did not appear nude, but posed provocatively in a four-page spread. "Unfortunately, this goes on in other businesses," says Mike Trager, former chairman of Clear Channel Entertainment Television and a former NBC executive. "If an attractive woman gets a top Wall Street job, there are always the male accusations that she did it with her womanly wiles. The issue here is if you want to be a serious journalist, then you have to decide on how you're going to portray yourself."

"It's disappointing," says Robin Roberts. "It's important that you don't use your sexuality, especially since so many women sportscasters like Gayle Gardner and Lesley Visser started the fight for acceptance of women in the business." Said Jeanne Zelasko of Fox Sports, who was not 1 of the 10 contestants, "When I talk to young women about careers in this field, do I advise them to get a solid background in sports and reporting, or do I tell them to enter a beauty contest?" Adds Lisa Guerrero, the Fox Sports anchor who appeared in a revealing pictorial in *Maxim* magazine, "We're damned if we do and damned if we don't."

The Color of Sports

Minorities in the Media

There has been no single bigger issue in the history of American society than race. Race dominates every facet of American culture and certainly the sports media are no exception. What makes race relations and reporting so interesting in sports is the fact that while people of color now dominate the sports themselves, they're still underrepresented in sports management, coaching, and reporting.

The problems related to minority representation in sports ownership and coaching have been well documented and do not need detailed analysis. Much has been made of the fact that even though minorities are now dominant in terms of their participation in sports, they have very little presence in coaching or team ownership. Despite the fact that most of the players in the National Basketball Association are black, not until 2004 did Bob Johnson of the Charlotte Bobcats become the league's first black owner. "Today's black athletes are just gladiators," says NFL Hall of Famer Jim Brown.

In terms of minority media ownership, there have been some spectacular success stories. Before he got into NBA ownership, Johnson founded the Black Entertainment Television (BET) network, which has greatly expanded the roles of minorities in media. BET produces much of its own programming and also has a sports division that produces and carries live sporting events. In 2004, BET began its 23rd season of televising college football involving traditionally black colleges. "BET has generated a loyal fan base for these games," said Jacque Coleman, BET Vice President of Specials and Sports Programming, "and we're committed to continuing our tradition of televising the best in Black College Football."

Another minority-owned company, New Vision Sports Properties, was founded in 2002 and specializes in both marketing and media. New Vision has partnered with other media outlets and several Fortune 500 companies to create more visibility for the historically black colleges. Part of the deal included exclusive licensing rights for the schools, and New Vision helped televise a 32-game college football schedule in the fall of 2004. The company notes that its primary mission is to "assist in the creation and maintenance of revenue streams to ensure the continued growth and viability of historically Black Colleges and Universities nationwide."

But overall, the representation of minorities in sports media follows a similar pattern to that of minorities in coaching and team ownership. Of the nation's 14,000 radio stations, only about 4% are minority owned, and for television stations the figure is less than 2%. Since television deregulation in the late 1990s, minority television ownership has dropped from 33 stations to 20. "Minority ownership is in decline," says Willie Davis, who owns four radio stations in two states. The former Green Bay Packer and NFL Hall of Famer says blacks, Hispanics, and other

Table 12-1

Blacks in Newspaper
Sports (2004)
Source/Courtesy: National
Association of Black Journalists

Name	Newspaper	Position
Caesar Alsop	*Philadelphia Daily News*	Sports Editor
Dwayne Bray	*Dallas Morning News*	Sports Editor
Leon Carter	*New York Daily News*	Sports Editor
David Humphrey	*Ft. Worth Star-Telegram*	Deputy Sports Editor
Garry Howard	*Milwaukee Journal-Sentinel*	Asst. Managing Editor, Sports
Lee Ivory	*USA Today Sports Weekly*	Executive Editor/Publisher
Gregory Lee	*Washington Post*	Deputy H.S. Sports Editor
Larry Starks	*St. Louis Post-Dispatch*	Asst. Managing Editor, Sports
Jewell Watson	*Cincinnati Enquirer*	Asst. Sports Editor
Gene Farris	*Akron Beacon-Journal*	Deputy Sports Editor

minorities need better access to capital and the return of regulations that encourage white owners to sell to members of minority groups.

Efforts in Congress died in 2003 to revive a program that provided tax breaks to broadcast owners who sold properties to minorities, and broadcast ownership rules put into place by the Federal Communications Commission in recent years have allowed for more consolidation within the industry at the expense of minority owners. Many black broadcasters were critical of the FCC under former Chairman Michael Powell. The commission eliminated nearly all the protections and programs aimed at promoting minority ownership going back to the Nixon and Ford administrations, according to David Honig, executive director of the Minority Media and Telecommunications Council. "This chairman tore down the civil rights infrastructure adopted during previous Republican administrations," Honig said.

Aside from ownership, minorities are making some headway in reporting and management positions. On the print side, many blacks have now taken key positions in sports media management and editing (Table 12-1). In broadcasting, recent figures indicate that minorities have made noticeable gains in both radio and television. The television minority workforce rose from 18 to 22%, with the gains split evenly between blacks and Hispanics. The minority workforce in radio almost doubled, from 6.5% to nearly 12% during the same time period. Nearly 84% of all television stations have some sort of minority presence on their news staffs.

Table 12-1 is by no means a definitive list, but it gives you an idea of the important positions now held by black sports journalists and editors at some of the biggest newspapers in the country.

Some minorities have become very successful, and highly visible, in the sports media. James Brown has won Emmy Awards for his work as host of the NFL pregame show on Fox, but also contributes in a variety of other media, including radio. Bryan Gumbel did sports work for several years at NBC before moving on to host his own show with HBO. His brother Greg Gumbel has become the longtime host of the NFL pregame show on CBS. But these men still represent a distinct minority in the sports broadcasting field. "I firmly believe people hire in their own likeness, so that's what network executives always have done," said Brown. "All we're asking for is an opportunity to succeed and fail like everyone else."

A more common avenue for minorities is to move from the playing field to the broadcast booth. Shannon Sharpe and Michael Irvin have all recently retired from the NFL and gone on to television work with national networks. Irvin is one of several former players who work for ESPN, along with Joe Morgan, Harold Reynolds, Tom Jackson, and many others. Perhaps because of the extraordinary amount of content it produces, ESPN has moved to the forefront in the hiring of minorities for on-air positions. Its stable of announcers now includes Asian-Americans, Hispanics, and blacks. The network also created ESPN Deportes in 2000 for its growing Spanish-language audiences, which gives more visibility to minority anchors and reporters.

The growth of the Hispanic population, which now is the largest minority population in the United States, has prompted sports media companies to branch out. ESPN Deportes is now a 24-hour network, distributed to 13 million subscribers on Sunday nights, and ESPN also offers Sunday Night Baseball games and Sunday Night NFL telecasts in Spanish. "Providing ESPN-branded content in Spanish is a major step forward in ESPN's commitment to serving a diverse, growing fan base," said George Bodenhemier, ESPN president.

In 2002, Telemundo signed a deal to carry NBA and WNBA games in Spanish— the first broadcast deal for one of the big U.S. sports on Spanish-language TV in the United States, which is usually dominated by soccer. "My mother and my father, they only speak Spanish," said NBA player Felipe Lopez. "To have it in their own language—and for millions of Latinos who tune in—it's going to be a lot easier for them to watch the games."

In his own way, Stuart Scott of ESPN is a definite attraction for minority audiences. Scott represents a new kind of minority presence in the sports media, in that he never tried to become the mainstream television sports personality. His style is very much his own, and very appealing to minority audiences. "I've tried to make it OK to have a more laid-back style that is a little more reminiscent of the African-American subculture" he said. "There haven't been too many sportscasters with a slant that way. But here's the thing about style: You have to be comfortable with it. I am not all this young hip-hop guy, but that's definitely part of me. If I'm watching a game with friends, I'm gonna say, 'Man, Mike's blowin' up.' What I'm doing here is part of me." According to one of the producers at ESPN, "Athletes really dig Stuart. He talks the language of the kids. He brings that attitude. He's opened up a lot of doors."

Opening doors is still the main challenge for minorities in sports media. The success of people such as Brown, Gumbel, and Scott has inspired other minorities to travel the same road. "I do carry this responsibility seriously," said Brown. "If the decision-makers see James Brown doing a good job, it will open the door for other brothers and sisters coming behind me and give them an opportunity to do well."

The Reporting of Race

Most sports reporting of race has focused in three main areas: lack of opportunities for minorities off the field, the alleged exploitation of minority athletes, and the continuing battle against racism. The 1980s and 1990s saw an increasing unwillingness on the part of the media or the public to defend prejudicial or racist statements in the sports arena. Dodgers executive Al Campanis and CBS broadcaster Jimmy "The Greek" Synder both lost their jobs after ill-advised on-air comments. Baseball executives suspended Cincinnati Reds owner Marge Schott in the early 1990s for her derogatory comments against minorities, and in the winter of 2000, baseball suspended Atlanta Braves relief pitcher John Rocker for similar comments he made in a *Sports Illustrated* article.

Institutionalized racism in sports has been challenged on different fronts, especially by Native Americans. Several groups have unsuccessfully tried to get the Washington Redskins, Cleveland Indians, and Atlanta Braves to change their nicknames. Colleges and universities have shown a little more sensitivity on this point; in recent years, Miami of Ohio, Eastern Michigan, and Marquette are just some of the schools that have retired potentially offensive nicknames for their athletic teams. But such changes usually ignite controversy, especially for a school with a long tradition. After Miami University officially changed from Redskins to RedHawks in 1997, trustee William Gunlock, an alumnus, cried. "I will always be a Redskin," he said.

Some media have also tried to exert a more positive influence. In the 1990s, the *Portland Oregonian* decided not to include any racially offensive sports nicknames in any of its headlines or stories. The newspaper was widely applauded, but hardly any other media outlets followed suit. What copying has taken place is the preoccupation with sensationalism, celebrities, and scandal. In that sense, minority sports reporting isn't really different from any other reporting, which might be the biggest problem of all.

Minorities also say they haven't come far enough in representation off the field and for the most part, the major sports leagues agree. "The NFL is on the verge of an awakening," said Carmen Policy, a former front office executive with the Cleveland Browns. "We sort of drifted off for a time when we felt there was no overt racism in the league and we got kind of lazy. We realize now there's a lack of opportunity created by a flawed process." In 2002, the NFL enacted new hiring policies that required teams to interview at least one minority candidate before selecting a head coach.

Many have hailed the NFL's decision, even though the new rules did not apply to general managers or assistant coaches. Others don't necessarily see the answer in quotas or affirmative action. Jim Brown advocates a permanent training ground for minority managers at the high school, NCAA, and professional levels. "You shouldn't go to the owner and say, 'hire some black folks'," he said. "It's the owner's money. He should hire the most qualified people."

One way or another, much of the debate comes down to the issue of money. Money drives everything in sports, including the race issue. The tremendous amount of money now available to minority athletes has defused the issue somewhat on the professional level, but it remains a contentious debate in college athletics. "The NCAA is corrupt," says former NBA star Charles Barkley. "There's exploitation of the black athletes and always has been. They use the players to make money for themselves and everybody knows it."

NCAA rules prohibit paying a college player for athletic competition, yet the organization makes millions of dollars off the same athletes. Every year, the recruiting process for high school athletes gets more intense, more competitive, and often more illegal. Fallout from the highly publicized football recruiting scandal at the University of Colorado in 2004 is still being felt.

A panel investigating the scandal criticized top officials for failing to monitor a runaway system that routinely used sex, alcohol, and drugs to entice high school prospects. The commission report says "there is no clear evidence that university officials knowingly sanctioned" inappropriate behavior. But it concluded "the university's leadership must be held accountable" for abuses that include nine accusations of sexual assault by recruits and players since 1997.

There's also another side to exploitation for those who chase the riches from an early age. Several prominent NBA players, including Kevin Garnett and Kobe Bryant, skipped college completely and went right from high school to the pros. In those cases, the players may have given up just as much as the millions of dollars they earned. "People are getting millions of dollars, but not growing up," said Olympic gold medalist Carl Lewis. "Here they are, people who never really learned what it's like to be 20, 21, 25 and have to earn everything. What about important life experiences?" Adds Brown, "The money they're making has no meaning from the standpoint of breaking down barriers or making more opportunities. It's wasted money."

References

Angell, Roger. (1982). *Late innings*. New York: Ballantine Books.

BET tackles black college football for 22nd season of hard-hitting action. (2003, September 3). *Viacom*. http://www.viacom.com/press.tin?ixPressRelease=80154038

Brietenbucher, Cathy. (2004, Spring). Selig to lead off in Milwaukee. *Association for Women in Sports Media Newsletter*. http://www.awsmonline.org

Carlisle, Jim. (2003, January 26). ABC lavishes talent on pregame show. *Ventura (CA) County Star*. http://www.insidevc.com/vcs.nfl/article/0,1375,VCS_140_1700319,00.html

Clinton needles sports world for not hiring minorities. (1998, April 15). *CNN*. http://europe.cnn.com/allpolitics/1998/04/15/clinton.town.hall/

Consoli, John. (2002, September 23). ESPN launches 24-hour Spanish channel. *Mediaweek*.

Cowboys receiver vents about Fox's Oliver. (2004, November 1). *ESPN*. http://www.sports.espn.go.com/nfl/news/story?id=1913928

Eischel, Larry. (2003, September 17). Lack of sponsors was fatal to women's league. *The Philadelphia Inquirer*. http://www.philly.com/mld/inquirer/sports/6790063.htm

Empowering women in sports. (1998). *Feminist Majority Foundation Task Force*. http://www.feminist.org/research/sports5a.html

Etling, Lisa. (2001). Missing in management. *Women's Sports Foundation*. http://www.womenssportsfoundation.org/cgi-bin/iowa/career/article.html?record=11

FAQ, Radio and Television Broadcasting. (2004). *Minority Media and Telecommunications Council*. http://www.mmtconline.org/FAQ_s/rtb/index.shtml

Gantz, Waler and Wenner, Lawrence A. (1991). Men, women and sports: audience experience and effects. *Journal of Broadcasting and Electronic Media*, 35, (2), 233-243.

Garber, Greg. (2002, June 6). Landmark law faces new challenges even now. *ESPN*. http://espn.go.com/gen/womenandsports/020619title9.html

Giobbe, Dorothy. (1993, December 11). Women sportswriters still face hassles in the locker room. *Editor & Publisher*.

Halberstam, David. (1989). *Summer of '49*. New York: Avon Books.

Holhut, Randolph T. (2000). Title IX: leveling the playing field for women. www.mdle.com/WrittenWord/rholhut/holhut43.htm

Hollobaugh, Jeff. (2000, August 30). 1,500 runner not just another pretty face. *ESPN*. www.espn.go.com/oly/s...ield/columns/hollobaugh_jeff/710008.html

Hottie topic. (2000, December 25-January 1). *Sports Illustrated*.

Kenworthy, Tom. (2004, May 19). Reports faults lax Colorado officials in scandal. *USA Today*. http://www.keepmedia.com/pubs/USATODAY/2004/05/19/470587?extID=10032&oliID=213

Kirchen, Rich. (2004, March 8). Tuning out: number of minority media owners declining. *Business Journal of Milwaukee*. http://www.freepress.net/news/article.php?id=2742

Lainson, Suzanne. (1998). *Sports news you can use*. http://www.onlinesports.com/sportstrust/sports44.html

Lopez, John P. (1997). Breaking the barriers. *Houston Chronicle*. www.chron.com/content/chronicle/sports/special/barriers/since.html

Martzke, Rudy. (2002, September 19). Telemundo gets jump with NBA score. *USA Today*. http://www.usatoday.com/sports/columnist/martzke/2002-09-19-martzke_x.htm

Martzke, Rudy. (2002, August 14). Arrington does disservice to herself, other female journalists as pinup. *USA Today*. http://www.usatoday.com/sports/columnist/martzke/2002-08-13-martzke_x.htm

McNutt, Randy. (1997, April 19). Miami adopts RedHawks. *Cincinnati Enquirer*. http://www.enquirer.com/editions/1997/04/19/loc_miami.html

Messner, M.A., Duncan, M.C., and Cooky, C. (2003). Silence, sports bras and wrestling porn: women in televised sports news and hilights shows. *Journal of Sport and Social Issues*, 27, (1), 38-51.

Mushnick, Phil. (2003, May 23). It's no 'one-shot deal.' *New York Post*. http://www.nypost.com/sports/35805.htm

Olson, Lisa. (1997, January 23). Hall of shame. www.theage.com/au/news/ ns970123a.htm

Olson, Walter. (1998, February). Title IX from outer space: how federal law is killing men's college sports. *Reason Magazine.*

Papper, Bob. (2004, July-August). Recovering lost ground. *RTNDA Communicator.*

Reply comments of diversity and competition supporters. (2003, February 3). *Minority Media and Telecommunications Council.* http://www.mmtconline.org/briefs/04/BroadcastOwn %20Reply.pdf

Romano, Allison. (2002, September 2). 'Dearth of women' in top spots. *Broadcasting & Cable.* http://www.tvinsite.com/broadcastingcable/index.asp?layout=story_stocks&articleid=CA241754&doc_id=100468&pubdate=09/02/2002

Sportscasters: behind the mike. (2000, February 7). [Television show]. *The History Channel.*

SportsCenter of the Century: the most influential people. (2000, February 20). [Television show]. *ESPN.*

The GolfWeb Q&A: Jim Ritts. (1996, January 12). http://services.Golfweb.com/library/qa/ritts960112.html

Top editors at U.S. Newspapers. (2004). *National Association of Black Journalists.* http://www.nabj.org/newsroom/census/story/556p-830c.html

Watkins, Calvin. (2002, February 20). SMU gives men's track team the heave-ho. *Dallas Morning News.* http://www.dallasnews.com/sharedcontent/dws/spt/stories/ 022004dnsposmulede.a28b127.html

Welcome to New Vision Sports. (2004). *New Vision Sports Properties.* http://www. newvisionsports.net/

Women sportscasters bristle at commentator's remarks. (2002, October 10). *ESPN.* http://www.espn.go.com/nfl/news/2002/1010/1443917.html

13

Employment

If you took an economics class at school, you know about the basic laws of supply and demand. As the supply of any product rises above demand, there is a "surplus" and the price charged for the product drops accordingly. The same situation applies in the world of sports media. Every year there is a tremendous "supply" of eager college graduates looking to make their mark in the business. Think of how many people just at your school alone are interested in sports and then multiply that by thousands of colleges, universities, and trade schools all across the country. According to a report in the *American Journalism Review*, more than one-half of all the males surveyed at three major broadcast journalism schools (Syracuse University, the University of Missouri, and Ohio University) wanted a career in sports broadcasting. That compares with just 27% who want to go into television or radio news. "It supports my gut reaction that most of the males come to Ohio University to be about sports," says Eddith Dashiell, associate professor in the university's E.W. Scripps School of Journalism.

Those who do graduate must compete with the thousands of other people already in the business, but looking to move on to a new situation. Unfortunately, the "demand" for such talent can never keep up with supply. Sports media positions, even in the smallest and poorest areas in the country, are rare and highly coveted. The growth of the Internet, cable, and other alternative outlets has eased the situation somewhat by creating more positions. But the fact remains that getting a job in sports media remains a difficult and frustrating endeavor.

The Bad News

Probably the most important hurdle to get over is your own perception of the sports media industry. Most people get interested in the business with the idea that they will become the next Rick Reilly or Dick Vitale. They envision themselves traveling first class to cover huge events, interviewing and hanging out with famous athletes, and becoming a household name.

Certainly that is the case for a select number of sports journalists who have reached the very top of their profession. But the reality is much different for the other 99.9%, especially those just starting out. Working in sports media is difficult and often monotonous work. Instead of covering the Super Bowl, you'll probably be covering high school swimming or tennis. The hours are long and the pay is low, leading to cases of "burnout" for many people in the business. Sports doesn't seem as much fun when it's no longer just a hobby and becomes a career. Television news director Griff Potter says, "It's about journalism, not sports. If you are in it for the sports, you're not a journalist but a fan. Get a job in another industry and buy season tickets." News director Dennis Fisher is even blunter. "Don't get in the business," he says. "There is too much competition and not enough jobs to go around. If you insist on going into it, then be resigned to hard work and little glory."

Dave Benz does both radio and television sports in Indianapolis. He adds, "These are tough times for sportscaster types. From the downsizing of sports networks (such as Fox Sports Net), to the total elimination of others (such as CNN/SI), to the reduction and, in more and more cases, elimination, of sports departments at local television affiliates, opportunities for sportscasters are vanishing at an alarming rate. The end result has left the sportscasting industry more cut-throat than ever, so much so, I know many experienced and talented folks who are either out of work or getting out of the industry all together. The road to sportscasting success will be long and hard, if not impossible."

The Numbers Game

As Benz suggested, despite the growth in technology and media options, many outlets are reducing or eliminating the amount of sports content they produce. In 2002, KDKA television in Pittsburgh revamped its sports segment and now provides only three and a half minutes of sports during its 3 hours of news programming. News director Al Blinke said the station was cutting the time allotted for sports almost in half in order to redesign its sports programming. "The reality of it is, what we're trying to do now is treat sports more as news," says Blinke. "There are so many sports channels out there that do hits, runs, and errors. We want to do the stuff that transcends sports."

KDKA joined stations in Tampa, Las Vegas, and all across the country in taking a new, hard look at sports programming. "You don't want to do anything that chases away [the sports] audience," says Dan Bradley, former vice president of news at WFLA in Tampa, which completely dropped sports from its 5 p.m. and 5:30 p.m. newscasts in 2000. "But you also don't want to spend too much time on something your audience could care less about." Rival station WTSP also dropped sports from both of its early evening newscasts. According to former station news director Jim Church, "Telling a story when nobody's listening is not a good use of air time."

The case of KCTV in Kansas City illustrates how the media are rethinking their local sports content. In February of 2004, KCTV completely eliminated its local sports department without giving up a local sports segment. The station moved away from producing local sports in-house and now contracts out the work to Metro Sports, a cable sports network in Kansas City. According to KCTV, "Metro Sports will gather, edit, and deliver the sports stories of the day." Ostensibly, contracting the work out will save KCTV money because it no longer has to pay for the salaries, equipment, and travel related to an in-house sports department. But it also eliminates the sports jobs at the station.

The result of all this is that many sports media outlets are hiring fewer people, and supply still far exceeds demand. Research shows that entry-level media applicants outnumber hirings by 3 to 1 in radio and a whopping 10 to 1 in television. And even that probably underestimates the situation in sports broadcasting. The numbers suggest that for every entry-level position in a television newsroom, the typical news director gets 60 to 70 resume tapes. Television news director Jeff Kiernan of WCCO in Minneapolis says whenever he has a sports opening, which is rare, he usually get around 200 resumes. It's a much brighter situation for behind-the-scenes personnel such as photographers or editors. For those openings, a news director might get only a dozen or so applications.

A survey of recent graduates confirms the problem. Only half of the journalism and mass communication students who graduated with a bachelor's degree in 2003 found work in the communications field, the lowest level of employment in a decade. A recent public relations graduate remarked, "Keep your head up—the economy is terrible right now, so try not to take rejection personally."

The Money Pit

Because there are so many people applying for positions and so few positions available, entry-level salaries remain depressingly low. Station management knows it can pay low salaries because it has an inexhaustible talent pool. As the market size and responsibilities increase, so does the pay. But entry-level sports journalists often find it difficult to survive the beginning years when they are expected to "pay their dues."

Ball State University professors Mike Gerhard and Bob Papper have confirmed this with their research into industry salary levels. Recent numbers show a slight increase in salaries, mainly to keep ahead of inflation. A closer look at the figures, however, reveals some disturbing information (Table 13-1).

Two things jump out immediately. First, sports broadcasters make a lot less than their counterparts in news and weather, a fact that is consistent at every television station in the country. As discussed previously, research shows that sports is the least-watched segment of the newscast. Because of its relative lack of respect and importance,

Table 13-1	Position	Median Salary	Minimum Salary
Broadcast Sports Salaries *Source: Ball State University/RTNDA*	Television sports anchor	$35,000	$16,000
	Television sports reporter	$25,000	$15,000
	Radio sports anchor	$29,500	$14,000
	Television news anchor	$50,000	$17,000
	Television weather anchor	$43,000	$16,000

sports broadcasters are generally not as highly paid as news or weather talent. This obviously does not apply to all-sports outlets such as ESPN or sports talk radio.

The second observation is that while some of the salaries seem impressive, keep in mind that most of the gains and the big numbers come from the bigger markets. Sportscasters in New York, Los Angeles, and Chicago make a very good living in the business, as do industry professionals in places such as Minneapolis, Nashville, and Miami. But it usually takes years to work up to such a professional level. Of greater importance are the figures for the smaller markets, places such as Tupelo, Mississippi or Lawton, Oklahoma, where entry-level graduates are likely to start out. In those markets, you can expect to start around $20,000 a year or less, no matter what the position.

Television news director Bill Evans started in 1982 as a sports director in El Dorado, Arkansas for $11,500 a year. Today, that's equivalent to about $20,000 or what Evans pays now for experienced reporters. "Many of the starting salaries today are what I was getting in the late '70s," says television news director Dean Adams. "That just amazes me." According to former news director Bob Freeman, who worked for years in the Evansville, Indiana market, "People getting out of school feel they shouldn't have to work for $18,000 a year. They think they should make $25,000 or $30,000. Frankly, a market this size can't bear that kind of starting salary." Television sports director Cory Curtis says young sportscasters can handle the low pay, if they're willing to make sacrifices. "I have a saying, 'short term sacrifices for long term gains.' That means moving to Billings, Montana if you have to. That means making $13,000 a year if you have to."

The Good News

Don't give up hope yet. While it's hard to find a job in the sports media business, it's certainly not impossible. In fact, finding job openings is very easy. Magazines such as *Broadcasting & Cable* and *Electronic Media* have weekly classified job listings that include information about the position and where to send a tape. Several Internet sites, such as *tvjobs.com, sportscastingjobs.com,* and *medialine.com,* have much of the same information. You can also access job openings by going to the Web site of the newspaper or broadcast outlet where you want to work. While there is sometimes an access fee to find this information on the Internet, you can get it for free by going to the local library. School placement services and professional contacts can also be helpful.

There's much to be said for persistence, ingenuity, and hard work when looking for job openings. It's quick and efficient to use professional job services or Internet sites to get leads, but none of these job openings is a secret. If you found them, chances are thousands of other job seekers know about them too. Sometimes it's better to pick a particular area or outlet where you want to work and focus your energy there. This could involve calling or visiting the outlet, even if it doesn't have an immediate job opening. By making an effort, you introduce yourself to the decision-makers and get your "foot in the door." It also communicates that you're serious about your work and are thinking about the future.

Gentle persistence in the form of occasional phone calls or visits to the same outlet can pay off down the line, but be careful not to overdo it. There's a fine line between persistence and annoyance, and news executives don't like someone who is a constant bother. You might be better off sending a resume and contact information every 3 months or so, just to let them know you're still interested. Many times, editors or news directors will stick that information in a file they keep handy for when they start a job search. It's no guarantee you'll be hired, but most employers will at least give you the benefit of the doubt.

Once you've found the job you want to go after, there are some concrete steps you can take to put yourself in the best possible position to get hired.

Experience

Most people don't realize that your job preparation begins long before you actually start looking for work. In the sports media field, as with almost all facets of media and journalism, employers are looking for people with experience. They want someone who can come in and start working right away with a minimum of training. Training costs time and money, and given the high turnover rate in the industry, it's not worth the costs to most outlets. Even newspapers and stations in the smallest towns now expect applicants to have some sort of media experience.

There are several ways to get experience, including work at college, summer work, or internships. If your school has a student media outlet, such as a newspaper or radio/television station, you should be working there. "There are very few overnight successes," says Charley Steiner, the radio voice of the Los Angeles Dodgers. "When I arrived at Bradley University, the first thing I did was go to the radio station and say, 'Folks, you better get used to me because you're going to see a lot of me over the next four years.' I played records, read news, did play-by-play, and managed the station."

Even if the school doesn't have such opportunities, there are still ways to get experience. Summer is a great time to go to the local newspaper or broadcast station and help out. You may not get paid, but you'll get invaluable experience learning how the business works from the inside. Media outlets are always looking for dedicated people who are interested in learning and contributing.

Many media outlets now have partnerships with schools across the country in which students can get college credit for summer internships. This helps the outlet in that it doesn't have to pay any money and it can expect that the students will come in with a certain amount of training. The advantages to the students are obvious in that they get a first-hand look at how sports content is gathered, produced, and presented. Depending on the size of the media outlet, students may actually get to help report or present some stories, so make sure your internship is one in which you get to learn and contribute. An internship at the *Washington Post* or with WCBS in New York sounds great, but it doesn't help you if all you're doing is answering phones and getting coffee.

Given the highly competitive nature of the industry, it's not surprising that competition for these summer internships has increased. Many media outlets have now created a fall application deadline for their programs, just to give them enough time to sort through all the applications. You can get a lot of information on what's available and when to apply from your school placement office. Most outlets also post their internship guidelines on their Web sites. In any event, if you're interested in getting an internship, you should probably start making plans the summer before you want to work. There's simply too much competition today to wait until the last minute and expect to find something.

Joe Grimm of the *Detroit Free Press* is considered one of the "gurus" in the newspaper internship field. He maintains a Web site (http://www.freep.com/jobspage/interns/intgrid.htm) that helps prospective interns with the planning process (Table 13-2).

Table 13-2	Date	What You Should Be Doing
Internship Planning Calendar	July	Talk to outlets you want to work for next summer; visit if you can
Source/Courtesy:	August	Evaluate and strengthen your portfolio
Joe Grimm, *Detroit Free Press*	September	Get your resume together and update your portfolio; learn about application deadlines
	October	Mail your first applications (the earliest deadlines are Nov. 1 and getting earlier)
	November	The busiest month for sending applications (most deadlines run until Jan. 1)
	December	Interview at a newsroom or two over break
	January	Write thank yous and start calling targeted outlets
	February	Phone calls to your prime outlets could help
	March-June	Begin lining up freelance work if no internships are available; look for another way to break in or maybe something unexpected will turn up

Even if your internship falls through, Grimm suggests you find anything where you can get experience, even if it's unpaid. "Experience may be more important than money," he says. The bottom line is that you need to do whatever it takes to get media experience, even if the hours are horrible and you're not getting paid. Today's sports media employers demand experience, and without it, your chances of getting a job are almost zero.

Portfolios and Resume Tapes

Once you get some practical experience, you can start thinking about putting together a portfolio, resume tape, or demo reel. These are all different names for the same thing—examples of your work that let employers evaluate your writing, reporting, and anchoring. The portfolio is a collection of printed stories, either newspaper or magazine, whereas the resume tape includes an anchoring segment and one or two broadcast reports. The demo reel is the radio version of the resume tape.

One of the first and most obvious rules is that you want to showcase your best work. Evaluating and judging the "best" is often difficult, but generally you know what work stands out. Your very best effort should go first—right at the front of the portfolio and the lead story on the resume tape. Prospective employers often have hundreds of applications to go through, and many news directors will sift out resume tapes by looking at each one for 10 seconds. The good ones go in one pile and the rejects in another, so don't ruin your chances by saving for a "big finish."

A portfolio or resume tape should give some indication of your skills, and especially your versatility. With so much of the industry now focused on the bottom line, media outlets are looking for ways to save money and stretch resources. One way they do this is by hiring people with a variety of sports media skills. For print reporters, this means covering a wide range of stories and subjects. The reporter with the ability to write features as well as game stories and who can cover several different sports is much more attractive than someone without those skills.

Almost all sports broadcasters want to become anchors, but stations are looking for people who can also write, shoot, edit, and produce. Your resume tape should showcase all your skills, so put on stories that you've also shot and edited. Television news director Ron Lombard says versatility is the number one thing he's looking for. "These days we need sports journalists who can do it all: write, report, produce, and anchor, along with shooting and editing their own material. (We want people with) the ability to do it all quickly and with attention to detail."

In addition to versatility, your portfolio should also reflect your ability to write, think critically, and, most importantly, work as a serious sports journalist. Too often, young sports journalists focus their stories on scores and highlights, but ignore solid sports reporting. More than anything else, news directors want to see creative, enterprising stories that appeal to more than just hard-core sports fans. They're looking for communicators and storytellers, not just someone focused only on last night's game. Television news director Joel Streed says, "I'm looking for someone who is possibly a cross-over from news. That means you can do more than just read scores and follow highlights. Show me the story you did on the hockey mom who gets up with her child at 4 a.m. to get to practice. Or how about the guy pitching horseshoes? I guess the keyword is different." News director Griff Potter says he wants "a journalist, not a rip-and-reader. Someone who understands that highlights, runs, and errors are boring television."

In putting together a resume tape, broadcasters face some challenges unique to the medium. Unlike print reporters, they must also demonstrate some sort of on-air "presence," usually defined by how they look and sound on camera. There are several elements to this, including the idea of control. Good sportscasters convey a sense of control on air in that they are relaxed, confident, sound mature, and can overcome mistakes. In some cases, the news director actually wants to see a mistake on your tape, just to know how you will react to it. Overcoming mistakes with a smooth transition or self-deprecating humor can be just as important as a sportscast with no mistakes at all.

Employers also want to know how you think on your feet. Live shots are a good way to demonstrate this because they demonstrate your ability to think fast and communicate with the audience and, in some cases, can be just as important as the other material on your tape. But it's important not to go overboard. Many sports broadcasters succumb to the temptation of putting dozens of live shots or standups together in a lengthy montage. News directors certainly want to see what you look like, but such montages tell them very little about your ability to report or communicate with the audience.

Above all, "presence" means the ability to communicate effectively. It's become something of a disturbing trend on national sports shows to turn the presentation into a comedic sideshow, complete with funny noises, sounds, and impersonations. While a select few sports broadcasters can carry this off, it certainly doesn't appeal to most television news directors. Lombard says he wants someone with "good writing and storytelling and a unique style. Too many sportscasters look and sound alike or try to mimic a particular style."

The growing convergence in sports media means that even print reporters now have to worry about their on-air presence and performance. For example, Peter Gammons covered baseball for two decades with the *Boston Globe*, but now is a regular contributor to ESPN. In these cases, print reporters are more valued for the information they have instead of their presentation styles, but a certain minimum level of quality is expected. A print reporter doesn't have to come across like Dick Vitale, but he or she can't put audiences to sleep, either.

The *Juneau County Star Times*, located in central Wisconsin, is seeking a Sports Editor to direct development of the sports section, create and write stories, layout, design and paginate sports pages, photograph sports events, coordinate coverage with other Central Wisconsin Newspapers sports editors, and maintain regular contact with editor. Minimum requirements include a degree in journalism, two years production experience in desktop publishing and experience in covering sports on a weekly newspaper. Qualified candidates will possess excellent writing, editing and photography skills, proficient computer skills in QuarkXPress, and Adobe Photoshop, a willingness to put team goals before individual goals, and the ability to work quickly and accurately in a fast-paced environment under deadline pressure. Additionally, the successful candidate must demonstrate an ability to work well with people in the community and on the newspaper staff, and be able to train assistants in covering sports and layout.

[a]This ad ran in September 2004, so please do not contact the newspaper.

Table 13-3

Typical Ad for Newspaper Sports Editor[a] *Source/Courtesy: Madison.com*

Employer Expectations

Part of knowing what to put on a resume tape or in a portfolio is determined by what the sports outlet is looking for. Sometimes the newspaper or broadcast station will give a very clear definition of what it wants. Consider the ad shown in Table 13-3 for a newspaper sports reporter.

It's obvious that the newspaper values versatility in that the prospective employee has to have a variety of different job skills. In addition to the traditional newspaper skills of reporting, writing, composition, and layout, this person should also have computer and photography skills. Experience is also required, in this case in both desktop publishing and sports editing. The days where someone could walk into a newsroom off the street and start working with no experience are over.

There's also an emphasis on working under deadline and getting along with others in the newsroom. No matter what media you're in, there's going to be deadline pressure, and outlets want employees who can work well and make critical decisions when the clock is ticking. The part about working well with others is also important. Employers want a "team player," and in many cases would rather hire a less experienced person with a good attitude rather than someone who will grouse and complain. When an outlet is deciding between two equally qualified candidates for a job, attitude often makes the difference.

You should go into any job with the expectation that it will involve long hours and low pay. There is no such thing as a 40-hour week or a 9-to-5 job. You will be asked to work overtime, work weekends, and work holidays, and if it's a salaried position, you won't get any extra pay. The most successful people in sports media have a good attitude because they have a passion for their work. They put up with all the headaches because it's something they really want to do. Those that don't have the passion can become extremely cynical and often leave the business "burned out." It might be hard to tell at this point whether you have a passion for the business, but at the very least you should have a realistic understanding of what the job is really like.

One of the things you don't see in the ad is any mention of salary. That's because the management of the station is in such a strong position that it can easily afford to give prospective employees a low, "take-it or leave-it" offer. Don't expect to go into an entry-level position and bargain for a higher salary. The management position is that there are dozens of other qualified applicants, and if you turn down the job one of them will surely take it. The large size of the sports media labor pool means that management can play a very successful game of lowball. That doesn't mean you have to take whatever is offered, but if you insist on bargaining, be prepared to walk away or lose the offer.

Resumes, Cover Letters, and Interviews

A less important part of the employment process involves cover letters and resumes. This is the material you send with your portfolio when you learn about a job opening. A good resume or cover letter doesn't necessarily get you the job, but if it's unprofessional, sloppy, or written poorly, it can surely lose you the job.

Typically, job applicants will send a cover letter, resume, and portfolio/resume tape when applying for a position. A cover letter is what introduces you to the person in charge of the hiring process. A cover letter should play it fairly straight—tell the media outlet who you are, why you want the job, and why you should get it. There are many different ways of creating a cover letter, but they should try to include certain things. It's very important to use names and spell them correctly. Including a name is not only courteous, but it also makes the news director or editor feel like the application is personal and not just some form mailing (avoid "Dear Editor" or "Dear News Director" at all costs). Find out how to spell the name correctly because a wrong spelling sends a signal that you're either careless or didn't do your homework.

News directors and editors are very busy and they probably have a hundred or so resumes to read through. Get right to the point with your cover letter and don't waste a lot of time on introductions or warm-up material. They don't care about your life history—just tell them who you are and why you're applying. If you've been recommended by someone who's connected to the station, that gives your application more credibility and you would certainly want to include that information at this point.

The next section should deal with the two things employers want to know most: how can this person help us and what skills/experiences does he or she have? Employers already know what they have to offer (salary, benefits, vacation, etc.) and it goes without saying that you shouldn't even ask about those things at this point. Instead, tell them what you have to offer and what you can do to make their product better. An emphasis of your versatility is especially appropriate because stations are looking for people with a variety of skills and experience. You might want to mention your combination of job-related skills or the experience you have that would help you in the job.

It's also important to show interest and let them know you really want the job. Graduates coming out of college certainly have different skill levels, but for the most part everyone's at about the same place. When employers have two or more candidates that are roughly equal, they often make their decisions based on who has the best attitude. One way of showing interest is to volunteer to meet the employer or travel at your own expense to the media outlet, and many jobs have been filled simply because people showed this type of persistence. But again, don't go overboard.

In many other jobs, the resume is the most important part of the hiring process. But given the importance of the resume tape and portfolio, it is not quite as important in hiring media positions. The resume should allow the employer to tell at a glance the important things about you—your education, work experience, skills, and contact information. Therefore, it should be concise, easy to read, and ordered in a way that makes it easy to find information.

Focus your resume on those things that media outlets care about and forget the things that don't matter. The only personal information you really need is your name and contact information. You do want to indicate if you have a college degree because it's pretty much the minimum requirement at sports media outlets, except for some technical positions. Grade point average is not really necessary because your GPA is not a true indication of how you would do on the job. It might be that you sacrificed grades in order to get valuable experience at the college newspaper or television station. If you have a good GPA, feel free to put it down, but it certainly isn't a requirement.

Work experience is absolutely essential, provided it somehow relates to sports media. Employers do not care if you worked at Pizza Hut or J.C. Penney's, and instead want to know about your media skills and experience. This is where you can describe not only what you did in college, but what specific skills you learned. The more things you did the better and don't be afraid to go into detail, including work at internships. If you have zero media experience, you might want to include some of your other jobs. But if you don't have any media experience, chances are you won't get hired.

As with work experience, you can list awards and honors you won in college, as long as it might pertain to the job you're seeking. Journalism honor societies and honors you've received for student media contests are fine, but employers don't care if you were fraternity pledge chairman or voted "most popular" on campus.

The use of references often depends on the media outlet and some will specifically request at least three. It might be a good idea to include references whether the employer asks for them or not as a sign that others think highly of you and your work. Remember that references should always reflect positively on you and that you should check with the person giving the recommendation. Many times, someone will ask for a recommendation and then be surprised to hear later that the recommendation was very poor. Don't assume that the recommender is always going to say good things about you.

Recommendations from those working in the industry carry a little more weight than recommendations from teachers because they indicate how well you can do on the job. You should always try to include recommendations from professional people and not rely solely on professors and college people, which is another good reason for doing internships. In addition to a professional recommendation, you should also get someone to write something about your character. As mentioned, attitude is a very important part of the job search process and employers want to make sure they're getting committed workers. No media outlet wants to spend the time and money on a job search, only to find out that it has hired a "troublemaker" with a bad attitude.

The resume shown in Table 13-4 was posted on Medialine (*www.medialine.com*), a company that specializes in media job placement. It's used as an example of how to create and maintain a professional media resume. At a glance, an employer can determine essential information about the prospect, including education and media experience. One of the important points intentionally left off the Internet version of this resume—probably for privacy reasons—was contact information. Make sure prospective employers know how to contact you by phone or e-mail.

Based on their evaluations of resume tapes and portfolios, news directors and editors will typically narrow down the list of applicants to two or three finalists. These people will be contacted by phone and, if both parties are interested, a personal, on-site interview will be arranged. Bringing in job candidates requires a lot of time and money, and stations don't like to waste their resources on unqualified prospects. But don't confuse station interest with commitment. There are no guarantees and, in some cases, stations have called off the process after interviewing all the candidates.

If a media outlet calls you for an interview, there are some things you can do to help your chances. One thing is to research your prospective employer. Find out about the outlet, who owns it, and what their content is like. You can also learn about the community, such as important businesses or local events. Thanks to the Internet, this type of research is now extremely quick and easy.

As mentioned, attitude plays a key part in the interview process. How you get along with others at the media outlet, the answers you give, and even the questions you ask reflect what kind of attitude you would bring to the work environment. At the very least, you should show a high level of interest in the position and a willingness to "do whatever it takes" to get the job. Interviewees who immediately start asking about vacation time, sick leave, and benefits usually raise red flags.

Salary is another area you should probably avoid until you're more sure of the station's commitment. Asking too early could be a sign of "jumping the gun" and

Personal
Chris Kane
Sports Anchor/Reporter, WAGT-TV, Augusta, GA

Experience
WAGT-TV (NBC 26) Augusta, GA
Sports Director, November 1997–present
- Produce and Direct Local Sports Coverage
- Produce and Anchor Informative and Entertaining Sportscasts
- Host and Produce Masters Week Golf Coverage
- (2002) Host of "Golfing Augusta" a half-hour golf show that airs on Comcast Cable
- (1998–1999) Augusta Lynx Radio Hockey Play-By-Play Announcer (ECHL Team)
- Weekend Sports Anchor, Aug. 1997–Nov. 1997
- Anchor and Produce Weekend Sportscasts
- Shoot, Write, Edit, and Report three days per week

WKEF-TV (NBC 22) Dayton, OH
Sports Anchor/Reporter, July 1995–Aug. 1997
- Shoot, Write and Edit Daily Sportscasts
- Report from 1996 Centennial Olympic Games in Atlanta, GA
- Weekly Feature "Kane's Kids" (nontraditional stories)

WFND-TV (UPN 47) Findlay, OH
Sports Anchor/Reporter, July 1994–July 1995
- Produce, Edit, and Anchor Daily Sportscasts
- Host and Produce Weekly Football Special "College Corner"

WPXI-TV (NBC 11) Pittsburgh, PA
Paid Intern, June 1992–August 1992
- Assists Producer during Nightly Sportscasts
- Associate Producer of "Steelers 51h Quarter Show"

Education
Ohio University, June 1993
- Bachelor of Science with a Major in Telecommunications

Awards
- Georgia A.P. Best Sports Program (2002)
- Georgia A.P. Best Sports Feature (2002)
- Georgia A.P. Best Sports Feature (2002) Honorable Mention
- Georgia Association of Broadcasters Best Sportscast (2002)
- Georgia A.P. Best Sports Feature (2000)
- Georgia A.P. Best Sports Reporting (1999) Honorable Mention
- Georgia A.P. Best Sportscast (1998)

Table 13-4

Typical Sports Media Resume
Source/Courtesy: *Medialine* [http://www.medialine.com/talentshop_demo.htm?page=1&resumeid=3479]

assuming that you've already got the job. Based on our discussions of the pay scale earlier in this chapter, you should have something of an idea of the outlet's salary structure. It's also fine to ask about a general salary range before you agree to visit the station. But most stations have a very definite idea of what the job will pay and often this is nonnegotiable.

You should also use the interview as a time to get a closer look at the station and the community. It could be that the situation is not just right for whatever reason—too far away, the staff seems too hard to work with, or other workers at the station warn

Table 13-5	Name	Location	Duties	Fee
	Robert Barnett	Washington, DC	Primarily negotiates network contracts	By the hour
Broadcast Agents	Sherlee Barish	Milford, PA	Job finder and contract negotiator	5 to 10%
Source:	David Crane	San Francisco	Consultant and job finder	7.5%
http://www.tvweather.com/	Steve Dickstein	Philadelphia	Finds jobs and negotiates contracts	8 to 10%
tv_talen.htm	Art Kaminsky	New York	Started as a sports agent, but also finds jobs and negotiates contracts in TV news	Variable
	Bill LaPlante	Burlington, CT	Finds and negotiates jobs	10%
	Bob Woolf	Boston	Primarily a sports agent who negotiates contracts in the Boston area	Variable
	Pam Pulner	Washington, DC	Finds jobs and negotiates contracts across the country; handles several sportscasters	Variable

you not to come there. Just because you've got an interview doesn't mean you have to take the job. At the same time, jobs in sports media are extremely precious and hard to come by. Pass on a job now and it might be months before you get another good offer.

Agents

In some situations, primarily for radio and television, sports media performers find it helpful to have an agent. An agent is someone who represents the professional interests of the broadcaster in return for a fee. Typically, agents charge by the hour or anywhere from 5 to 10% of a broadcaster's yearly salary. Table 13-5 gives a listing of some of the agents and their fees. Many specialize in handling sports broadcasters or anchors.

Agents generally offer three kinds of services: talent consultation, fee negotiation, and job placement. Some agents will solicit tapes from young sportscasters and give them a critique of their work. This helps the agent "scout out" young talent on the rise and establishes business relationships with people who may end up in high-paying jobs down the road. Be warned that agents can be brutally frank in these critiques and may refuse to represent you. Agents also scout talent by looking at thousands of tapes from local newscasts all across the country.

If an agent agrees to represent you, he or she will try to move you up into a bigger, higher-paying market. The agent will take a tape of your best work and shop it around with news directors across the country. Many of these stations don't have immediate openings, but the agent gets the word out that you're available should an opening come up. Stations like to fill openings as soon as possible, so having these tapes on file gives the news director or manager instant access to an available labor pool. The agent also makes periodic contact with station managers just to remind them of your availability.

When you decide to take a new job or you need to renegotiate a contract at your current station, the agent helps in that process. The negotiable parts of the contract are usually salary and benefits, with everything else determined by the station, including conditions for termination. The "no-compete" clause, which prevents a broadcaster from going across town to work at a competing station in the same market, is a contract standard for both radio and television. When challenged in court, the legality of broadcast contracts and the no-compete clause have been upheld, so be careful of what you sign. More and more, the contract is a condition of employment at broadcast stations, and most on-air performers simply can't get the job without signing one.

For many reasons, sports broadcasters in small markets and those just starting out don't use agents. Many agents will limit themselves to clients in "big" markets and not even look at tapes from anyone else. It makes financial sense for the agent, who makes much more money from broadcasters in the bigger, wealthier markets. Chicago agent Jeff Jacobs represents Oprah Winfrey among others, and it's unrealistic to think that he would bother with students just coming out of school.

Hiring an agent can also be a financial burden for young sportscasters, who usually don't make a lot of money to begin with. It hardly makes sense for someone earning $15,000 per year to give $1500 off the top (10%) to an agent. There's also the issue of high turnover in smaller markets, which is why stations typically don't bother to sign broadcasters to contracts. They understand that entry-level positions are usually held for only a year or so before the broadcaster wants to move up to a bigger market and make more money. Agents don't get involved at the small market level because there's often no contract to negotiate and there's no guarantee the sports broadcaster has the ability or desire to move up. Agents usually enter the picture when the broadcaster is already established and working in a bigger market.

Despite all this, many young sportscasters turn to agents to help them break into a highly competitive field. Agents are generally people who have worked in the industry and have developed an impressive list of contacts. Because they make more money when the broadcaster makes more money, they're motivated to work hard. They can also devote more resources to the job search process, relieving broadcasters of the time and cost of mailing out resume tapes, checking job lists, and making phone calls. At the very top levels of sports broadcasting, for networks and very large markets, almost all on-air performers are represented by an agent.

The decision of whether or not to use an agent is a difficult one and is often based on the individual goals and needs of the people looking for jobs. But agents are an established fact of life in the business, especially in the high-profile sports jobs.

Final Comments

Even with all this terrific advice, the sports job-hunting process is frustrating and difficult. Obviously, some hiring decisions are out of your control. The media outlet may be looking for a particular type of person, such as when television stations want to hire a female to complement a male anchor. The outlet may prefer to hire someone locally and save the money it would cost for an extended job search or it could be grooming someone already working at the outlet and merely going through the formality of advertising the job.

News directors like Paul Conti admit, "There just aren't that many jobs openings at local TV stations. Be prepared to start very small." And that's probably the most difficult thing people in sports media have to accept. When they finally get that first job, it will probably be at a very small media outlet doing very unglamorous work. Kenny Mayne of ESPN says that the biggest problem job seekers have is impatience. "They get out of college at 21 or 22 and they expect to be in the big time in 2 years. They get impatient and maybe give up on it too soon because they don't attain whatever goal they set for themselves." Mayne admits he failed several times. He was out of television for 5 years and it took him three interviews to hook on with ESPN.

Other sports reporters have similar stories. One of the main things that separate them from those who don't make it is persistence and a willingness not to give up. "I've had doors slammed in my face and news directors tell me I wasn't good enough for sports," says Rich Eisen, who left ESPN for the NFL Network. "It's not the most fun activity in the world. But do some research, choose an area where you want to live and go. And keep at it."

Dave Hotard (Figure 13-1) of WJTV in Jackson, Mississippi is one of the thousands of people who have recently gone through the job search, interviewing, and hiring process in sports media. Hotard graduated college in 2003 and took a position with WCBI in Columbus, Mississippi. He has since moved on to become the number-two sports anchor at WJTV.

In terms of what students should be doing while they're still in school, I would say get as much experience as you can, either through an internship or student media at your school. When you get ready to graduate and start looking for that first job, just remember to stick with it. Two months after I graduated I had no prospects, no jobs leads, no nothing, and I was really starting to think about a different career. But people in the business told me to be patient, and right after that I got two different job offers.

It's important to be persistent because there's so much competition out there. I started work in Columbus, which is the 132nd television market. When we advertised for a new sports director, we got 400 resume tapes, including 100 on the first day. When we had an opening for a number three sports person, we got 200 tapes.

With so much competition, you've got to try hard to make yourself known. A lot of times I would send out tapes and get no response, so I started e-mailing or calling the stations every day. You run the risk of getting annoying, but it also forces them to acknowledge you.

Figure 13-1

Dave Hotard, WJTV,
Jackson, Mississippi.
Courtesy: Adam Chapman

You also have to be willing to work anywhere and for low pay. Even if you have to go to a small station in a terrible town, do it. If someone offers you a job, take it, because those offers are very hard to get. Even if it's a job you don't really want to do, it gets your foot in the door at the station.

References

Becker, Lee B. and Vlad, Tudor. (2004, November). 2003 annual survey of JMC graduates. *AEJMC News*, 1, 4-7.

Careers in sports: play-by-play announcer." (1999, September 7). *ESPN*. http://www.espn.go.com/special/s/careers/anno.html

Careers in sports: TV sports anchor. (1999, September 7). *ESPN*. http://www.espn.go.com/special/s/careers/anchor.html

Deggans, Eric. (2000, April 27). Local TV eliminating some sports reports. *St. Petersburg Times*. http://www.sptimes.com/News/042700/Sports/Local_TV_eliminating_.shtml

Employment listings: news and editorial. (2004). *Madison.com.* http://www.madison.com/jobquest/listjobs.php?cat=news

Finder, Chuck. (2002, July 18). The big picture: KDKA-TV alters sports approach. *Pittsburgh Post-Gazette.* http://www.post-gazette.com/sports/columnists/20020718thebig5.asp

Grimm, Joe. (2004). The jobspage internship calendar. *Detroit Free-Press.* http://www.freep.com/jobspage/interns/intgrid.htm

Metro sports report to premiere on KCTV5 news February 9. (2004, February 5). *KCTV.* http://www.kctv5.com/Global/story.asp?S=1633489&nav=1PugKfDG

Papper, Bob and Gerhard, Michael. (2002). 2002 radio and television salary survey. *RTNDA Communicator.* http://www.rtnda.org/research/salaries02.shtml

Round the horn. (2004). *Sportscastingjobs.com.* http://www.sportscastingjobs.com/roundhorn20.asp

Stone, Vernon. (1999). News operations at U.S. TV stations. http://web.missouri.edu/~jourvs/gtvops.html, 1999.

Glossary

Abbreviated game story A short, simplified account of a game that includes the essential 5Ws—who won, the score, who played well, and how did it happen.

Active voice The writing construction in which a subject acts upon a situation. It is preferred to writing in which the subject is being acted upon (passive voice).

Actuality Radio term for a sound bite, or short interview segment.

Ad-libs Unscripted portions of an on-air broadcast performance.

Advertiser driven Sports shows that are created and presented based mainly on their ability to attract advertisers or sponsors.

Agent Person who represents the financial interests of on-air sports media talent. Agents scout for new talent, negotiate contracts, and critique clients' performance, usually for a fee of 10%.

Alliteration The writing technique of using the same sounds in two or more neighboring words or syllables, such as "Jimmy Jackson juked his way to three touchdowns."

Analyst Broadcaster on radio or television who assists the play-by-play man in describing the game; concerned primarily with adding explanation or context to the events. Also called "color man."

Approach How the media choose to present sports content to their audiences. Generally, media outlets treat sports either as serious business or as inconsequential.

Associate director In terms of live sports production, the person in charge of timing the show and coordinating commercial breaks.

Attribution The journalistic technique of crediting the source or speaker of a quote or other piece of information. In broadcast, attribution goes at the beginning of a sentence, whereas in print it typically goes at the end.

Audio personnel   The people responsible for making sure the sound elements of broadcast sports are working properly, at the right levels and at the proper time.

Axis   A term that refers to an imaginary 180° line that goes through a videographer's field of vision. Videographers should not cross the axis and shoot back on the action from the other side.

Beat game story   A developed game story written by a beat writer or someone who covers a team on a regular basis. It includes many elements of the developed story, but also assumes that readers have a continuing interest in the story and don't need a lot of background details.

Billboards   Related to an Internet site, the posting of and response to messages by audience members.

Boosterism   The tendency of media to be supportive of local athletes, teams, and events because it's good for the local community (see also, *Homer*).

Carriage fees   Fees charged by sports cable outlets for local cable companies to carry their programming.

Cellcast   Method of sending back live radio transmission based on cellular phone technology.

Character generator   Graphic information that accompanies a television story. It usually involves complicated numerical or statistical information that requires more explanation. Also commonly referred to as "chyron" or "super."

Cliché   A phrase that has been written or repeated to the point of overuse.

Commercialization   According to sociologists Frey and Eitzen, the movement of sports in the United States toward an emphasis on more advertising, profit, and revenue, generally at the expense of public service. Also referred to as "Corporatization" (see also, *Public Service*).

Comrex   Radio transmission method based on digital compression of signals.

Conflict of interest   A situation in which the sports media person covering an athlete, event, or story has some connection to the situation that could compromise his or her journalistic integrity.

Conglomerate   A large media company that owns dozens or even hundreds of outlets as a result of consolidation (see also, *Consolidation*).

Consolidation   In the media industry, the concentration of more and more media outlets into the hands of fewer and fewer companies (see also, *Conglomerate*).

Context   In terms of a sports feature story, the overriding human or social importance that makes the story interesting and relevant to the audience. Common feelings such as joy, frustration, despair, and pride make for good human contexts. Social contexts include issues that are commonly understood and shared, such as injustice, discrimination, and the like.

Convergence   A movement in which the various media will blend together or "converge" in terms of production and distribution of content. For example, a sports reporter might cover a football game by writing a story for newspaper, writing a different version for the Internet, and giving a radio report on the game.

Copy editors   Newspaper people who look over written sports stories to make typographical and factual corrections.

Corporatization   see *Commercialization*.

Cover letter   Letter sent to a prospective employer that introduces the applicant and tells about his or her qualifications.

Cross talk   On-air conversation between different broadcast anchors, usually to introduce one another or a different segment of the show. Also called "tosses."

Critic   A style of sports media reporting in which the reporter purposely engages in attacks or criticism, primarily to provoke a reaction among the audience.

Cutaway   When shooting a sporting event, these are the nonaction shots taken of the crowd, other players watching, the scoreboard, etc. They can add depth and emotion to the story and can be used in television to help edit several plays together.

Deadline   The time at which a reporter's story must be finished and turned in order to be distributed through the sports media.

Demo reel   A collection of a radio reporter's best stories and anchor work for use in helping find a job (see also, *Portfolio, Resume Tape*).

Depth of field   The relationship between foreground and background elements in a picture.

Developed game story   Goes beyond the abbreviated game story in that it includes reaction, analysis, perspective, and context.

Digital divide   The difference in access to Internet content, which has been dominated by the white, young, and highly educated in comparison to other groups.

Director   In terms of live sports production, the person responsible for executing the producer's plan for the show. The director primarily determines camera shots and inserts graphics.

Downsizing   The reduction of resources, both human and technical, at sports media outlets.

Edit in the camera   The process of television videography in which raw footage is shot in sequences or in a particular order that makes it easier to edit the final product.

Engineer   Person responsible for the maintenance and repair of broadcast equipment related to the production and distribution of sports media content.

Feedback   In a sports media sense, the ability of the audience to communicate with sports content providers. Examples would include audience polls, e-mails, and phone calls.

First-person   A style of sports media reporting in which the reporter takes an active part in the story, whether as a participant or through direct observation.

Format   The way a broadcast sports story is presented, such as package, voiceover, and reader.

Fragmentation   The splintering of previously mass audiences into smaller, "niche" audiences (see also, *Niche*).

Framing   The photographic technique of arranging the proper context for viewing the elements in a picture. Framing determines how wide (far away) or tight (close up) the action appears to the viewer.

Golden moment   An interview technique in which the sports reporter keeps quiet after a question has been answered in hopes that it will encourage the interview subject to keep talking.

Graphics operators   The people responsible for making sure the printed, on-screen information related to broadcast sports is working properly, in the right location, and at the right time.

Hard-core audience   Those audience members that have a very deep interest in sports and will consume sports content no matter what is offered. It is contrasted to "casual" audience members who will only watch sports if they are particularly interested or if the content is presented in an interesting way.

High-definition television (HDTV)   A new television transmission system that depends on digital rather than analog signals. The technology is important to sports broadcasting because it delivers ultraclear pictures.

Homer   A sports media personality who openly supports the local team in his or her reporting. Many homers are employed by the teams they cover instead of independent media outlets (see also, *Boosterism*).

Hyperlinks   The underlined portions of Internet text that allow viewers to jump to different content.

Infotainment   The term, often used derisively, that refers to the growing focus on entertainment in the reporting of news and sports.

Interview objective   The overall purpose the sports media person has in conducting an interview. There are typically three different types of sports interview objectives—informational, entertainment, and confrontational.

Layout   A newspaper term referring to how the paper is arranged physically in terms of composition and placement of individual elements.

Lead   The beginning line or first few lines of a media story.

Localism   The effort of sports media outlets to concentrate on local athletes and events. National stories can also be "localized" in that they serve as the basis for a local story.

Made-for-TV sports   Term used to describe athletic events that were created only for their ability to attract television audiences. Examples include the Superstars events of the 1970s and the golf "Skins" games of the 1990s.

Marti   Microwave relay system that allows radio stations to broadcast live from certain locations.

Mixer   Radio technology that lets a station "mix" or combine sounds at an event by manipulating different microphone inputs.

Natural sound   A broadcast term for sound that occurs "naturally" at the scene of a story. For a football game, the natural (or "nat") sound would be crowds cheering or booing, coaches yelling on the sidelines, and pads crashing against one another.

Niche audiences   Smaller, specialized audiences that have generally replaced the mass sports media audiences. For example, the "X Games" programs to a niche audience of young (12–24), extreme sports fans (see also, *Fragmentation*).

Opinion   A style of sports media reporting based more on commentary and analysis than on objectivity and impartiality.

Outcue   For a broadcast story, the last few words of a taped report. It gives the anchors and technical director a better idea of exactly how the story will end and when to go on to the next one. The most typical outcue is "standard," which means the reporter ends with a standard phrase, such as "I'm Jim Smith for Channel 12 News."

Package   A self-contained, taped story that includes some combination of video, audio, graphics, and natural sound. Usually done by a reporter and introduced by the anchor.

Perks   Gifts, food, or other services extended to the sports media in the course of covering a particular game or event.

Personalization   The technique of communicating the sports story through a person or individual, which makes the story more appealing and interesting to the audience.

Play-by-play announcer   Person who describes the action of a particular sporting event for either television or radio; concerned primarily with describing the events as they unfold.

Plugola/Payola   Illegal and unethical situation in which sports media members trade favorable coverage for goods or other services. Traces back to the 1950s and the beginning of music radio when performers would pay disc jockeys under the table to get their records played on the air.

Portfolio   A collection of a print reporter's best stories for use in helping find a job (see also, *Resume Tape, Demo Reel*).

Preinterview   A technique of putting an interview subject at ease by engaging him or her in idle nonthreatening conversation before the real interview begins.

Preproduction   In terms of live sports production, the work that is done before the broadcast goes on the air. It includes such things as creating graphics and producing commercials.

Producer   For a broadcast outlet, the person in charge of the creation and production of sports content on a regular basis. Producing responsibilities include creating story ideas and content, directing staff, writing, and managing the newsroom. For live sports, producers are responsible for every aspect of the production.

Product placement   A technique in which advertisers get exposure for their products by putting them in highly visible places in stadiums or sports media content.

Public service   The belief that the media, including the sports media, should have a philosophy of serving the public good in some form or fashion. In terms of the sports media, an example of public service is the transmission of positive cultural values, such as teamwork, sportsmanship, and hard work.

Ratings   A measurement that gives a general indication of how many people are watching or listening to a particular broadcast channel. In television, one ratings point represents a little more than a million U.S. television households.

Reader   A written story with no video, audio, or graphic elements.

Resume tape   A collection of a broadcast reporter's best stories and anchor work for use in helping find a job (see also, *Portfolio, Demo Reel*).

Rights fees   The amount of money paid by networks and media outlets for the right to transmit or produce certain sports media content, most notably live sporting events.

Rule of threes   A journalistic technique of writing or reporting pieces of information in groups of three, such as "He ran for 125 yards, scored two touchdowns, and caught six passes." Based on the idea that people remember things better in groups of three.

Rundown   A representation of how broadcast stories will appear in a certain show. The rundown includes the order of the stories, how they are to be presented, who will be presenting them, and how long they last.

Sexploitation   The hiring and promotion of female sports media members, primarily in broadcasting, because of their physical attractiveness.

Script   A written version of a sports story used by the broadcast media to deliver on-air.

Shovelware   The technique of simply copying or "shoveling" sports media content directly on to an outlet's Internet site.

Sidebar   A story that accompanies and is related to a game day story. While the game day story focuses on the details of the game, a sidebar is more of a feature and focuses on a single element related to the game.

Slug   One- or two-word title of a story in a broadcast rundown.

Social commentary   A style of sports media reporting in which the reporter addresses some sort of social issue, taking the position that the issue is important, a problem exists, and some sort of corrective action needs to be taken.

Speed card   A card used by play-by-play broadcasters that has a listing of important information that is instantly accessible.

Sponsorship   The direct or indirect financial support of sports media content by advertisers.

Sports communication process   A three-step process for those who create sports media content. Such content should be based on a simple theme or message, should be presented using the best available elements, and should be easily understood by the audience.

Sports information director   Person at a college or university responsible for promoting athletic events at the school, providing media members with information, scheduling interview access with players and coaches, and coordinating media coverage of events.

Spotter   Person in a broadcast booth who helps the play-by-play person identify players, numbers, and other statistics.

Spotting board   A visual representation of players, numbers, names, and positions that are arranged for easy access to help a play-by-play person during a broadcast.

Standup   A reporter putting himself or herself on camera as part of a taped broadcast story.

Still store   Common television term used to refer to the graphics or pictures that appear on screen over the shoulder of the sports anchor.

Story outline   A rough sketch created by a sports reporter before he or she goes out to cover a particular story. The outline is essentially a blueprint of how the reporter wants to cover the story and should be flexible to allow for changes.

Streaming   The inclusion of moving video, usually in the form of highlights, interviews, or game action, on sports Internet sites.

Superstation   A television station, usually in a large city or market, that distributes its signal to a national cable audience. WGN in Chicago and WTBS in Atlanta are examples of superstations.

Synergy   The coming together or meshing of various elements of the sports media process to work as a coordinated whole.

Tape producer   In terms of live sports production, the person responsible for assisting with replays and taped elements.

Technical director   For a broadcast outlet, the person in charge of technically distributing content. For a live sports production, the technical director executes and coordinates the technical elements of the show.

Teleprompter   A technical device that allows television anchors to read their scripts while looking directly into the camera.

Time-out coordinator   For live sports production, the person who is a liaison between the production truck and on-field personnel. One of the responsibilities includes informing officials when broadcast time-outs need to be taken.

Title IX   Federal legislation passed in 1972 that prohibits athletic gender discrimination in universities and colleges that receive federal funding.

Utility personnel   Volunteer workers who assist with a variety of behind-the-scenes work at a live sports production.

Video news release   Taped material sent to broadcast stations by companies hoping to promote visibility of their products or services.

Virtual billboards   The digital manipulation of images to create ads or promotional announcements at stadiums and other sports venues. Such billboards are visible only to television viewers.

Voice over   A television story in which the anchor reads a portion of the copy over video, usually in the form of highlights.

Voice over/Sound on tape   A television voice over with the added element of a short interview on tape (sound bite).

Zoom   The photographic technique of moving in closer on a subject.

Index